AF305335

On Courage

On Courage

How to Be a Dissident in an Age of Fear

Julia Angwin and Ami Fields-Meyer

MARINER BOOKS

New York   Boston

Without limiting the exclusive rights of any author, contributor or the publisher of this publication, any unauthorized use of this publication to train generative artificial intelligence (AI) technologies is expressly prohibited. HarperCollins also exercise their rights under Article 4(3) of the Digital Single Market Directive 2019/790 and expressly reserve this publication from the text and data mining exception.

ON COURAGE. Copyright © 2026 by Julia Angwin and Amiel Fields-Meyer. All rights reserved. No part of this book may be used or reproduced in any manner whatsoever without written permission except in the case of brief quotations embodied in critical articles and reviews. For information, address HarperCollins Publishers, 195 Broadway, New York, NY 10007. In Europe, HarperCollins Publishers, Macken House, 39/40 Mayor Street Upper, Dublin 1, D01 C9W8, Ireland.

HarperCollins books may be purchased for educational, business, or sales promotional use. For information, please email the Special Markets Department at SPsales@harpercollins.com.

The Mariner flag design is a registered trademark of HarperCollins Publishers LLC.

hc.com

FIRST EDITION

Designed by Jen Overstreet

Library of Congress Cataloging-in-Publication Data has been applied for.

ISBN 978-0-06-349194-6

Printed in the United Kingdom

26 27 28 29 CPI 10 9 8 7 6 5 4 3 2

For Mira,
my brave one

—J.A.

For Ima and Abba,
with surpassing gratitude

—A.F.M.

Contents

Prologue: A Stress Test for Democracy — xi

Introduction: Forget Your Perfect Offering — 1

PART I: On Inner Life

1. A Moral Collision:
   A Small Feeling and a Big Choice — 19

2. Bear Witness:
   You Are the Watchful Eye of History — 31

3. Look for Your Options:
   When Doors Are Closing Fast, Try to Wedge One Open — 46

4. Practice and Prepare:
   Resistance Takes Discipline, Training, and a Plan — 61

PART II: On Finding Your People

5. Make a Minyan:
   Find a Political Home — 79

viii   *Contents*

6. Don't Start from Scratch:
    Repurpose Your Networks   90

7. Bring the Blankets:
    People Need an Invitation to the Movement   110

8. Share Your Fate:
    The Power of Accompaniment   122

PART III: On Threats and Violence

9. Write Down Your People:
    *You Can't Prepare for Every Threat, but You
    Can Improve Your Conditions*   135

10. Make a List, Check It Twice:
    Opposition Research and the New Vigilantism   146

11. Stack Your Defenses:
    The Swiss Cheese Theory   158

12. Win the War of Persuasion:
    Nonviolence Is More Convincing than Violence   173

PART IV: On Growing the Ranks

13. Seize the Story:
    The Pleasure of Agency and the Joy in Defiance   189

14. Find the Double Thinkers:
    *Bring Others to the Brink of Their Own
    Moral Collisions*   201

15. Start a Belief Cascade:
It's Scary to Be First, but No One Wants to Be Last   219

16. "Get the Jeep Out of the Mud":
The Art of Imperfect Coalitions   230

Conclusion: For the Long Run   243

Acknowledgments   249
A Note on Sources   256
Notes   257
Index   293

A Stress Test for Democracy

IN THE SUMMER OF 2024, a few dozen people gathered in a hotel conference room near Washington, D.C., to game out what would happen if an American president attempted to seize authoritarian power.

Seated around the table were retired U.S. military generals, former cabinet secretaries and governors of both parties, business executives and faith leaders, a former federal judge, and a handful of activists. Each person was assigned a team to join—administration, pro-democracy forces, or those not aligned with either camp. Some took on the role of White House staff or members of the president's cabinet. Others acted as part of a pro-democracy coalition that included the opposition party, faith leaders, and grassroots activists. Judges, members of the news media, and military personnel were on the nonaligned team.

The goal of the exercise was to stress-test American democracy. Over the course of five long days, facilitators presented the group with a series of dark scenarios: What would happen if the president initiated illegal mass deportations? If he defied Congress or the courts? If he broke the law to fire career civil servants and replace them with partisan loyalists? If he sought to use government power to punish his political enemies? The participants did their best to respond realistically to each scenario.

It wasn't pretty. In an early scenario, the president was so enraged by protesters swarming the streets of cities nationwide that he invoked the Insurrection Act, which allows the president to suspend the prohibition on deploying the military domestically. "Tell the troops to use all the force they need to clear the streets," he demanded.

The opposition party attempted to stop the troop deployment by filing a lawsuit, but the judge dismissed the complaint. Congress tried to stop it by halting funding, but the president found a way to use existing budgets. The military objected that mobilizing every state's National Guard would leave the country vulnerable to attack. The president fired his top general, and then another, and another, until he found one who would comply.

In nearly every round of the simulation, the White House eventually sent the military into the streets of American cities—and the group of exercise participants sitting in the hotel conference room soon understood how difficult it would be for counterforces to stop a president who was set on blazing past constitutional guardrails to amass power.

"The results were not encouraging," read the official report from the Brennan Center for Justice, the nonpartisan think tank that organized the simulation. "The games demonstrated repeatedly that an authoritarian in control of the executive branch, with little concern for legal limits, holds a structural advantage over any lawful effort to restrain him."

Late in the afternoon, when all efforts had failed, one participant grew frustrated. "This is new," he said. "We don't have any tools for this."

In the months and years since the exercise took place, many in the United States and around the world have experienced some version of this sentiment—the notion that this is new, that it is without precedent, and that, under extraordinary assault by antidemocratic forces, individuals are largely without the tools to guard our democracies against rapidly encroaching authoritarianism.

But it isn't true. Amid circumstances far more repressive, with fewer freedoms, and without access to the deep reservoirs of movement knowledge we now have, people throughout history have found ways to fight for liberation and democracy. And they have won.

This book is about what our collective nonviolent power can look like, what it takes to succeed, what gives individuals the courage to fight back—and how you can do it, too. People have been fighting for their rights, for their dignity, and for each other for a long time. Let's study at their feet.

On Courage

Introduction

Forget Your Perfect Offering

NOT LONG AGO, MANY AMERICANS thought of dissidents as being of another place and another time. Dissidents were overseas heroes—figures like Alexei Navalny and Malala Yousafzai, who stood up against tyranny in our time, or people like Nelson Mandela and Mahatma Gandhi, who hovered above history in a kind of mythical realm. Their noble struggles were the stuff of history textbooks and biopics, far from our everyday lives.

But in the days following the 2024 election, a dark mood fell over the United States. The American president started punishing his political enemies, disappearing and deporting people for their political speech, and bending commercial businesses to his will. His masked agents rolled into our neighborhoods in unmarked vehicles, terrorizing families in racist, indiscriminate immigration roundups. Fear began to roam freely, reaching into nearly every corner of our public life. In each month after January 2025, it became more apparent that Americans would need a clearer picture of what dissent could and should look like in our country and in our time.

This book began as a personal project. A longtime investigative journalist, Julia has spent decades covering the abuses of the tech industry, using data and statistics to uncover systemic bias and writing books and articles counseling Americans on how to guard against surveillance in the era of big data. Ami has spent his career advising local, state, and federal leaders, shaping policy and communications strategy on issues from civil rights and housing access to artificial intelligence. Neither of us would have topped anyone's list to undertake a study of fear or risk, much less courage.

But as the policy pronouncements out of the West Wing grew more brazen and the administration's actions more distressing, neither could we see a path forward for the issues we had long worked on. The promise of a country where all people are treated with equal dignity already seemed miles away. Now the path had become shrouded in a fog thicker than at any moment either of us could remember.

It was in this fog that we found each other, like so many Americans, dazed and disoriented. It all felt like something out of a foreign autocracy. *This was new.* So we decided to attempt an experiment: We would call up people who had bravely stood up to authoritarianism around the world and see if they had any advice for staying safe and preserving democracy.

"You Are in a New Reality"

For nearly a year, we investigated what to expect in this new authoritarian reality. As the president was unleashing fear in the streets of America, we were talking with dissidents—activists and opposition leaders, scholars and movement strategists, journalists and faith leaders, humanitarians, corruption watchdogs, and leaders of human rights groups.

Our earliest conversations with dissidents from Russia, Venezuela, Hungary, and Nicaragua had a strange quality to them. We conducted our first interview at 3:00 p.m. on January 20, 2025: Inauguration Day. For the first few weeks, our inquiries were met with amused detachment. Two earnest Americans had found a sudden interest in their longtime struggles—*that's rich!* Most interviewees politely answered our questions in abstract terms but rejected comparisons between the United States and the repressive regimes they called home.

But as the U.S. president began enacting many of the scenarios anticipated in the authoritarian simulations, the dissidents' skepticism lifted. What replaced it was acute alarm, as well as practical advice delivered at a rapid clip. "You are in a new reality," one former Venezuelan opposition leader told us, "and you need to behave like it."

We broadened our conversations to include U.S. dissidents, recognizing that for some the fight in America was not new, while others had joined it only recently. In the end, we spoke with more than one hundred people on five continents who have cut through fear to preserve their values: A student activist from Hong Kong who risked everything for democracy. A mom in a working-class neighborhood in Caracas who broke with the political movement that had raised her. Twentysomethings in Cairo who staged a gutsy stunt to try to bring down an autocrat. A mild-mannered immigrant in Washington, D.C., fighting to save a landmark civil rights law. And we spoke to Americans who are living under acute threat—because they are undocumented, because they are transgender, or because of their political activism—and who have faced risks as they dissent in their workplace, their community, or their family. Each did it anyway.

We also dug into the history of nonviolent dissident movements at home and abroad. We read the works of Soviet dissidents whose writings undermined the communist narrative in Russia. We absorbed the accounts of *campesinos* who smuggled tortillas to the rebels during El Salvador's brutal civil war. We studied the civil resistance techniques of the U.S. civil rights movement, the efforts of California farmworkers who organized for humane conditions, and the fight of Guatemalan women to win justice for the atrocities committed against them.

We pored over research across academic disciplines, from political philosophy to theology and psychology. We scoured the memoirs of movement leaders, from Black anti-apartheid activists in South Africa to student civil rights leaders in the American South and beyond—with an eye toward both their enduring lessons and their useful mistakes and regrets.

Each is a part of the same story—of where courage comes from, how it is sustained, and how taking personal risks can help save the free world.

A Taxonomy of Dissent

We began to notice patterns. People in different regions of the world and across a wide range of historical and political contexts described remarkably similar experiences with the mechanics of fear and courage.

When we asked if they were afraid, they discussed weighing the immediate consequences of dissent against deeper fears of abandoning their values. When we asked how they protected themselves, they returned again and again to community. When we asked about tactics, they talked about the power of persuasion. When we asked what kept them motivated, they spoke of the joy and agency that came with seizing control of their life's narrative. Many rejected the term "dissident" as too negative; almost no one was comfortable being called courageous.

But under various gradients of repression—standing, as the twentieth-century theologian Howard Thurman put it, "with their backs against the wall"—these people seemed to be relying on a shared set of principles, practices, and tools in order to live out their values.

We were reminded of a phenomenon in the history of science in which researchers across the world have often arrived at the same discovery independent of one another. The Pythagorean theorem was independently developed in ancient Mesopotamia, India, and China centuries before it was canonized by a Greek philosopher in the sixth century BC. More recently, physicists Richard Feynman in California, Julian Schwinger in Boston, and Sin-Itiro Tomonaga in Tokyo—each working separately—discovered a theory called quantum electrodynamics in the late 1940s.

These events illustrate a form of collective intelligence that can emerge in the pursuit of science, according to the renowned sociologist Robert K. Merton. In his 1963 paper on "multiple discoveries," Merton wrote:

> For scientists, even the most lonely of lone wolves among them, are all "members of one another." The study of multiples shows how scientists are bound to the past by building upon a deposit of accumulated knowledge. . . . The community of scientists extends both in time and in space.

Something comparable can be said of the dissident experience. Our reporting showed that dissidents are building on a deposit of accumulated knowledge. They are inspired by each other and by history to confront and overcome their fears in the pursuit of justice. They are a community in both time and space. And yet, so much of the dissident literature we encountered focused on histories of a single heroic person, or of a single movement. So we tried to weave together cross-movement, cross time-and-space lessons from our inquiries.

"Dissident" is often invoked in reference to a specific kind of person, defined narrowly as one who has taken the greatest physical risk, put the most on the line, or endured an extraordinary cost. While some such people are covered in this book, that definition of a dissident can be limiting. Here we instead use the term to describe anyone who is taking a meaningful risk in their own context by fighting for the principle that all people are worthy of equal rights, dignity, and opportunity. We explicitly include the often unheralded behind-the-scenes work of community care as a dissident practice. By using "dissident" to include a more expansive set of experiences and people, our hope is to ease the path for anyone to step into the logic of dissent and utilize these tools in the name of societies that reflect that basic ideal.

Violent resistance is not the subject of this book. We locate ourselves in the tradition of principled nonviolence in service of democratic movements. Though there are dissidents who use violence to achieve their political aims, and others who work toward antidemocratic ends, neither model is our focus in these pages.

We also are not making expansive or comprehensive claims

in this book. Our sample size of one hundred–plus experiences is small, and we are not social scientists. Our findings are descriptive, not determinative, more testimony than academic study. This book also does not contain a definitive accounting of the transgressive actions of the current U.S. presidential administration, nor of any other authoritarian government. What it offers is a set of insights that capture the common experiences of the nonviolent dissidents we interviewed and a vocabulary that we hope will give language to what our readers might already be feeling.

Authoritarianism can be disorienting. Amid unfamiliar feelings, it can be hard to even diagnose what you're going through, whether in your family, your community, your workplace, or your country. Our goal is that this book will give you a shorthand for these experiences that can clarify your next steps—through terms, concepts, and a set of examples of how to do it.

In the first section of the book, we focus on the individual dissident—their inner life and internal calculus, their fears, their core values, and their motivations. We map their trajectory from the "moral collision" that spurs them to action to the ways they transcend their fears by confronting them honestly, beginning with small steps, managing anxieties with careful planning, and focusing doggedly on what they can control.

In the second section, we focus on dissident communities—how people find one, how they make one, and the transformative power of *regularly* being with others who share their values. Here we describe how dissidents find a political home, how they repurpose their networks, how they grow their circles, and how they build what can be called a "community of fate."

The third section tackles the unfortunate side effects of being a dissident—the threats and violence that can stalk one's life. We describe both spiritual and technical ways by which dissidents defend themselves, including a deepening of relationships with neighbors and mentors and a "Swiss cheese" approach to layering protections against both digital and analog threats. We also investigate the literature of nonviolence and explain why this approach can be a powerful tool even when the other side is violent.

The final section is about growing a dissident movement—how to bring more people into the work. Here we describe dissidents' use of both patience and pressure to move "double thinkers" to enlist in their cause and the tactics they employ to ignite a "belief cascade." We examine the power and perils of building imperfect coalitions and reveal the "pleasure of agency" that many dissidents feel doing their work.

Many of these terms come from our conversations with dissidents around the world and from scholars and thinkers whose literature we encourage you to dig deeper into and whose work is cited in the source notes. We offer their language as guideposts that can help you navigate this dizzying new terrain.

On Courage is not a manual so much as it is an invitation. We invite you into the room with these dissidents, and into their heads and their hearts, as they weigh hard choices and confront the fear of losing their jobs, their freedom, their way of life, or all three. This book presents countless tools that they offer us—practical, spiritual, and strategic.

Authoritarianism, Evolved

The United States is only the latest country to fall into the seductive and noxious embrace of a would-be autocrat. Since the 2024 election, our righteous grief has sometimes taken on the peculiar character of American exceptionalism. But the truth is that liberal democracy is now the least common form of government: Nearly three out of four people on earth live under some form of autocracy. Authoritarianism isn't a rare condition. It's a virus afflicting the majority of the world's population—a reversion to the hierarchies of race, class, caste, and gender that long governed humanity. After all, at the birth of the United States in 1776, no other wide-scale representative democracy existed on earth; some might forget that this form of government is history's great exception.

And yet many people need no such reminder. Even in the world's multiracial democracies, freedom and equality remain only provisional. There are millions of Americans, for example, whose very identities make daily life feel like an act of dissent. People of color in the United States have long been disproportionately subject to tracking, unwarranted surveillance, aggressive prosecution, incarceration, and suppression—a set of conditions that the scholars Vesla M. Weaver and Gwen Prowse have called "racial authoritarianism." Look to the people who lived and labored in bondage for America's first century; the emancipated men, women, and children who endured vigilante violence for attempting to redeem the promises of Reconstruction; the civil rights activists stalked and intimidated by federal agents at the direction of J. Edgar Hoover; the Muslim and Arab Americans across the United States who have been surveilled since September 11, 2001; and the Black Americans who continue to disproportionately bear the brunt of state violence and racial discrimination.

These are, of course, only a few noteworthy debts in the ledger of American history. For the millions who await a multiracial democracy that truly fulfills its foundational promises, simply living from day to day can be a struggle for freedom and equality. These voices are also found in these pages, each a link in the same chain and an author of the same story of the fight against global repression and authoritarianism.

Today's authoritarianism, though, looks different than in the past. It no longer rides into town on the back of a coup or revolution. Instead, autocratic leaders like Vladimir Putin in Russia, Viktor Orbán in Hungary, and Daniel Ortega in Nicaragua hold elections, but they use state power to crush dissent, manipulate election rules and results, and control the media.

Harvard political scientists Steven Levitsky and Daniel Ziblatt have described how today's democracies erode in ways that are subtler and less perceptible. They offer a four-pronged test of warning signs in an emerging authoritarian leader. They write:

> We should worry when a politician
> 1. Rejects, in words or actions, the democratic rules of the game
> 2. Denies the legitimacy of opponents
> 3. Tolerates or encourages violence
> 4. Indicates a willingness to curtail the civil liberties of opponents, including the media

These indicators are today supercharged by tech tools, which give authoritarians surveillance powers far beyond the wildest dreams of their predecessors. These autocrats—ever cozier with the world's tech oligarchs—are themselves learning from one another about crushing dissent in new and creative ways: networks of cameras and drones that surveil populations; cell-phone location tracking that monitors individuals' minute-to-minute data-mining to find those who have expressed dissent on social media; and network graphing to map people's friends and contacts.

The good news is that authoritarians can be defeated, but it takes more than just politics as usual. In a 2025 paper, scholars Jonathan Pinckney and Claire Trilling calculated that the probability of an average country going through democratic backsliding being able to halt it is about 7 percent when it relies exclusively on institutional methods such as elections, litigation, and legislative action.

When a population engages in nonviolent civil resistance activities, such as boycotts, protests, and strikes, the chances of success increase, but even then it's a toss-up at 51 percent, Pinckney and Trilling calculated. Tipping the balance means that Americans—accustomed to showing up every few years to cast their ballots and make their voices heard—will have to learn a different mode of activism beyond the familiar cycles of electoral campaigns.

"Civil resistance 'works' by raising the costs of tyranny and systematically removing the sources of power for an autocrat and his enablers," writes Maria J. Stephan, a leading scholar and organizer, whose seminal book with Erica Chenoweth, *Why Civil Resistance Works*, provides a fundamental data analysis of civil resistance movements during the past one hundred years.

In 2017, the historian Timothy Snyder put a concise and accessible guide to resistance work in the pockets of millions. The manifesto, *On Tyranny*, provides twenty rules—such as "Do not obey in advance"—that have now become articles of faith for pro-democracy movements worldwide.

This book builds on these and other important contributions to the genre of democratic resistance—works that have persuasively made the case that what we are witnessing *is* authoritarianism and that call on us to fight back. This book is for the individual who is trying to answer the question: "Now that I object, what do I do next?"

In these pages you will not find a comprehensive theory of how to topple a tyrant or a foolproof way *out* of this current mess, but rather a collection of ways *in*—stories and lessons of ordinary people who showed extraordinary courage that invite readers to the work of principled dissent.

If you look closely, you'll also spot a major contradiction in this book: Many of its characters told us their stories—and offered us their advice for successful democratic movements—from their new homes in exile. Others we could quote only from their writings, or from news reports, because they are imprisoned or dead. At a moment in history when the world is growing less democratic every year and the world's oldest democracy is stepping back from its commitments to human rights and democratic movements abroad, *On Courage* is full of advice on how to win from people who have lost—at least for now.

But events can change quickly, for the better and for the worse. This book itself was researched and written on an intensely accelerated timeline, a product of the emergency in which our free societies have found themselves. Often, when we shared with someone that we were writing this book, they would reply: "Can you write faster?" We did our best. As a result, it is possible that by the time you read these words, the conditions we describe will have changed in America or around the world.

In presenting our findings in all their contradictions, we were also following a piece of advice we heard frequently from dissidents. Over and over again, they cautioned us about the dangers of waiting to act until you have the perfect plan, the perfect coalition, the perfect moment. Instead, dissidents argued for an approach that was rigid in principle but flexible in approach.

In 1992, the songwriter Leonard Cohen released his longest album to date. It was a time of extraordinary upheaval and change. The Soviet Union had just collapsed. The streets of Los Angeles had erupted in a civil uprising. Apartheid was taking its last gasps in South Africa. The world was still in the clutches of the HIV/AIDS crisis. On the album, which he titled *The Future*, Cohen grappled with the totality of these events—some good, some bad, all transformative. Perhaps you are familiar with the famous chorus of the album's haunting ballad "Anthem":

There is a crack, a crack in everything / That's how the light gets in.

But it is the couplet that precedes those celebrated lyrics that, though less well known, calls out to us in our time:

Ring the bells that still can ring / Forget your perfect offering.

On Courage is an invitation to the imperfect work of dissent. It is a guide that is equal parts practical and spiritual, a resource for anyone, anywhere, who feels the walls of history closing in on them. Through the haze, and through the dark, there is a way forward. It is not accessed through a blueprint, a perfect offering. It is not found in the expediency of abandoning core values. It is found by clutching tightly to those values as a lantern in the depths. That's how we find each other and find the path.

That's how the light gets in.

I

On Inner Life

1

A Moral Collision

A Small Feeling and a Big Choice

ON A CRISP, BRIGHT DAY in February 2025, a mild-mannered civil rights lawyer named Paul Osadebe came to the terrible realization that a cornerstone of Dr. Martin Luther King Jr.'s legacy was not likely to survive.

The Fair Housing Act had passed the U.S. House of Representatives in 1968, just seven days after an assassin's bullet ended King's life. The law barred landlords from advertising or renting to "Whites only" and made housing discrimination illegal for the first time in U.S. history.

President Lyndon Baines Johnson had already signed the Civil Rights Act into law, guaranteeing equal treatment for Black Americans seeking a job, a meal, or a hotel room. Housing was the next frontier, a bid to redeem the "promissory note" of equal rights that King had invoked. Its passage, Johnson declared at the signing ceremony, finally meant that no one in America in search of shelter would "suffer the humiliation of being turned away because of their race."

But Osadebe believed all that was at risk. He had worked since 2021 in the federal office tasked with enforcing fair housing rules. It was his job to help fulfill Johnson's promise by prosecuting violations of the landmark law. If a landlord told an immigrant family that no units were open so that they could lease to an English-speaking couple instead, or if they denied a disabled tenant's request for a service animal, Osadebe's office could step in to sue the landlord.

But since January 2025, when new management moved into the Washington, D.C., headquarters of the U.S. Department of Housing and Urban Development, Osadebe had noticed that his new bosses seemed uninterested in enforcing civil rights law. It was an indifference that verged on hostility.

The trouble began with a "gag order" blocking him and his colleagues from communicating with anyone outside the agency about civil rights complaints. A few weeks later, HUD officials abandoned a case against a predominantly White homeowners association north of Dallas that had tried to push low-income Black residents out of their neighborhood. Then, on February 14, the new administration carried out a mass firing across the government—a "Valentine's Day Massacre," the media called it. Twenty percent of the fair housing office was terminated in a single day.

After the firings, Osadebe realized that enforcement of the Fair Housing Act was in peril. The law would still exist on paper, but not in practice.

They're not going to let us do our jobs, he thought.

But the crisis was not understood beyond the walls of the HUD offices, much less breaking through to the outside world. Poor tenants across the country didn't yet know that their housing rights had shrunk considerably. Even members of Congress, tasked by the U.S. Constitution with oversight of the executive branch, appeared to be unaware that the new administration was bulldozing these basic protections. There was information, however, that could alert all of them to the emergency unfolding beneath their feet, and Osadebe could be the one to deliver it.

Still, he recoiled at the thought of sticking his neck out. Though he was a union steward at the federal agency, he didn't consider himself an activist type, preferring to spend his free hours playing video games and going to concerts. His parents— working-class Nigerian immigrants—had always counseled their son to work hard, go to church, and keep his head down. When he told his younger sister about what was going on at the office, she urged him to stay quiet: "We are not people with a safety net to fall back on," she warned.

His family's voices battled his own conscience. Blowing the whistle would almost certainly mean facing retaliation. The end of his employment. The end of a stable income. Given the political climate, he wondered if it might even trigger a more acute threat—people finding his parents' address, tracking them down, and harassing them.

But Osadebe was a civil rights attorney. He had committed his career to protecting vulnerable people against discrimination and exploitation. "I was able to go to a law school that used to be segregated. I am living in an apartment that would have been segregated in the past. I have been able to live the life that I've had because the civil rights movement made real gains," he says. "I just don't want to live in a country that doesn't have civil rights."

He cleared out his office so that there wouldn't be much to carry if he was eventually frog-marched out of the building. And then he began to talk. He spoke to a local television station one day after the mass firing. The next day he gave his first live television interview to MSNBC.

Wearing an olive green sweater and holding his head still, the attorney told a national TV audience what he had seen at work. "We're losing the ability to protect people in their day-to-day lives," he warned. "Unless people take action and respond, we're going to be seeing a lot of pain."

Two Kinds of Fear

Around the world and across generations, dissidents describe weighing two fears against each other. The first fear is more immediate: losing a job, money, social standing, safety, or physical freedom. The second is more fundamental: living a life that doesn't feel honest or dignified, abandoning tightly held values, or being judged in the eyes of history or even a higher power.

This moral collision is where dissident life often begins—with a small feeling and then a big choice: to fill the crack with caulk or to wedge it open wider. To quiet the nagging voice or to follow it.

—

Adriana Gomez decided to follow it. A social services worker in a working-class neighborhood in Caracas, Gomez began to have serious doubts about Chavismo, the left-wing populist movement of longtime Venezuelan president Hugo Chávez, about a year after his death in 2013.

Gomez was still a teenager when the local branch of Chávez's party took an interest in her. One of eighteen cousins, she had always had a knack for leadership and was a natural mentor to younger children. "Since I was a kid, I've been drawn to community work and changing realities like violence," Gomez says. The Chavistas put her talents to use in their local organizing work, dispatching her to parishes across Caracas to organize field days for schoolchildren. Gomez felt seen by the charismatic president's followers. "They noticed my potential," she recalls.

Many in Venezuela were having a different experience under Chavismo: The regime was jailing its critics, suspending news outlets, and using its sweeping system of patronage to enforce political loyalty. But the very same political machine gave Gomez opportunities and access to spaces to run programs that became her calling, such as vocational workshops, after-school sports groups, and a soup kitchen to feed the hungry. She saw how teenagers needed structure to stay out of gangs and students needed food to focus on learning.

Gomez became the picture of loyalty. For years a sticker greeted visitors at her front door: "If you don't love Chávez, you don't love your own mother." When Chávez died in 2013, she wept in his funeral procession. But in the years after his death, Venezuela awakened to a long-slumbering economic crisis. The gas stopped arriving in her neighborhood. So did the food. "We had to sleep outside a supermarket just to buy flour," Gomez recalls. She had recently given birth to her fourth child. The sudden scarcity felt humiliating—and the whiplash infuriating. "You start to realize that it was all just talk," she says.

Gomez faced a decision: Was she willing to protest the government helmed then by Chávez's chosen successor, Nicolás Maduro? To do so would be choosing estrangement from the people who populated her daily life, many of them friendships that stretched back to childhood.

But the scales had fallen from Gomez's eyes, and she wasn't entirely alone. She found a few friends who were equally outraged. "We neighbors would ask ourselves, 'How long are we going to put up with this?'" she recalls. "Eventually, we said, 'Enough is enough.'"

To Be a Dissident Is to Be Who You Are

This is a conflict often faced by people in authoritarian societies: a collision between the head and the heart, between values deeply held and an outside world unfolding in dramatic divergence. It can happen over decades, or in an instant. It comes of morality, or it arises out of necessity.

To dissent is to risk being wrapped in a kind of negative identity—defined by what you are not. But it's the environment, the external circumstances, that recast these individuals in oppositional terms. Dissidents don't choose to be dissidents. They simply choose to be who they are.

In his 1982 essay "Dissent as a Personal Experience," the Soviet-era writer Andrei Donatovich Sinyavsky described his experience of Joseph Stalin's brutal mid-twentieth-century crackdown on culture in the Soviet Union. In the late 1940s, Stalin forbade musicians, writers, and other artists from producing art outside a set of strict Communist Party criteria. Those who broke the rules were designated as anti-Soviet and in turn sent to the gulag, tortured, or executed.

From his apartment in Moscow, Sinyavsky quietly grieved. "To my misfortune, I loved modernism in art and everything that, as a result of the purges, was subject to destruction,"

Sinyavsky wrote. "I saw the purges as the death of culture and the end of any original thought in Russia."

A life without free expression was not a life that interested Sinyavsky. To his mind, that was not a life at all. He resolved to find a way to continue his work. Under the pseudonym of "Abram Tertz," Sinyavsky began writing fiction satirizing Stalin's increasingly repressive rule. Soon he was smuggling his manuscripts out of the Soviet Union to be published in the West.

Sinyavsky had not intended to be an activist, much less a dissident. He was a free thinker. Without writing, he had no identity. "I just did not see any other way for my literary work to be published than this slippery path which was condemned by the state," Sinyavsky wrote. "It was necessary to choose, in one's own mind, between one's existence as a human being and one's existence as a writer."

He chose to be a writer.

———

Adriana Gomez chose to be a steward of her community.

The consequences came fast. When she broke with public narratives that everything was fine and began organizing protests demanding more resources for the neighborhood from the regime of Chávez's authoritarian successor, Maduro, old friends started to refer to her by the slur *escuálida*, meaning feeble, weak, or neglected—a term that Chávez had long used to demean his opponents. Gomez's social invitations dried up. For a time, an uncle stopped talking to her. She was banned from the facilities where she ran her recreation programs, and her relatives were removed from the local food subsidy list.

The environment in Venezuela had changed. Gomez, however, had not. She still believed that teenagers needed structure. She still saw that students were hungry. "Just because kids are from the barrio doesn't mean they're delinquents," she reflected. She continued her work.

Looking for alternatives, she began partnering with opposition figures to support her recreation programs and soup kitchen. Eventually she volunteered in poll-watching efforts ahead of the July 2024 presidential election.

Around 5:30 a.m. on July 29, 2024, after Maduro declared victory despite strong evidence that he'd lost the election by millions of votes, Gomez's phone rang. She had spent the previous days helping to collect tally sheets. When she picked up the phone, it was a member of the police force, a friend, calling with a warning. "If you're in [the neighborhood], get out," said the voice on the other side of the phone. "You're first on the list, and they're coming for you."

Gomez went into hiding for a while. But she soon returned to the neighborhood, which she swears is the best in Caracas. "There are good people—hardworking, educated, kind, fun, everything. It's a beautiful place," she said in a 2025 interview.

Gomez says she doesn't miss the Chavistas. She is who she

is. "I'm on the right path," she said. "All I want is a better life—for my kids, for my family. I want to live with dignity."

———

Paul Osadebe chose to be a civil rights attorney.

His television appearance criticizing his bosses was seen by more than a quarter of a million viewers, but if his supervisors at the federal housing agency were among them, they didn't let on. "They never said a single word," he recalls. "No warnings, no pressure, nothing." So he kept going. He gave interviews to local news stations and other national outlets. He minced no words in explaining that housing companies now had carte blanche to break fair housing laws and discriminate against potential tenants. "No one is watching," he told a ProPublica journalist. "No one will hold them accountable."

Osadebe was careful to always identify himself as a union leader and to say he was speaking in his personal capacity, not on behalf of the agency. It was a thin shield, though, and he knew he was likely to be fired at any time.

Meanwhile, the pressure on his work continued to mount. In June, Osadebe's boss was terminated after objecting to a proposal that would reassign nearly everyone in the fair housing office to other duties. His boss had argued that the reassignment would cripple enforcement of not just fair housing laws but also the Violence Against Women Act, which protects domestic violence survivors and helps them find safe housing.

With his boss gone, Osadebe would have to fight on his own. He spent the summer organizing a handful of colleagues to compile a whistleblower report—a dispatch from the inside of an agency under siege, detailing its death by a thousand cuts, including staff layoffs, stop-work orders, reassignments, and retaliation against dissenting employees. The letter was signed by two anonymous staffers and two named HUD employees: Osadebe and a colleague, Palmer Heenan.

When the report became public in September—they shared it with *The New York Times*—Osadebe and Heenan were called in to separate meetings and ordered to hand in their badges and laptops. As Osadebe had predicted, they were escorted from the building. The perp march was seamless, just as he'd planned, having cleaned out his office months earlier.

Standing outside the brutalist-style concrete headquarters of the housing agency, Osadebe turned to look into the camera on a reporter's iPhone and kept talking.

"This was done not because they thought it was actually legal, or that I did anything wrong. It was to silence me and anyone else who would speak out about the truth. But I'm just not going to let that happen," he said, two union pins fastened to his suit lapel. "People are currently homeless that don't need to be homeless. There's people *currently* in physical danger, mortal life or death danger, that don't need to be."

Osadebe hasn't stopped speaking out. He and some of his colleagues are suing the administration to undo the dismantling of their office and lobbying Congress to save the Fair

Housing Act. If his life has changed in meaningful ways, his low-key demeanor doesn't show it. "I have a really weird relationship with the word 'courage,'" he says. "I think it's just doing what's necessary."

———

It took KGB agents six years to track down the identity of the seditious author "Abram Tertz." When they did—by matching several pages of Sinyavsky's typewriter's unique spacing and letter shapes with a Tertz manuscript—the writer was convicted in a show trial and sentenced to prison labor camps.

He was not sentenced alone. Sinyavsky was tried and condemned alongside Yuli Daniel, another writer who had also published abroad under a pseudonym. The pair were two among hundreds of artists and intellectuals who comprised the Soviet dissident movement, a group who understood their work not as a fight against a regime but as a struggle to defend the rights they were granted in the Soviet constitution.

The authorities branded them as criminals, and history cast them as revolutionaries. But Sinyavsky maintained that it was the regime's intolerance that had forced them into these roles. A dissident "is not only a man who disagrees with the system and has the courage to express himself," he wrote. "He is also a man who does not consider himself guilty."

2

Bear Witness

You Are the Watchful Eye of History

IT'S NEARLY IMPOSSIBLE TO FIND accurate visiting hours for the Immigration and Customs Enforcement (ICE) detention center in Newark, New Jersey.

The agency's website states that visitors are allowed on-site between 8:00 a.m. and 9:00 p.m., seven days a week. But families are frequently turned away during those times. Another website—for the private prison company that owns the facility—lists a different slate of time slots. But those seldom match the actual visitation hours, which change frequently. The changes are rarely announced or posted online or at the building. Sometimes guards at the gate share schedule updates with visitors. Sometimes they don't.

Even when families get lucky and arrive on the right day, they can't be sure what time they'll get in. Visits are allocated in time slots based on the unit number of the person they've come to see. The only way to look up a unit number is to call a phone number that is answered infrequently. So relatives often arrive at 6:00 a.m. and wait in line for six, eight, ten hours outside the gates of the detention center.

They line up in the driveway, stooped over concrete barriers or beach chairs. In the summer, there is no shade, no water, and no access to bathrooms. Eighteen-wheeler trucks roll by every few minutes. And then there are the smells that waft from the nearby sewage treatment plant, asphalt-mixing operations, and animal fat–rendering plants—a putrid blend of marinating sewage, burning rubber, hot exhaust, and rotting flesh.

When the wind picks up, it can trigger a gag reflex for the people waiting—the brokenhearted siblings, spouses, and children of people who might have walked across continents to come to a country that has now disappeared them into a giant windowless concrete box.

"The cruelty is the point," says Kathy O'Leary, a fifty-eight-year-old mom from a nearby suburb who volunteers outside the facility.

O'Leary sees her role as bearing witness to the unnecessary callousness of this waiting game. On visiting days, she and other volunteers in the coalition she helped build—called "Eyes on ICE"—arrive at 6:30 a.m. and set up a tent on the sidewalk outside. They provide the visiting families with water bottles, snacks, umbrellas, sunscreen, extra clothes, and art supplies for the kids who have come to see their parents inside. They do what they can to support the families navigating an inhumane bureaucracy.

A visit to the detention center revealed these scenes:

A woman arrived at 7:20 a.m. for a 7:30 time slot, hoping to see her daughter. There was room for her, but the guard said she should have arrived an hour before her time slot and turned her away. She fell to her knees in grief.

A woman who spoke no English showed up without knowing her husband's unit number, and the guard refused to talk to the volunteer interpreters who tried to convey her request for his number. Eventually volunteers were able to write down his name so she could hand a piece of paper to the guard, so he could provide her with the unit number.

A fourteen-year-old girl whose mother and father were both detained by ICE showed up with an aunt to see her father and try to arrange for her aunt to take legal custody of her. While waiting in line, she got a phone call that her mother had been deported from a different ICE facility. She screamed in agony. A volunteer who was a therapist sat with her until she could calm down enough to go inside and inform her father of the news.

A woman who showed up dressed for church in a silky blouse, dress pants, and bejeweled slide sandals was turned away because the guard said the ban on open-toed shoes (which is written down nowhere) also apparently applies to shoes with closed toes that show the heel. Volunteers found her an extra pair of shoes she could wear, enabling her to enter.

Three kids ages sixteen, fourteen, and eleven showed up accompanied by a priest. (Kids can't go in without an adult.) But when the priest found out he would have to wait outside all day before entering, he said he couldn't stay. A volunteer offered to go in with the kids, and they were able to visit their family member.

While a group of families was inside for a visiting session, the Newark police arrived to ticket and tow cars that were illegally parked. There is no visitor parking lot at the facility, and no legal street parking within three-quarters of a mile. O'Leary paid the towing fees for the visitors from her own funds and spent the following week negotiating with the city to try to get the police to reverse the tickets.

O'Leary became interested in immigrant detention when she was pregnant with her son, who is now in high school. An observant Catholic, she was moved by a talk she attended some two decades ago at a parish hall about a mother who was ripped away from her breastfeeding infant to be placed in immigrant detention. O'Leary began volunteering at another immigrant detention facility in Elizabeth, New Jersey.

Over the years she grew more and more outraged by the abysmal conditions inside the detention centers, and by the private prison industry that profits from the misery. Her volunteer work expanded beyond just vigils and protests to lobbying the governor to ban immigrant detention centers in the state. In 2021, the governor signed into law a measure prohibiting private companies in New Jersey from contracting with the federal government to detain immigrants. But two years later, a federal judge struck down the law. In May 2025, ICE repurposed a halfway house in Newark as a privately run detention center.

O'Leary showed up to protest as soon as Delaney Hall opened its doors as an ICE facility. Soon she realized she was witnessing a humanitarian disaster: Visiting families lined up in the hot sun, wilting in the heat, were turned away for one petty reason after another. So she recruited volunteers to help her provide material, logistical, and emotional support to the visitors.

Most Americans will never see any of this. But O'Leary's crew, present from the time the sun rises until the skies darken over Delaney Hall, documents it all.

Information is power, and O'Leary fights for every scrap she can get. She stops many of the service cars that come through—food delivery trucks, postal vans—and asks their drivers about the conditions inside and what can be done to improve them. She uses her phone to film the transport vans that shuttle in and out of the facility and waves to the detainees that she can't see behind the tinted glass. She makes a note of whether guards are being helpful, which phone numbers are being answered, which local immigration lawyers are taking clients, and which lawyers are overwhelmed. (Most of them are.)

O'Leary and her fellow volunteers have found answers to some of the questions that ICE has kept from visiting families. Week by week, they piece together the visiting schedule. They learn which guards are permitting what kinds of clothing. Every time a new visitor successfully overcomes the obstacles to make it inside to see their loved one is a triumph.

When new volunteers arrive, O'Leary warns them that they should not try to make sense of all the arbitrary rules.

"The point is to get people to be so miserable and to create so many of these little insults and injuries that they just give up and go home, that they sign the voluntary departure papers and leave," O'Leary says. "Witnessing what they're doing, letting them know that we're not going to let them do what they're doing in the dark—I think that's resistance."

"Your Children Will Be Ashamed"

It is a fact of history that justice after state abuses is the exception, not the rule. For thirty-six years, Guatemala was torn apart by civil strife that has come to be known as La Violencia (The Violence). In a frenzied hunt for insurgents, the state military conducted a scorched-earth campaign, flattening villages and massacring tens of thousands of people.

Death squads roamed the countryside and conscripted rural men to participate in torturing and killing their own families and neighbors. Commandos murdered and disappeared people with impunity, displacing over 10 percent of the population in the process.

When peace finally came in 1996, brokered by the United Nations, many Guatemalans were desperate to forget the terrors.

But the indigenous Mayan women did not want to forget. They had been raped en masse. They had seen their children murdered and tortured in front of their eyes, their husbands conscripted and killed, their parents starved. They wanted the truth about their sufferings to be known, and their tormentors held to account.

After a repressive regime has collapsed or a period of acute state injustice has passed, political leaders and courts are often in disarray and must use their limited resources to rebuild. International criminal courts can only do so much. The Nuremberg Trials of the Nazis, for example, represented a high point for post-atrocity justice, and even so, many Nazis died comfortably in their beds many years later.

"Where there are trials, they are usually few in number and sometimes fail to convict even those who everyone 'knows' are guilty," the human rights activist Priscilla Hayner reflected in her 2001 book *Unspeakable Truths*. "Despite loud demands for justice from victims and rights advocates, post transition justice is rare."

And yet some survivors refuse to be silenced. In Guatemala, victims of La Violencia lobbied the United Nations to establish a truth commission to investigate and bring to light an honest accounting of what had happened. Argentina established the first well-known truth commission, the National Commission on the Disappearance of Persons, in 1983, following the end of its military dictatorship. Dozens of similar tribunals have since been established.

"In some countries, rights activists insist that a truth commission does not find new truth so much as lift the veil of denial about widely known but unspoken truths," Hayner wrote of these efforts. "In effect, the report of a truth commission reclaims a country's history and opens it for public review."

The staff of Guatemala's Commission for Historical Clarification collected thousands of testimonies, examined troves of documents, and hiked muddy mountain trails to interview survivors and exhume human remains. In the end, they estimated that two hundred thousand people had been murdered or disappeared during the conflict—more than 90 percent of them by the military and its paramilitary squads.

The commission also validated the Mayan women's claims that they had been the victims of genocide between 1981 and 1983. Though the commission did not name a single perpetrator, all who read the report knew that the two-year period had unfolded under the rule of General Efraín Ríos Montt.

Ríos Montt was immune from prosecution at the time the report was published because he was a sitting member of the Guatemalan Congress. But the women filed a lawsuit anyway, and they waited. Shortly after his immunity expired in 2012, eighty-six-year-old Ríos Montt appeared in a Guatemalan courtroom to stand trial. After months of vivid testimony from the women, he was found guilty of genocide and crimes against humanity and sentenced to eighty years in prison.

Justice wasn't a straight path. A few weeks after his conviction, the constitutional court annulled the verdict on a technicality. When Ríos Montt was finally retried five years later, the women were still there, waiting for justice.

Patrick Ball, a human rights statistician who worked on the original Guatemalan report, recalled the scene in the courtroom as he awaited his turn to testify. Dozens of women sat in the audience in their colorful *traje*. One by one, they stepped up to the stand to tell their stories. The testimony of the women, Ball says, offered something that printed pages could not: moral witness.

"They were just sitting there silently with these implacable looks of insistence," Ball recalls. "That's power. That's nonviolent power."

Ríos Montt, by then ninety-one years old, died during the retrial.

Ball says he has worked with eleven truth commissions and testified at six atrocity trials. He has learned over his decades in the human rights field that bearing witness is crucial even if justice takes a long time. For the perpetrators of state violence, the crimes they committed were usually all in a day's work. But for the victims and their families, these crimes represent the worst day of their lives. They will never forget. "While most people will react to that by hiding or withdrawing, not all of them will," Ball says.

The few who don't withdraw—the Mayan women in Guatemala, the victims of apartheid in South Africa, the Argentinian mothers who long searched for their disappeared children— often relentlessly pursue accountability. And detailed witness accounts give them the ammunition to obtain the acknowledgment and justice they seek, whenever it may come.

"We will know who you are," says Ball, who has spent his career cataloging perpetrators of state violence. He assembled databases that recorded the names of every senior Salvadoran military officer who served during the country's civil war. He helped compile profiles of thousands of Congolese military and police officers credibly accused of serious human rights violations.

"You are not going to be anonymous," he says. "You can wear cute little balaclavas. It may protect you from a few minutes of social media shame, but people are never going to give up their pursuit of you because you've destroyed their lives.

"The things you're doing now will haunt you for the rest of your life," he says. "Your children will be ashamed."

Fighting the Long Defeat

In his 1978 essay "The Power of the Powerless," the Czechoslovakian playwright and poet Václav Havel offered a roadmap for speaking honestly even when authoritarians punish truth-telling. An outspoken dissident, Havel had seen his life shrink and his days become quieter under the watchful eye of the Soviet-aligned secret police.

"The lack of free expression becomes the highest form of freedom; farcical elections become the highest form of democracy," he wrote. "Banning independent thought becomes the most scientific of world views; military occupation becomes fraternal assistance."

Through surreptitiously distributed newsletters called *samizdat*, he and other dissidents sought to tell the story of what was actually playing out in the Soviet Union and its satellite states.

Addressing readers both in the West and behind the Iron Curtain, Havel observed that, "because the regime is captive to its own lies, it must falsify everything." But lies are delicate structures, he wrote:

> For the crust presented by the life of lies is made of strange stuff. As long as it seals off hermetically the entire society, it appears to be made of stone. But the moment someone breaks through in one place, when one person cries out, "The emperor is naked!"—when a single person breaks the rules of the game, thus exposing it as a game—everything suddenly appears in another light and the whole crust seems then to be made of a tissue on the point of tearing and disintegrating uncontrollably.

Disintegrating the crust has historically been the work of journalists, writers, and artists. Dissidents like Havel wrote plays in which thinly veiled characters acted out the crimes of the state and the vacuousness of life in a cruel government bureaucracy. In modern Russia, musicians have played a role in speaking truth to power, with members of the band Pussy Riot even serving prison time for performing a song about Russian President Vladimir Putin. Art can convey truths that a repressive state won't allow in the official record.

Today nearly everyone has a sophisticated audio and video recording device in their pocket, and the work of witness is shared among the citizenry. Truth can be conveyed in cell-phone footage, not just in official media reports.

At the Delaney Hall ICE detention center, one dedicated chronicler is Sister Susan Francois, who lives nearby in a convent run by the Congregation of the Sisters of St. Joseph of Peace. Most weekends she swipes open her Android phone, pulls up TikTok, and tells the stories of the indignities, such as those perpetrated by an especially capricious guard whom the volunteers have nicknamed "Mr. Sunshine."

When Mr. Sunshine denied entry to a woman trying to visit a family member for not being early enough, Sister Susan reported on it to her TikTok audience. "I saw her drop to her knees literally in prayer and supplication with her arms outstretched praying to God for mercy," she told her viewers. "Unfortunately today mercy was not provided by that guard."

One morning in August, two girls, ages eight and fifteen, arrived at Delaney Hall on their own, hoping to see their father, who was behind the concrete walls. The sisters had come to see him one last time before he was slated to be deported back to Ecuador. Their mother couldn't come because she was at work, cleaning restaurants on weekends to make rent. Mr. Sunshine turned the girls away.

"Nah, you're not coming in today," the guard barked at Stephanie Campos, a volunteer with Eyes on ICE, who had chaperoned the girls on prior weekends. "You came in with three kids yesterday. Now you're coming in with these kids. No, I don't like this. You're not coming in."

As a bilingual volunteer, Campos sometimes accompanies children who arrive alone. Campos is an anthropologist who did her PhD dissertation on a women's prison in Peru, so she is familiar with issues related to families and incarceration. And as a daughter of Peruvian immigrants, she also understands the immigrant experience in America. She has a day job, but with her adult children now grown and out of the house, she has time to spend weekends volunteering at Delaney Hall.

Campos knew that fighting Mr. Sunshine was usually not worth it. She tried briefly to explain to the guard that the girls' mother was working, but he cut her off. "Well, she should have taken the day off."

Retreating to the sidewalk cluster of volunteers, Campos burst into tears. When she had composed herself, she sent texts to all her local immigrant rights group chats with a request: She needed a Latino man who could volunteer to act as if he was a relative of the girls. A fellow volunteer recruited a Peruvian man who lived a short drive away.

The Peruvian man agreed to meet Campos and the volunteer down the street, away from the detention center. When he arrived, her heart sank. He was light skinned. The girls were darker skinned. But it would have to do.

They workshopped his story: He was to say he was the girls' uncle who had come to America at seven years old and hadn't been in touch with the family but had showed up now because it was an emergency. "Just walk straight to the girls, don't talk to the volunteers," Campos advised him.

Mr. Sunshine was skeptical. He wanted to interview the girls on their own. But the "uncle" was adamant: These children were minors. They would not talk to him unaccompanied. Mr. Sunshine backed off.

Hiding behind the nearby bushes, Campos watched the girls waiting in line. When they finally walked through the gates of the detention center, she again began to cry—deep relief.

Campos often repeats the words of one of her heroes, the medical anthropologist Paul Farmer, who explained why he kept going amid setbacks while fighting infectious disease among the world's poorest people. "We want to be on the winning team, but at the risk of turning our backs on the losers, no, it's not worth it," Farmer said. "So you fight the long defeat."

It is a fight that can be excruciating. Sometimes it takes Campos days to recover and refortify her emotional reserves after a weekend of chaperoning children into Delaney Hall. But she tries to savor each win.

"We're going to lose a lot in this fight," she says. "But they didn't lose the opportunity to see their dad one last time. They didn't lose their opportunity to say goodbye."

Then she began to weep.

3

———

Look for Your Options

When Doors Are Closing Fast,
Try to Wedge One Open

ON MONDAY, MAY 31, 2021, two heavyset men wearing suits boarded a plane that was preparing to take off from Pulkovo Airport in Saint Petersburg, Russia, en route to Warsaw. Once onboard, the men conferred quietly with a flight attendant, who frantically switched on the public address system and, after a moment of static silence, made an announcement: "Passenger Pivovarov, please come to the front of the plane."

Andrei Pivovarov, a former leader of the pro-democracy opposition group Open Russia, had just downloaded a movie to his laptop for the flight. Set to announce his run in the upcoming parliamentary elections, Pivovarov had booked the Warsaw trip to clear his head and calm his nerves ahead of what promised to be a risky campaign.

As Pivovarov approached the cockpit, the men reached into their pockets, revealing a pair of matching badges: they were FSB, agents of Russia's secret police. "You are on the federal wanted list," they told Pivovarov. "There is no use resisting."

Pivovarov was marched off the plane and eventually charged by Russian prosecutors with carrying out activities on behalf of an "undesirable organization." As evidence, the government presented thirty-four posts on Pivovarov's Facebook page, which included information about opposition candidates running in the upcoming municipal elections.

He was sentenced to four years and sent to Russia's northwest region to serve his time in a notorious prison: Penal Colony No. 7.

The Politics of Fear

"Russia isn't as oppressive as people imagine," says Maria Kuznetsova, who worked with Pivovarov before his arrest. "It mostly runs on fear."

By the numbers, Kuznetsova is right. Seven countries have a political prisoner population at least twice the size of Russia's. And nine other countries appear before Russia in the world rankings for political prisoners per capita. In Russia, one in nearly 193,000 people is a political prisoner, a small number relative to the country's vast population. Today a Russian citizen is nineteen times more likely to die in a car crash than to be jailed on politically motivated charges.

And yet the message gets across. Since Vladimir Putin's return to the presidency in 2012, the Kremlin has relied on a relatively inexpensive set of tactics to cause millions of citizens to think twice about breaking with the regime—part of a strategy dubbed by Vladimir Gel'man, a political scientist and former Russian democratic activist, as "the politics of fear." Evolving from the late Soviet strategy based on "monitoring disloyalty among the country's citizens and on intimidating those who manifested it," Gel'man writes, the Putin regime blends well-publicized intimidation and public discrediting of the Kremlin's opponents with selective persecution.

The state's logic is straightforward: "They basically make an example in each industry," Kuznetsova says.

It doesn't take many cases to create an environment in which ordinary citizens question everything. The Russian government began arresting and prosecuting protesters after clashes with police during demonstrations in Moscow's Bolotnaya Square in May 2012. What came next was a series of repressive laws, passed under the cover of protecting law enforcement and preventing violence.

The laws focused on undermining the financing of oppositional nonprofit organizations, an effort the Kremlin wrapped in allegations of supporting violence, as well as on new consequences for holding rallies and public actions. Soon three top campaign associates of the Putin rival Alexei Navalny were accused of financial crimes under the new laws, and one was forced to flee Russia. And in February 2015, two days before planned anti-Putin marches, the Russian opposition leader Boris Nemtsov was assassinated under mysterious circumstances in Moscow.

The combined effect was to create an environment in which ordinary citizens came to understand that taking even small risks could have enormous personal consequences—inside or outside the law.

Over time the politics of fear has bled beyond the letter of the law and into Russia's social fabric. At universities, for example, students and faculty can file reports about behavior they deem not sufficiently patriotic—a formal process known as "denunciation." According to the independent human rights watchdog OVD-Info, denunciations have emerged as a "systematic tool of coercion" since Russia's invasion of Ukraine in 2022 and are often facilitated formally by university administrators. A 2025 survey found that while fewer than two in ten Russian students personally knew someone who had been subject to denunciation, more than six in ten said they were afraid to share their views on their campus.

The war also gave the Kremlin a pretext to expand the scope of repressive laws and pass new ones under the cloak of national security. They included a law allowing the government to seize property from anyone who publicly broke with the state's narrative on the war; a law requiring the registration of all Telegram channels with over ten thousand people, which would inhibit digital organizing and mass communication; and a law making the spread of "fake news" about the army an act of extremism.

Fear, a high-leverage investment, is cheap to produce. It creates a threat that, even if only implied, is foundational. This threat supports a sweeping infrastructure of fear that lives between the lines and is often enforced outside the legal system.

"Modern autocrats have no need to rely on massive repression as a means of maintaining their dominance," Gel'man writes. Fear does most of the work.

"Fear in Your Kitchen"

Raised in a working-class family in an industrial Siberian city, Kuznetsova moved to Moscow in 2016 to attend university. There she became active in Russian politics, eventually working with Pivovarov to support independent candidates across Russia in the run-up to Russia's 2020 local and regional elections.

Kuznetsova was arrested for activism often—five times in 2020 alone, she estimates. In July of that year, a few days after the passage of a constitutional referendum allowing Putin to remain president until 2036, she was detained in the offices of Open Russia with Pivovarov and held for almost ten hours. She was held again later that year in a hotel lobby in the far eastern city of Khabarovsk after taking part in antigovernment protests.

"Fun times," Kuznetsova jokes.

The frequent confrontations with the security police served as a kind of exposure therapy. Kuznetsova knew she wasn't breaking any laws, and she was always released in the end. Of course, not everyone who interacted with the security police walked away unscathed. She had heard horror stories from friends about encounters that had resulted in physical battery, sexual assault, or imprisonment.

But whenever she was released, Kuznetsova felt emboldened, even obligated, to use her safety as a down payment on more dissent. "The system of fear works just for a moment, for the first time," she recalls. "Then you realize, 'Oh, it was just fear.'"

———

In early 2021, Kuznetsova began hearing rumors that the Russian president was planning big changes. She had sensed a shift in the tenor of politics. Strange signals had begun to emerge—repressive measures that felt disproportionate and extreme even for Putin's Russia. The cost of dissent seemed to be rising.

On January 17, the FSB detained Putin arch-opponent Alexei Navalny at Moscow's Sheremetyevo International Airport. Pivovarov was removed from the Warsaw flight about five months later. Both men had been planning to run in the upcoming parliamentary elections. Both received trumped-up charges. Putin was picking off his rivals one by one, neutering the opposition in the lead-up to the war.

Every day, the crackdown appeared to get closer and closer to Kuznetsova. Police carried out raids in the Open Russia offices, seizing megaphones and laptops. Then they searched her central Moscow apartment, leaving her roommates spooked. Kuznetsova began having panic attacks whenever she stepped into the Moscow Metro. This time her fear was warranted.

Back in Siberia, her family was getting worried. The execution of Kuznetsova's great-grandfather in the 1930s during Stalin's purges had left a family wound that never fully healed. Her mother knew her activist daughter wouldn't give up politics entirely, but she pleaded with her to take a step back. Maybe, she suggested to her daughter, it was safer to stop writing to Pivovarov in detention; the correspondence could draw unwanted attention.

"That's not prohibited, even in Russia!" Kuznetsova protested over the phone one afternoon. This fact did little to ease her mom's concerns.

Pivovarov's family also adapted to the times. His mother's social circles had shrunk considerably by the time her son was apprehended at the Saint Petersburg airport, Pivovarov recalls.

"It's fear in your kitchen," he says of the political realities that lead some Russians to withdraw into a smaller life. "That's the kind of fear that spreads."

Deeper than Any Law

The mood was dark in Penal Colony No. 7. Pivovarov had been sentenced to total isolation for his first three months. In the evenings his mind would race through the rumors that authorities planned to manufacture new criminal charges and extend his sentence indefinitely.

In the mornings, a camera surveilled him from the mandated 5:00 a.m. wake-up time. Not being out of bed by 5:01 a.m. was considered a violation. Even a single button open on his prison uniform was a violation that threatened to add time to his sentence and prolong his three-month stay in isolation.

Pivovarov assessed his options. In Penal Colony No. 7, prisoners were disenfranchised, and yet in a sense, so were the colony's staff, who were tiny sprockets in the boundless machinery of the state. Pivovarov, by contrast, was one of the highest-profile political prisoners in the country. Any news about his detention would surely travel up through various levels of administration, first to the prosecutor's office that oversaw the penal colony and then all the way to Moscow.

"They don't like it when there's a lot of attention on them," Pivovarov observed of the prison staff. He resolved to make noise, to cause some bureaucratic headaches, and began by contesting one of his citations. It was a gamble: If he won, his conditions might improve. If he lost, who knew what fresh sanctions awaited him?

The bet paid off. One day Pivovarov was called to the warden's office. "Why are you complaining, Andrei?" the warden asked. Pivovarov explained his concern that he would be left in these isolating conditions beyond the mandated three months. His appeals, he told the warden, were a bargaining position. But he would call them off if his conditions improved.

The warden looked Pivovarov in the eye. "When the three months are over, I'll transfer you," he said. "I promise."

—

Inner freedom has long been a tool of survival for people living under repressive conditions.

The Black Christian theologian Howard Thurman, whose work on spiritual discipline influenced the leaders of the U.S. civil rights movement, grew up in the American South at the start of the twentieth century. Later in life, in his travels to other parts of the world—to colonies like Burma and India, where he met nonviolent leaders who were living as British subjects, including Gandhi and the Nobel Prize–winning Bengali poet and activist Rabindranath Tagore—Thurman came to believe that at the heart of all freedom is the idea that people always have options, even when they can't act on them.

In 1976, he was invited to deliver a lecture at the University of Redlands in Southern California, where he demonstrated his point with a story from his childhood.

Once, as a boy in Florida, he went for a walk in the woods

with his older sister. The young Thurman felt, as younger siblings often do, that his sister was always trying to control him. So when he spotted a baby snake in the woods, he saw an opportunity to demonstrate his independence. Knowing how she felt about anything that slithered, Thurman stopped to point out the critter. His sister reacted predictably. Then, to show her that he was not afraid,

> I put one of my feet on top of this little creature and the weight of my body made it impossible for him to move. Then I felt a series of simple, quiet, rhythmic spasms under my foot. The snake couldn't move, but he could do this wiggle. He kept alive the sense of option.

For Thurman, the snake offered a parable on the nature of freedom. The dark magic of "all dictatorships, all tyrants," the theologian argued from the lectern, is to make ordinary people feel as if they have less and less space to maneuver. In a society facing repression, pathways always seem to be disappearing, one's options constantly shrinking. It can feel as if there is no turn left to make and no place left to go. Fear makes a person feel stuck.

This civic claustrophobia is why freedom struggles so often take up the language of enclosure and encroachment. In the United States, these calls have risen out of diverse traditions and contexts. Delegates at the Continental Congress raised a yellow flag with a coiled snake to caution the British crown not to "tread" on the rights of the colonists. Some two centuries later, Black activists in the United States seized on the dying words of the Staten Island man Eric Garner as a rallying cry against police brutality and ongoing racial inequality in America: "I can't breathe."

Thurman often used a similar language of constraint, addressing his writings on liberation to people, both at home and abroad, who lived "with their backs against the wall." But by focusing on options, the theologian was also challenging oppressed people to derive their sense of possibility not from the conditions imposed on them by governments, but from what they knew innately was compatible with the human spirit.

Luther E. Smith Jr., a professor emeritus at Emory University's Candler School of Theology, has researched Thurman's life and writings. "For Thurman, there's a freedom you experience that's deeper than any law," Smith says. "You experience it as you're about to head out of the church or head out of your home, onto the protest line—and you're already free in that sense."

In other words, no autocrat, no colonist, and no president can make a living being abandon their deepest sense of right and wrong. In Thurman's understanding, if authoritarianism is an ever-narrowing line of vision, freedom is a sweeping horizon that can be accessed with only a little more space, an unlocked door, or a few more options.

———

Pivovarov now had a few more options. The warden had capitulated, and things were better in the new section—marginally. He now received an allowance of 2,000 rubles, which he could spend each day in the prison shop. Part of the first 2,000 rubles went to buying lemons, in the hope that the vitamin C would boost his immune system after many months confined indoors.

But some prison privileges remained strictly off-limits. Pivovarov and his longtime partner, Tatiana Usmanova, had never married, and though they had built a life together, their partnership was not recognized by the state. As a result, Pivovarov was prohibited from calling her, and she from visiting him in prison.

But he had received a letter from Usmanova during his first days in the penal colony that included a pamphlet on the procedures for getting married in prison. Aware that the colony administration had been known to react to pressure, Pivovarov put in a request to prison officials that he be allowed to marry, while Usmanova worked with lawyers to press their case from the outside. But officials stonewalled.

There were other problems, too. The official television set in his new barrack, controlled by the colony administration, had been programmed to tune in to nothing but sports. Pivovarov longed for any word from outside the walls of Penal Colony No. 7. Sensing that he may have already used up his complaints, he would have to try another tactic, play a different card.

An opportunity came one afternoon when a prison inspector came by his cell on routine rounds. The regular check-ins had begun after Pivovarov demonstrated his willingness to complain to the risk-averse prison staff. The inspector wanted to know whether the prisoner had any complaints.

There was one thing, Pivovarov said politely. Without access to the news channels, he had no way to follow the Russian army's invasion of Ukraine. "I would like to be given more information about the progress of the special military operation announced by our President Vladimir Putin," he told the inspector, careful to invoke the government's official language for the invasion.

That's how Andrei Pivovarov got his own TV set.

———

In the late summer of 2023, more than a year into his sentence in the penal colony, Pivovarov was mopping the floor of his cell during a mandatory cleaning hour when an officer said to follow him. They marched a few minutes to the prison administration building, where he was left to wait alone in a sparse room.

In the hallway outside he heard a familiar voice. It was Tatiana, his partner, walking briskly with a prison-ordered wedding officiant. "Andrei never officially proposed to me," she later recalled in an interview with Holod, an independent Russian news outlet. "We discussed the wedding in the form of 'we need to solve this problem.'"

They were married in a cavernous prison commissary. The

bride wore a white flowing cotton dress with long billowing sleeves. The groom donned his prison uniform. They held each other in a long embrace, their first in over a year. The whole affair lasted less than ten minutes.

When Pivovarov returned to his cell, a guard handed him a mop.

"I came back," he recalls, "and there was still time for cleaning."

A Way in Your Mind

Pivovarov is no longer in Penal Colony No. 7. In the early hours of August 1, 2024, he was awakened by the warden and told to pack his things. On a plane several hours later, in the airspace between Russia and Turkey, Pivovarov learned that he had been included in a prisoner swap between his home country and the United States—the largest such exchange since the Cold War. As part of the deal, he says, he was banned from returning to his homeland.

Kuznetsova left Russia, too. In April 2021, she reached a breaking point and moved west to Georgia, the destination of many opposition activists amid the prewar crackdown. She didn't stop in Siberia to see her family. "I thought it would be for a few months," she says. Then Russia invaded Ukraine.

Kuznetsova has never gone home. In May 2025, she graduated with a master's degree from Harvard University's Kennedy

School of Government. She says she is at peace with her decisions. "I saw people pretend everything was okay," Kuznetsova remembers of her activism in Russia. "It eats them alive. They feel powerless. They also feel like they're betraying something inside them."

She shrugs: "Better to participate than pretend not to be alive."

Pivovarov has started a new life in Berlin, where he is helping to build a Russian civil society in exile. He makes social media videos addressing conservative Russians who may have become disenchanted with the human and economic toll of the Ukraine War and rampant corruption in the army's upper ranks. He says he is filling a gap in the information space, giving voice to a narrative he believes many in Russia feel but can't voice out of fear of meeting his own fate.

Despite Russia's continued descent into even more centralized rule, Pivovarov still hopes to return and help steer the nation toward democracy. "Maybe it's strange, but I really believe that in the future I'll come back to Russia."

Strange, perhaps, coming from someone else. But from the political prisoner who searched for a door still barely cracked, then wedged it open to escape solitary confinement, it sounds more like a promise.

"You have to create your way in mind," Pivovarov says. Focus on your options, he says, and "a person can do anything."

4

Practice and Prepare

Resistance Takes Discipline,
Training, and a Plan

It was only after the masked figures drove off that Mike Mathis realized they had been parked in front of his house all day.

It was a brisk afternoon in late March 2025. Mathis, a software engineer, was working in his home office on the second floor of his townhouse on a quiet block of Somerville, Massachusetts, just outside of Boston. At about 5:30 p.m., he finished his workday and wandered downstairs.

That's when he noticed the lights flashing outside. He peered out the window. Police cars were lining the street. When he opened his front door, there was his neighbor, giving a statement to the Somerville police.

The neighbor had witnessed a kidnapping, he said. In broad daylight. Right there, in front of the house. "We think we know what happened," Mathis recalls the officers saying. "But we're trying to get the stories of what people saw."

Mathis had moved to Somerville a few years before, and he and his wife had grown fond of their neighborhood. The restaurant life was vibrant and the leafy streets were calm, their stillness broken only by the occasional traffic accident. Sometimes a car sped down the hill past the speed limit, taking the turn too wide and sideswiping cars parked on the street in front of the Mathis residence. It had happened twice in recent months.

He had installed a security camera to catch the next hit-and-run on film. Standing on his porch, watching the police lights glow against the tree-lined street, he wondered whether the camera had picked something up. Mathis stepped back inside, sat down at his computer, and uploaded the security camera footage.

5:15 p.m.: A young woman in a white puffer jacket is walking down the street and talking on her phone when six figures emerge from the periphery and surround her. All of them wear street clothes—hoodies, sunglasses, baseball caps. Several have pulled neck gaiters over their faces. For a moment, the young woman seems to protest. Then the masked figures place her in handcuffs and lead her into a black sport utility vehicle parked nearby.

Mathis played the footage again. Then again. "I was confused. I didn't know what I was looking at," Mathis reflected later. "It looked frightening."

He scrolled back even further—an hour, then two hours, then more. The figures had arrived early in the morning and had spent the day camped out on the street in two separate unmarked vehicles.

The whole thing was disorienting. What he had captured on camera wasn't clear. But he had observed the political environment in the United States darken in recent weeks amid threats by the newly inaugurated president. He had heard when Tom Homan, the tough-talking "border czar," threatened to bring immigration raids to Boston. "I'm bringing hell with me," Homan had vowed.

Mathis had caught a glimpse of this promised hell. He uploaded the footage to the websites of two local television stations and sent it to the generic email address listed on his congresswoman's website.

He awoke the next day to a media firestorm. Journalists had identified the woman as a Tufts University graduate student, Rümeysa Öztürk, who was in the country on a student visa from Turkey. The State Department had revoked Öztürk's visa without notice, apparently because she had coauthored an op-ed in the university newspaper urging Tufts administrators to "meaningfully engage" with calls to divest from companies tied to Israel.

The doctoral student had been taken into detention by agents of U.S. Immigration and Customs Enforcement. And Mathis had provided the nation with its first glance of a future the president's supporters had been waiting for.

"It's just kind of an odd feeling," Mathis recalls. "Like, is this actually happening?"

It was happening right there, in front of his house: A Somerville neighbor had been snatched by masked agents and spirited off to an out-of-state detention center without any due process. And now people could see it happening on news websites, social media feeds, and television channels around the world.

What Did People Do?

When the news came that the U.S. government had begun arresting students who were involved in pro-Palestinian activism, Nadje Al-Ali was out of the country visiting her elderly mother.

She had feared this might happen. A professor at Brown University, Al-Ali has spent her career studying the challenges faced by women across the Middle East. Numbered among her scholarly works are articles on feminist mobilization and gender-based violence in Egypt, Iraq, Turkey, and Lebanon, as well as essays on the Kurdish region.

In the winter of 2023, Al-Ali had stepped in to support student demonstrators at Brown who were facing legal action after refusing to leave a university building. The Hamas attack on Israel earlier that year, on October 7, had killed some 1,200 people, with more than 250 taken hostage, and was followed by an Israeli military response that would stretch over the next two years and leave more than 70,000 people in Gaza dead. The protesting students had called on the university to support a ceasefire and to divest its endowment from companies that they said "enabled war crimes in Gaza."

Al-Ali often disagreed with the students' protest tactics. "On both sides, there are things that I find too crude and not nuanced enough," Al-Ali says of the campus protesters. But the professor felt that the undergraduates had been acting within their constitutional rights. "I wanted to support students' ability to do activism on campus and not be punished for it, as long as it is not any kind of hate speech or violence."

Al-Ali is not a citizen of the United States. She holds a green card. So she took note in January 2025 when the new administration issued a warning to noncitizens who had taken part in pro-Palestinian campus activism: "We will find you, and we will deport you." Sitting in Europe, it struck her that the White House had made good on its promise.

Al-Ali cut her travel in Europe short. Concerned that her support for campus activists and causes might trigger alarms at passport control, she contacted an immigration lawyer to track her return flight. She arrived home without issue, but her reality had changed.

The White House was punishing people like her. All of her professional commitments, she felt, would have to be reconsidered, measured against a dark new standard: Could they make her a target for deportation?

By late March, the nation had seen a series of graduate

students and scholars arrested, incarcerated, denied entry to the country, or deported from the United States. Many were of Muslim or Arab descent, and some had expressed pro-Palestinian views. Then came the video of Öztürk, disappeared by masked agents on the basis of an op-ed. Like Öztürk, Al-Ali had been written up on a website claiming to monitor media and academia for "anti-Israel bias." She considered changing the route she took to get to work.

One by one, Al-Ali took commitments off her calendar. Months earlier she had begun work on an article examining and critiquing the role of gender in the experiences of women living under both Israeli occupation and Hamas rule. That would have to go back on the shelf. More travel was on her docket—a fellowship in Beirut and then a research visit to Baghdad. She canceled both. Then there was the matter of the annual Middle Eastern Studies Association (MESA) conference. Since coming to Brown in 2019, Al-Ali had almost never missed a MESA gathering. But that now felt like a soft target for ICE. She decided to skip it.

"It really had a detrimental impact on my ability to engage in research and focus," Al-Ali recalls. Weeks into the new climate, her life in academia had changed beyond recognition. And she wasn't alone. Thousands of others at American universities were now thinking twice about what they wrote and what they said—the very work of academia.

———

It was all too familiar.

The daughter of a German mother and an Iraqi father, Al-Ali had come of age in a postwar Germany that was reckoning with the complicity of ordinary people in its recent past. "The Holocaust and Nazi Germany were really so much a part of my consciousness, this idea of 'what did people do?'" she says.

Her father's side had tasted tyranny, too. Relatives in Iraq lived in fear of being picked up on the street and disappeared by the Ba'ath regime. In 1980, her uncle, Majid, was executed for his defiance of Saddam Hussein.

So by the time she got the call from the president of MESA asking whether she would consider testifying in a federal court case challenging the White House policy of ideological deportation, Al-Ali felt that she didn't have much of a choice. The pressure came not from the MESA colleague, but from within. "I never want to be that person who is silent and thereby complicit," she says. "It didn't take me long to know deep inside that I needed to do it."

She was taking a risk. The government's trial attorneys had refused to swear off witness retaliation, and the professor's imagination was dense with dark scenarios: detention, green card revocation, and deportation all seemed within the realm of the possible. She told her real estate agent to prepare to sell her house in the event she had to leave. "I was scared," she says.

But history weighed on her. "It's now normal that there are masked men and women on the street picking up migrants. It's now normal that the government can interfere in university business," she says. "What I'm more scared of than being thrown in prison or deported is normalizing all this."

Al-Ali called up a couple of close friends on the Brown faculty for a gut check. They were encouraging. Her final call was to a lawyer with the Knight First Amendment Institute, the free speech legal team that had agreed to take on the professors' case.

She had never before taken the stand at a trial. The little she knew of depositions was from the movies. But she would do it, she said, on one condition: The legal team had to do everything possible to make sure she was prepared.

How do you prepare to do something that could very well go wrong—and change your life forever?

You Control the Rhythm

The September 19, 1960, issue of *Life* magazine devoted eight full pages to the civil rights struggle that was roiling the United States. The text of the article was brief; the photos did most of the talking. One portrait in the spread is especially striking: It depicts three Black men in starched white button-down shirts. Two of them lean in toward the head of the third, blowing a cloud of cigarette smoke into his face. They were preparing for the Nashville sit-ins.

By the fall of 1960, the nation had gotten a taste of the nonviolent direct action that would come to define the next decade of social change. Lunch counter protests in Southern cities had arrived earlier that year, drawing national attention to the daily realities of racial discrimination and helping to desegregate many commercial businesses across the South.

But for millions of Americans, the sit-ins hit like a bolt of electricity. The nation watched the young people staying exquisitely, almost preternaturally still as restaurant patrons smeared them with food, verbally assaulted them, and in some cases beat them until they bled.

Like any shrewd strategic act, civil disobedience campaigns generally come as a surprise to their targets. For the media, government, restaurant owners, and the general public, the sit-ins appeared almost spontaneous.

But the *Life* images showed what should have been obvious to any onlooker: that these actions were planned and practiced; that precious few acts of extraordinary political courage happen in a vacuum; and that a deliberate methodology must have been used to enable hundreds of people to do something so unnatural to all human beings.

Among the chief architects of that methodology was James Lawson, a Methodist minister who in 1959 began holding nonviolence workshops every Tuesday night in the basement of a Nashville church.

A conscientious objector during the Korean War, Lawson had spent a year in prison for refusing military service. He later made his way to India, where he worked as a teacher and missionary for three years while studying the movement for Indian independence. Returning to the United States, Lawson had felt a "call" to bring what he'd learned of Gandhian nonviolence to the struggle for Black freedom.

Lawson's trainees had never experienced anything quite like the Tuesday night workshops. He taught about the history of nonviolence, Christian pacifism, and Eastern philosophy. But he also focused on pragmatic matters, like the importance of sitting up straight during sit-ins and how to get out of town after a protest.

Role-play exercises were key. Trainees would simulate day-of actions, taking turns acting as either the protesters or their harassers. Those playing the role of antagonist might shout racial slurs at the demonstrators, force them off their stools, or even drop ashes in their hair. Lawson believed that if activists could realistically face the challenges in the offing, they would be able to endure greater pressure during the protest itself. "Try to feel the person you're playing," he would instruct his students.

Over time the teacher transformed the church basement into a spiritual and practical training ground, the type of space the sociologist Aldon Morris calls a "movement halfway house": Pews were not pews, but lunch counters. The team was not a group of activists, but part of a "soul force" ordained by divine providence.

"We had a nonviolent academy equivalent to West Point," said the activist Bernard Lafayette—who, as a student, participated in Lawson's early sessions—in the 2000 documentary short *Nashville: We Were Warriors.*

Nadine Bloch, a strategic nonviolent action trainer who collaborated with Lawson in the mid-2000s, has brought the model of role-play exercises pioneered in Nashville to workshops on at least five continents; participants range from sex workers advocating for their rights in Brazil to activists fighting a repressive regime in Myanmar. Bloch compares practice runs to the kind of training required of firefighters and other first responders.

"If we're serious about people power and nonviolent resistance, we are going to train ourselves and prepare ourselves," says Bloch, who is a director with Beautiful Trouble, an organization that trains political activists around the world in creative protest tactics. "It gives us information about what works and what doesn't, and it prepares ourselves, not just as individuals, but as a community to understand roles and responsibilities."

What comes of the exercises is a group not ignorant to threats—whether a burning building or searing social tensions—but better able to tamp down the feelings of anxiety and focus on the work at hand.

"People feel much more prepared," Bloch says. "Practicing doing the things that you think you might encounter really can give you a way to manage your own fear."

—

On the afternoon before she took the stand against the government of the United States, Nadje Al-Ali was sitting on a sofa in a Boston Hyatt surrounded by twelve attorneys who were all pretending they were in a federal courtroom. If not for their Sunday casual attire and the minimalist hotel furniture, you might have even believed them.

"You want to make sure your witness feels comfortable enough that they can tell their story honestly and directly," recalls Ramya Krishnan, a senior staff attorney with the Knight Institute who served as lead counsel in the case. "One of the most important things that we seek to do through preparation is to ensure that [the people testifying] aren't taken by surprise."

For four hours, the lawyers ran Al-Ali through what seemed like every conceivable scenario that might emerge at trial. They practiced her answers to each question, then revised them, then practiced again. The climax of the day came when a fast-talking litigator on the Knight team stood up to play the Department of Justice attorney who would cross-examine Al-Ali the next day.

The questions came at her, rapid and nasty: *Professor Al-Ali, are you aware of reports that you have abetted antisemitism? Do you believe women are better off under Hamas?* The questions—delivered at a pace that might throw her off—were designed to cast the professor as an extremist and force her into a defensive posture.

They did throw her off. So the Knight Institute litigator broke the fourth wall and paused to offer some friendly advice: *You don't have to answer the questions at the same tempo they come to you*, he said. *You control the rhythm.*

It had been like this for weeks, one prep after another, in person and over video. The sessions had not vanquished Al-Ali's fears; at night she still endlessly perused the documents on the court docket. But the uncertainty she had felt earlier had been replaced by a quiet confidence—the product of good counsel, thorough preparation, and a growing sense of where she fit in the lawsuit's strategy.

One of the goals of the lawsuit, says Krishnan, was "forcing the government to have to explain what it is doing, to answer questions, to reveal to the public what is being done in their name."

There was only one real way to achieve that: by showing the specific ways in which the ideological deportation policy had harmed real people. And real people—living, breathing noncitizens—would have to take the stand.

"Without them," Krishan says, "there is no case."

A Very Specific Task

On the morning of her testimony, Al-Ali arrived early at the John Joseph Moakley Courthouse of the U.S. District Court in Boston, a stone's throw from the city's storied harbor.

She walked through the lobby, a canyon of red brick and speckled granite, passing under the wood-paneled X-ray machine. She passed a genial guard in a bulky bulletproof vest.

At the end of the hall, she hit the elevator call button, and it glowed white. As she waited, she caught a glimpse of one more face in the alcove, a photograph inside a mahogany frame. Narrowed eyes, straight-on scowl. It was a photograph of the man whose administration she had come to testify against: the forty-seventh president of the United States.

Al-Ali could see the strategy and understood her role in fulfilling it. This wasn't about beating back the winds of authoritarianism on her own or confronting the echoes of her family's past. All she had to do was talk and tell the truth. That was one discrete job, a manageable project.

"I was scared, but I also felt focused," Al-Ali recalls. "I was doing a very specific task—and that felt good."

———

She was in her office on campus when the texts started coming, first from a Knight Institute lawyer, then from friends who had seen the news: Judge William G. Young of the U.S. District Court for the District of Massachusetts had ruled that the government had used the threat of deportation to silence noncitizens on campuses across America who spoke out in support of Palestinians. They had won.

Young's ruling characterized the administration policy as a "full-throated assault on the First Amendment," describing the ideological deportation issue as "perhaps the most important ever to fall within the jurisdiction of this district court." The case, the Ronald Reagan appointee wrote, "squarely presents the issue whether non-citizens lawfully present here in [the] United States actually have the same free speech rights as the rest of us."

Young determined that they do—and that the professors had shown that the policy violated their constitutional rights in real and meaningful ways. The testimony of Nadje Al-Ali, he declared, was a window into the profound impact of the threat of ideological deportation on a noncitizen's protected speech.

Between meetings and classes, Al-Ali didn't have time right then to read the 161-page ruling. It wasn't until she got home later that evening that she finally sat down on her bed and opened her laptop. She read carefully, highlighting passages in yellow as she scrolled through the PDF.

At the end of the document, the judge posed a question. The president "believes the American people are so divided that today they will *not* stand up, fight for, and defend our most precious constitutional values so long as they are lulled into thinking their own personal interests are not affected," the judge wrote. "Is he correct?"

II

On Finding Your People

5

Make a Minyan

Find a Political Home

PATRICE LAWRENCE HAD BEEN LIVING undocumented in the United States for years when a childhood friend made a suggestion: "There's someone you need to talk to."

A student visa had brought Lawrence from Jamaica to study political science and government at a small college on the East Coast. But sometime after graduation she had become "out of status." The intervening years were a maze of anxieties and impossible choices, her immigration status looming over nearly every aspect of her daily life.

Ordinary events were a nightmare: signing up for a bank account, getting a driver's license, filling out forms. Even working was a risk. The public policy jobs for which Lawrence had studied required authorization from the federal government. But without the right documentation, she made her way as a tutor and babysitter. She was working as a nanny when the friend of a friend called.

"I thought she had a brother for me to marry," Lawrence jokes. Instead, she soon found herself on the phone with another young woman—also undocumented, also from the Caribbean. The woman wanted to pitch Lawrence on an idea: establishing a network for people like them who had come from the same region and were now moving through the same struggles, so they could navigate those struggles together.

It wasn't that Lawrence opposed the idea. She just found it difficult to compute. Long ago, she had trained herself to speak as little as possible about her immigration status. Nothing good ever came of that. Friends and relatives would pelt her with unwanted advice or chastise her about how she'd gotten into this situation in the first place. She went to great lengths to conceal her status: When asked about her family background, Lawrence would demur, careful never to get too specific. She even developed multiple accents in order to toggle between the various territories of her life.

It was a smaller life—one of caution, isolation, and profound limitations. That was what it meant to Lawrence to be undocumented in America: going it alone. "I didn't think of this as a communal problem," she recalls. "I thought of it as a me problem."

But now one of the only other Black undocumented people Lawrence had ever met was on the other end of the phone, talking through an idea that would take shape slowly, over years of conversations. What if there was a gathering? What might it look like for more people like them to meet one another? As Lawrence moved in and out of these discussions with her friend and others, she was troubled by safety concerns. "Aren't we targeting ourselves?" she wondered.

Life continued apace. Lawrence moved to Ohio and took on a new nannying gig. Eventually a concrete plan emerged: Scores of Black undocumented people living across the United States would meet up in Miami. Lawrence still wasn't sure it was a good idea.

A few days before the gathering was to finally take place, another call came—a final nudge from one of her friends in the planning group: "You're coming to Miami, right?"

Lawrence hadn't seen a beach in years. She gave in and booked a flight. She laughs now as she recalls what ultimately pushed her to get on that plane: "It was snowing in Ohio."

Broken, but Not Alone

There's no consensus among the world's ancient religions as to what constitutes a community, but some faith traditions use the prayer quorum as one measure. For the Friday Jummah prayer, for instance, Islam traditionally requires at least three residents—not travelers passing through town, but locals. The Book of Matthew offers Christians a more flexible threshold: the divine dwells "wherever two or three are gathered in my name," a verse often invoked in smaller worship gatherings.

For Jews, the number is ten. A group of ten worshipers, called a *minyan*, is required for public prayer.

It's not that prayer can never happen without a *minyan*. Centuries of Jews have prayed, for example, in transit—the peddler on the road between villages mumbling the words of the morning blessings, or the student tuning out the noise of the subway to make it through the evening prayers as the train hurtles uptown. And in other extenuating circumstances—in famine, in war, under various shades of persecution that make gathering impossible—many have prayed in smaller cohorts, or alone.

But the ideal, according to Jewish law, is clear: There are just some things—the holiest things, the hardest things—that can't be done alone. Without ten, a community cannot perform the call to prayer or read from the Torah scroll. Perhaps most significant, without ten people, a person grieving the death of a loved one can't recite the *kaddish*, the mourner's prayer.

In her 2024 book *The Amen Effect*, Sharon Brous, a prominent American rabbi, raises a natural question about the *minyan* requirement: "Isn't that an unfair burden to place on a mourner? In the midst of your grief, now you have to wake up early, leave work meetings, and fight traffic to join nine other people, some of whom you may not even know, in prayer? Can't I just grieve alone in my home?"

No, Brous says, and explains why a person cannot do any of those things on their own:

Your couch can't say "Amen" to your broken heart.
Your fireplace can't hold your silence, can't hand you a

tissue, and can't bear witness as you struggle and search for and sometimes find comfort in your grief.

Tradition demands that these most important acts happen among a group of people, in the context of community, Brous writes. "The one who suffers is invited, repeatedly, into the recognition: I am broken, but I am not alone."

———

On her first morning in Miami, Patrice Lawrence was listening to people say things out loud that she had only ever said in the safety of her own head, and she couldn't take notes fast enough.

Some presenters were academics. Others were activists. Most of them were undocumented. All were Black. One speaker talked about mental health: *There is a psychological toll of living without papers*, he explained. Lawrence wrote that down. *Being undocumented makes everyday racism even worse*, said another speaker—*like driving while Black, but with an added layer of risk*. She jotted that in her notebook, too.

The real breakthrough came at lunch, over a spread of curry goat, peas, and rice. The room smelled like home. Winding her way through the buffet line, Lawrence started making small talk. But it wasn't the normal kind of small talk. Something had come over her. She felt energized. People shared their immigration status—and so did she. They spoke in their authentic accent—and so did she. No one was lecturing. No one pointed fingers.

Elsewhere, she recalls, "when people asked me about myself, I'd find some way to talk about who I was without talking about who I was." Here, though, over food she loved and sounds she knew, she wasn't posturing. "I could finally breathe."

Lawrence had resigned herself, many years earlier, to a life in the shadow of her status. "I had so much fear and shame and anger and grief inside of me," she remembers. But in the lunch line, those powerful feelings had met their match.

"It was the first time I felt free," she recalls. "I realized I wasn't alone."

Small Circles

What Lawrence had discovered was a political home—the kind of landing place most of us never find.

We exercise, shop for healthy food, and visit the doctor regularly to gird ourselves against health scares—a new diagnosis, a heart attack, an unexpected illness. Personal crises happen, too: A loved one dies, a relationship ends, a job falls through. Most of us do our best to be ready, to be resilient in such moments, relying on personal and perhaps spiritual community to ground us, as well as other practices to protect and promote our mental health. All of it makes us stronger if the bottom falls out of our personal life.

But what can we do when society is spinning out of control? When the world no longer functions as we've known it to? When we can't take for granted long-standing civil and human rights—or when our country lurches toward authoritarianism? In a moment of prolonged and cascading political crises, forgoing political community is like opting to go without health insurance, exercise, or a core group of loved ones. It leaves a massive gap in our personal safety net.

There is a time-worn practice for these circumstances: gathering regularly with a group of like-minded people. Activists around the world offer two reasons—one psychological, one practical—for why this practice can be a hedge against illiberalism.

The first may be more obvious to anyone who has lived in a country that has felt the frigid air of totalitarianism: Repressive leaders move the goalposts of normalcy. Peaceful cities are reframed as "war zones." Activists are cast as terrorists. What was previously profoundly abnormal suddenly seems tolerable, even ordinary—another fixture in the backdrop of daily life.

Organizing within a political home can be a tool of mutual accountability, a way to enlist one another in what the Russian American writer M. Gessen calls "moment(s) of recognition"—reminders from people of shared moral fiber of what is and isn't normal. The goal of these groups isn't to stop having moral collisions, but to have people with whom to process them, to give them structure, and to push back.

The active cohort of Soviet dissidents who eventually

helped topple the Soviet Union's Communist regime never grew much larger than about one thousand committed activists. They gathered around shared interests like poetry and literature, music, playwriting and film, visual art, and philosophy. Amid pervasive government surveillance, these clusters lived and operated across an archipelago of apartments and communal dormitories where friends would meet, share work, and stay when they needed a bed for the night.

"The dissident movement was built on small circles of people who really trusted each other as friends," says Benjamin Nathans, a history professor at the University of Pennsylvania and the author of a book on Soviet dissidents. "That created powerful bonds and loyalties."

Tatsiana Astrouskaya, a historian who has studied Soviet underground culture, found that this social trust had the effect of creating spaces where dissidents could feel safe encouraging each other to get bolder and sharper in their criticism of the communist system. "The quest for individual autonomy, free-thinking, and creative expression, somewhat paradoxically, was often only achievable as a part of a collective undertaking," she writes.

The works that emerged from these circles—poems, plays, and other powerful testimonies to Soviet repression—often made their way out into the broader world, helping to undermine the Soviet Union in the eyes of both the international community and its own citizens.

This is the second reason to find a political home: None

of us can be expected to absorb the shocks of authoritarianism on our own, or to face rapid-fire changes in laws, norms, and institutions alone. Resistance requires risk-taking and strategy, and the best way to nurture noncooperation is to join a group of people who share values and organize together.

In 2021, Félix Maradiaga, a prominent figure in the Nicaraguan opposition, was imprisoned after announcing that he would challenge Daniel Ortega for the presidency. Maradiaga had come to prominence as a vocal critic of Ortega's corrupt practices, like channeling state funds to his family and allies through government contracts and private business ventures.

Maradiaga, who was released from prison in 2023, says that dissent was most difficult for him when he felt like he was doing it alone. "I spoke openly against crony capitalism," he says. "To my surprise, there were very, very few who spoke up." He credits his ability to advocate against Ortega's dictatorship in the years before his imprisonment to the community of support he cultivated—both locally, through family and friends, and globally, through international networks such as the World Liberty Congress, an alliance of pro-democracy activists from authoritarian regimes, including China, Iran, Rwanda, and Russia.

Now living in the United States, Maradiaga, as president of the Congress, leads the organization and helps to train activists fighting authoritarian governments. Among the protest tactics that he teaches, he says, none may be as important as finding your people: "Having a community is a powerful tool of resilience."

A Little More Freedom

Today Patrice Lawrence is the executive director of the UndocuBlack Network, an organization with members in over thirty U.S. states that grew out of the Miami convening. She leads a small staff in advocating for the needs of people like her inside a U.S. immigrant rights movement that she says tended to place Central and South American experiences at the top of its agenda.

The need for a new, dedicated effort became especially clear to Lawrence at the first immigration reform gatherings she attended after her Miami experience. "No one was talking about the countries we come from, the languages we speak, the experiences we're having," Lawrence says of those events. "Now that I knew there were more people like me, I wanted to change that."

The work is not without risk. In 2019, after the U.S. president revoked the legal status of up to ten thousand Liberian refugees, UndocuBlack mounted an aggressive campaign on their behalf. The organization led a coalition in applying pressure on federal lawmakers through civil disobedience actions, lobbying, and even a lawsuit aimed at stopping the president from ending the protections. Ten state attorneys general signed on to an amicus brief.

But inside the halls of Congress, UndocuBlack's leader was negotiating more quietly, drawing on her own experiences to make sure that legislation met the real needs of the kinds of people she had met in the lunch line. "When I sit in that room, I'm never just representing myself," Lawrence says. The woman who had once shared her status with no one was now taking the risk of disclosing it to some of the most powerful people in the country.

It worked. Despite the long odds, the bill passed on December 17, 2019, delivering legal status to thousands of Liberian refugees in the United States.

Through building the network, Lawrence also met lawyers who helped find her own way forward. "I figured out a way that's possible after everyone told me it was impossible," she says. "For so long I have wanted freedom, and I have a little bit more of it now."

The work is different now. The calls she gets from network members are more bitter and more frequent: Someone who can't endure the pressure and has decided to "self-deport." An organizer who is having trouble locating someone who's disappeared into detention. A friend who dutifully showed up for his ICE check-in and left with instructions to return with a list of three countries that would accept him for deportation.

"There are some days I just want to run away," Lawrence says. But it's those days when she is clearest about her mission. "I want to come out on the other side."

6

———

Don't Start from Scratch

Repurpose Your Networks

NEVER ONCE DID DAVID SALAS–DE la Cruz imagine that his appointment to the Rutgers University Senate would change the trajectory of his life.

Faculty governance bodies—where professors share decision-making responsibilities with trustees and administrators—have dwindled in power in recent years. Salas–de la Cruz, an associate professor of chemistry, imagined his appointment would entail some combination of bureaucratic duties alternating between the ceremonial and the administrative.

And for a while, that's what he got. Every other week, two dozen colleagues from across campus—from the medical school to arts and sciences—gathered to discuss a list of mundane issues, like parking on campus or where students could purchase course books. One of Salas–de la Cruz's first assignments was putting together a master calendar on the university website that harmonized the calendars from Rutgers' three campuses. Such was the work of the university senate.

But in February 2025 the tenor of the meetings changed. Conversations became more urgent. No longer did parking and scheduling top the agenda. A national campaign of federal coercion, wielded through university research funding, threatened to undercut professors' research across all disciplines. Salas–de la Cruz saw a crisis unfolding for his students: Without research credentials on their résumés, their careers would stall out. "I'm a dad, you know," Salas–de la Cruz says. "What came to me is, 'I need to protect my students. I need to do something about this.'"

There was no clear path forward. The cuts had triggered a panic at Rutgers, but Salas–de la Cruz quickly understood that something bigger was playing out across higher education. The White House was threatening institutions directly; freezing federal funds, officials reasoned, would force universities to adopt long-sought changes to school policy to align with conservative ideological priorities. Columbia University, with its private endowment of over $16 billion, capitulated quickly to a monitoring and surveillance regime overseeing admissions, campus protests, and even a small university department that studies much of the non-Western world.

It was an extraordinary attack by the federal government on academic freedom, and it had been met with astonishingly little pushback from a powerful higher education institution. Columbia had seemed to respond from a place of vulnerability. "Nobody came to the rescue," Salas–de la Cruz says. Sure enough, the federal government was soon targeting additional institutions, trying to strike "deals" with schools across the country. "I realized that universities are silos," he says.

Those days were dizzying. The chaos on campus was unfolding against the backdrop of other alarming headlines, from immigration raids in U.S. cities to dramatic shifts in American foreign policy. The new president was railing against the North Atlantic Treaty Organization (NATO), the post–World War II alliance between the United States and several European nations that had long served to deter aggression against its individual member states.

One afternoon, when Salas–de la Cruz was attending the American Chemical Society's national conference in San Diego, he went deep down an internet rabbit hole on the history of NATO. "I realized, 'Oh my God, these people share resources. They protect each other,'" he says. "They quickly send messages if something is happening."

Could the same model work for higher education institutions under assault by their own government? Salas–de la Cruz was soon on the phone with Paul Boxer, a Rutgers psychology professor with whom he had worked on the senate calendar project. Realizing that their senate positions afforded them a powerful tool of pushback against government bullying, the pair wrote up an all-for-one-and-one-for-all pledge, modeled after NATO, for the eighteen members of the Big Ten Conference, of which Rutgers is a member.

The Rutgers Resolution was short and sweet, just one page of commitments around a central theme of solidarity: "Whereas, the preservation of one institution's integrity is the concern of all, and an infringement against one member university of the Big Ten shall be considered an infringement against all." The resolution urged the president of Rutgers to propose a "Mutual Academic Defense Compact" to the leaders of the other Big Ten universities, which would require each university to pledge to share legal and financial resources in the event of a political or legal assault on its autonomy.

It passed 62–17 in the Rutgers University Senate and was adopted enthusiastically within weeks by most of the other Big Ten universities. Dozens of other faculty senates around the country also voted to adopt the pledge. As of December 2025, faculty members from more than 175 campuses had joined the movement and set up local campus teams to defend academic freedom. They have formed an organization, Stand Together for Higher Ed, that allows faculty to speak with one voice even when their universities do not; the network has been repurposed into a nationwide movement and a bulwark of faculty organizing and solidarity.

None of the universities had officially adopted the compact by the end of 2025. But while faculty senate votes are more like recommendations than binding policy, the groundswell of support for solidarity generated by these votes had already changed the national conversation about higher education.

In October 2025, when the White House issued letters to nine universities demanding that they commit to its political agenda in exchange for federal dollars, the move was greeted very differently than when Columbia acquiesced earlier in the year. Seven of the universities, including the one Big Ten member on the list, rejected the proposal immediately, and the other two had still not signed when the November deadline passed.

"We started something," Salas–de la Cruz says. "It belongs to everyone now."

A Dramatic Revolution

Campaigns, movements, and political efforts rarely start from scratch. They are built on the foundations of existing relationships, out of groups of people who have known each other in a different context and who decide to repurpose their relationships for a new, higher purpose.

Any network will do: In November 1989, a community of actors, playwrights, and theater companies helped bring democracy to Czechoslovakia.

It began on a Friday evening in Prague's university district. Students had gathered for a vigil to commemorate the death of Jan Opletal, a Czechoslovakian student killed by Nazi forces half a century earlier.

The student vigil made communist officials in Czechoslovakia nervous. And for good reason: Change was in the air. At that moment, across Eastern Europe, Soviet Bloc countries were collapsing. The Berlin Wall had fallen the previous week. And as the sky grew dark over Prague, the memorial vigil transformed into a peaceful protest march, spilling beyond the area where authorities had approved the gathering. Passersby could hear chants for democratic reform.

The gathering was large enough to provoke a brutal backlash. As police unleashed violence on the demonstrators, a tidal wave of outrage swept across the country. Czechoslovakian students were horrified by the violence that had befallen their friends and classmates. Their parents recalled the Nazi crackdowns from the early days of the Second World War.

Another group of Czechoslovakians was also paying attention: the underground theater movement that had sprung up in the late days of communism. A leader among them, the dissident playwright Václav Havel, had just been released from prison, where he had been serving a sentence for his activism. Havel's plight had become a cause célèbre for the country's arts community, a symbol of the Soviet war on free expression. Long suppressed by Soviet censorship, Prague's theater artists were ready to join the movement.

"It was impossible to go on acting while blood was being shed in the streets," the Czechoslovakian playwright Petr Oslzlý later wrote. "It was impossible to go on acting in a country where all divergent views were brutally suppressed."

On the day after the police crackdown, theater and film

students at Prague's Academy of Performing Arts called for a student strike. The city's performers gathered, too, and agreed to join the efforts. They would pause all theater performances and open theaters across the city only for the purpose of public discussion.

Theaters across the country became de facto hubs for the rapidly growing movement for democracy. Printers usually used for promotional materials pushed out leaflets and posters. Performance halls became salons for moderated discussions where citizens could share ideas and process the changes happening outside. The dramatists were making ample use of their technical skills, as well as the physical capital at their disposal.

But in relying on an intellectual infrastructure to motivate others to join the growing movement, the dissident artists were also tapping into something deeper. These were actors and playwrights, after all, people with a penchant for the dramatic. Dispatched into the community to spread the word, they performed banned plays and directed protest speeches to optimize their emotional impact. "We prepared all demonstrations as great theatre performances," Oslzlý wrote. "And yet—time and time again these great demonstrations were also great improvisations."

Their masterwork came a few weeks later, on New Year's Eve. Under intense pressure from growing crowds, the regime had agreed to end one-party rule and had installed its first noncommunist president in forty years: Václav Havel. Seated at a desk in front of a simple bookshelf, Havel looked directly into a camera and spoke to his countrymen:

> Everywhere in the world people wonder where those meek, humiliated, skeptical and seemingly cynical citizens of Czechoslovakia found the marvelous strength to shake the totalitarian yoke from their shoulders in several weeks, and in a decent and peaceful way. . . . Where did the young people who never knew another system get their desire for truth, their love of free thought, their political ideas, their civic courage and civic prudence? How did it happen that their parents—the very generation that had been considered lost—joined them? How is it that so many people immediately knew what to do and none needed any advice or instruction?

The new president offered his own answer: Despite the repression of communism, ideas of democracy and humanism had slept quietly in the hearts of the people. "Each of us could discover them at the right time and transform them into deeds," Havel told his people. Those beliefs had moved a nation long helmed by apparatchiks and bureaucrats to put its destiny into the hands of a poet. But as he concluded his address, the poet handed that power back to his fellow citizens, proclaiming, "People, your government has returned to you!"

Get Your Neighbors in a Group Chat

In September 1968, amid widespread child hunger and gaps in federal nutrition programs, the Black Panther Party announced plans for a new initiative: Free Breakfast for Children. The first site opened a few months later at a church in Oakland, and by the end of the school year the group reported serving over twenty thousand children. The militant Black power group went on to launch a raft of bold experiments in social welfare in cities across the United States, from sickle cell anemia testing and free clothing drives to a bus service to visit incarcerated relatives. Initiated and staffed mostly by women volunteers from the local community, the programs often included political education elements and aimed to meet the needs of African Americans where the state had failed them.

"We all had these kinds of programs with the intent of serving the people," Elaine Brown, a party activist who helped establish the Oakland breakfast program, said in an interview for the 1988 documentary *Eyes on the Prize*. But meeting basic needs also served the twin purpose of building political consciousness, and eventually collective power, among the people served, Brown said. "If they could get food, then maybe they would want clothing, and maybe they'd want housing, and maybe they'd want land, and maybe they would ultimately want some abstract thing called freedom."

Spend any time in Bushwick Ayuda Mutua (BAM) circles

and you're bound to hear some talk about the Panthers. "They're a heavy influence," says Dee, a volunteer with the mutual aid collective and a resident of the neighborhood in the northern part of Brooklyn, New York. "This work is about building shared understanding and breaking isolation through it."

In the spring of 2020, a group of Bushwick neighbors began soliciting donations for locals who were struggling amid the early weeks of the COVID pandemic. Designed at first to meet the needs of those who were ineligible for emergency government assistance, the effort rapidly evolved into a sophisticated social safety net, a kind of administrative state supporting thousands in the neighborhood.

With its pooled contributions, the group bought up groceries in bulk, and people dropped off donated nonperishable food at Mil Mundos Books, a multilingual bookshop that had opened in 2019. Neighbors in need could call a Google voice number and request essential goods like food and clothing. If the item was in stock, a caller could make an appointment and drop by the store to pick it up. The early days were chaotic as dozens of volunteers unloaded government-supplied food boxes from trucks, some sorting them into plastic shopping bags while others manned the hotline.

Out of the initial chaos emerged an organization with systems and protocols and a roster of over 150 monthly volunteers. Today BAM boasts a fundraising arm and an administrative team. One group of volunteers facilitates doctor's appointments and helps with health insurance. Another arranges pop-ups where neighbors can pick up items like tampons and pads, clothes, and groceries. Others are enlisted for "food rescue," making U-Haul runs to supermarkets in other boroughs to salvage fresh produce that would otherwise go to the dumpster.

"People can request support for basic and evolving needs of daily life in New York," says Maria Herron, a founding member of the mutual aid collective and the founder and codirector of the neighborhood bookshop. One objective of the mutual aid work, she says, is to lighten the burden of what she calls "life admin"—the daily demands of health, family, and school, which fall especially heavy on the shoulders of immigrant families and those whose first language is not English.

But the collective also serves a much broader swath of Bushwick. Abuelas, food truck vendors, and local political organizers are part of the BAM community. Lawyers, doctors, and journalists are, too. There are documented and undocumented people, twentysomethings who just moved into the neighborhood, and elders aging in the apartments where they were born. There are Cantonese speakers, Quechua speakers, and West African migrants dropped in New York by Texas Governor Greg Abbott's buses.

"At the end of the day all anyone wants to do is live with dignity," Herron says. "Do you want to live in a community or a strip mall?"

———

Today's Bushwick mutual aid organizers benefit from at least one tool for their work that the Black Panthers never had: a constellation of digital messaging channels that are home to some five hundred participants. And on some days, as phones across Bushwick light up morning to night, it can feel as though all of them are using it.

One hour might bring requests for work, for a job, or for help connecting with a placement program. Soon after, an invitation to a community picnic or an ESL class at Mil Mundos. People pose questions to the group ranging from the benign (*Anyone have a good dentist?*) to the urgent (*A mother of three who's recently arrived in Brooklyn. She has a budget of $1,200 a month. Does anyone know of an apartment?*). Someone else might chime in to share that a room is available in their apartment.

The BAM group chats, part of a latticework of similar texting channels in the area, are a real-time heat map, an early warning system for community needs and concerns. They're also a place where arguments occasionally break out, a reflection of the thorny communal dynamics of the analog world. Those conflicts can be explicitly racial—like accusations that one or another ethnic group is hoarding items or stealing from community events. Neighbors also express a wide range of perspectives on law enforcement: In the winter of 2024, after a woman threatened to call 911 when her phone went missing during a clothing drive, the organization decided to pause all community distributions.

Over the next two months, a group of forty BAM members met weekly to draft a set of community agreements. Among them: We don't call law enforcement, we don't tolerate racism—fourteen tenets in total, printed in English and Spanish on a form that all new volunteers must now sign.

For some members of the collective, participation is a choice—an expression of a kind of politics of interdependence. For many others it is a necessity. That's the case for neighbors living in poverty, with illness, or with a complicated immigration status, who use BAM and its many manifestations as a lifeline to resources and security.

But all of it draws neighbors in a segregated American city into each other's homes. All of it situates the people living between Cypress Avenue and Broadway as characters in the same story, and trusted intimates in a shared life.

———

In December 2024, group chats across Bushwick were blowing up.

Amid rumors that the incoming administration was planning mass roundups, a new level of anxiety was gripping the community. Lawyers in the neighborhood offered "know your rights" sessions. Others organized meetings to teach the differences between the insignias of various immigration-enforcement agencies—Immigration and Customs Enforcement (ICE), Customs and Border Protection (CBP), and Homeland Security Investigations (HSI).

A shared understanding quickly emerged in the community: *Only a judicial warrant could require you to open your door to the person presenting it.* New subgroups formed to coordinate responses to confirm sightings, alert the neighborhood, and provide legal support to those who were detained.

On a hot afternoon in the summer of 2025, a message hit the Bushwick group chats: Two plainclothes ICE officers had been spotted near the northern border of the neighborhood. The agents were walking south and moving deeper into Bushwick proper.

As the minutes passed more details came in: The agents were knocking on doors and trying to get into buildings. They did not appear to have the judicial warrant required of ICE officers to enter a home or make an arrest, but instead carried with them a piece of paper printed with the photos of individuals they said they were trying to find.

A text went out to group chats in the area with basic "know your rights" information. Seeking to avoid panic, the texts made no reference to the specific agents who had been spotted but emphasized a general message: *Unless there is a judicial warrant, do not open your door.*

Within minutes, the channels were flooded with screen grabs from Ring cameras and photos from inside buildings. A few neighbors confirmed in writing: "La migra está aquí, cuidado, ojo" (Immigration is here—be careful, watch out); "ICE está afuera" (ICE is outside). Others reported that people were asking the men questions: Who are you? What agency? Are you ICE?

There have been many days like this in the north Brooklyn neighborhood. Many end in heartbreak. On at least one occasion, armed agents took a neighbor off the street. Sometimes BAM members spend their lunch breaks on the ICE floor of New York City's byzantine federal building, 26 Federal Plaza, seeking information about their neighbors who have disappeared.

But that afternoon in Bushwick, the officers got back into their vehicle and drove off. No neighbors were taken into custody.

In the Hands of Women

In her work leading an embroidery collective, Niveen Mosleh, a Palestinian woman from Gaza, is carrying on an art form that combines cultural heritage with steadfast resistance, but she is hardly the first. The tradition took on new significance after the Arab-Israeli war of June 1967, as Israel occupied the West Bank and Gaza and prohibited Palestinian residents there from raising the Palestinian flag.

"It is forbidden to hold, wave, display or affix flags or political symbols, except in accordance with a permit of the military commander," read Israel Defense Forces Order No. 101 Prohibition of Incitement and Hostile Propaganda Actions. More than a decade later, as Israel asserted tighter control over the territories, the military lowered the threshold for political expression, forbidding works of art that simply combined the flag's colors—red, green, white, and black.

Palestinians on the other side of the Green Line separating Israel from the West Bank had already been facing profound restrictions and discrimination. The Israeli government had pursued an aggressive policy of confiscating land from Palestinians and reallocating it for new Jewish settlements. Israelis who moved to that land were governed by Israel's civil legal code and enjoyed full political rights, while Palestinians in the same areas lived under military law, leaving them with little recourse to stop home demolitions or the harassment and violence of settlers and the soldiers dispatched to protect them.

By the time Israel banned the flag colors, it seemed obvious to many Palestinians that the new prohibitions aimed to slow the political resistance that was emerging in the West Bank and Gaza. One artist recalled an Israeli intelligence official stopping by his art gallery in the early 1980s to warn that even "a flower with the different petals showing each color of the flag" would be unacceptable under the rules. The deep discontentment in the occupied territories grew into a wave of both nonviolent and violent demonstrations in the mid and late 1980s.

When Israeli authorities responded to the demonstrations by rounding up, arresting, and even deporting thousands of Palestinian men, the women of the occupied territories picked up the reins of the movement for self-determination. Some organized labor strikes and called on their communities to stop buying Israeli products. Others took over the leadership of prominent political factions like Fatah and the Democratic Front for the Liberation of Palestine, which had historically excluded women from holding leadership positions. But another group—quieter, behind the scenes—saw an opportunity for dissent in a role they had long played.

For centuries, Palestinian women had kept alive the art of *tatreez*, an ancient style of embroidery in which symbols of narrative and culture are woven into colorful traditional garments. Creating the bright, eye-catching patterns in dyed silks and cotton had long been a repository of Palestinian cultural memory and a means for women to support themselves. Motifs changed with the political currents and the conditions of the embroiderers themselves. Now, amid a surge of popular resistance, some wielded *tatreez* as an instrument of dissent.

"These women did not surrender to states of fear and panic," Niveen Mosleh, the director of the Sulafa Embroidery Centre in Gaza, said in a 2024 interview. Instead, embroiderers repurposed the traditional art form to assert their own agency and tell the story of their people. "They reached psychological stability and high levels of ability to concentrate and create [art], despite pain and suffering," Mosleh said.

Their creativity took a subtle, if intentional turn. Across the West Bank, women began secretly replacing traditional louder hues with the colors of the flag. They sewed into their *thobes* (the traditional Palestinian dress) black and red embroidery, with fuchsia and green stripes on the sides. They added symbols like date palms and cypress trees, sites of historical significance like the Dome of the Rock in Jerusalem, verses of poetry, and names of towns and villages from which their families had been expelled in the 1948 period that Palestinians refer to as the Nakba, or catastrophe. Some showed up at demonstrations wearing garments that testified to their connection to the land and their vision for statehood.

The *thobe* became a communications technology, a canvas on which to project Palestinian narratives in defiance of the Israeli military's orders. In a time before social media, "these protests might have been visible in newspapers internationally, or on television," said Rachel Dedman, a curator at the Victoria and Albert Museum in London, in a 2025 interview with *The Oxford Student*. The women would occasionally stitch English words into their dresses, a measure that Dedman says was intended to make their message of resistance clearer to people watching the Palestinian struggle from afar. "They were about forging a whole new language for *tatreez* that made the *thobe* and a woman's body sites of national identity and political resistance," Dedman said.

The women of the embroidery collectives are often associated with *sumud*, the Arabic word for steadfastness—and a principle that has long animated Palestinian life and resistance. But for many Palestinians, *sumud* also lives in the daily act of seizing a narrative many feel has been appropriated by the world. It means pushing back on a mainstream culture that some say portrays them as caricatures and asserting an alternative image: ordinary, alive, historically rooted in the land, and not going anywhere.

That insistence on Palestinian permanence is reflected in the evolution of *tatreez* itself. The long-standing practice of passing techniques from mother to daughter has shifted to a formal training and mentorship system in which women refine their skills over several months. This rigorous, communal structure has enabled groups of women to mobilize collectively under successive waves of repression.

As Israeli warplanes began to level Gaza following the Hamas attack of October 7, 2023, the women of the embroidery shops, drawing on their networks, continued to work on *tatreez* orders until the centers were destroyed in airstrikes that winter. The Sulafa collective "was able to accomplish this with the cloth and silk threads [we] had in the hands of women, which kept us going for a limited number of months," says Mosleh, who eventually left Gaza for Egypt.

She is pragmatic about the role *tatreez* plays as a source of much-needed income for women embroiderers. But amid the destruction of Gaza—entire bloodlines wiped out, universities and cultural institutions destroyed, and at least twenty Sulafa artists killed in the horrors—Mosleh suggests that the practice may also carry within it the seeds of a Palestinian future.

"It is necessary to strengthen these meanings and memories for our daughters and sons. To encourage them to revive them," she says. Such is the tradition of generations of women who carried on in the face of repression, marginalization, and extreme violence, she says. "Embroidery stood in solidarity with their steadfastness."

7

———

Bring the Blankets

People Need an Invitation to the Movement

THE HONG KONG POLICE FORCE'S official website lists the reward for Nathan Law's apprehension at one million Hong Kong dollars.

The pro-democracy activist stands prominently in several scenes in the island city's cultural memory: burning a copy of a Chinese Communist Party white paper, alongside fellow activist Joshua Wong, in 2014; clutching a microphone and leading chants onstage as students prepared to occupy Hong Kong's Civic Square in the city's financial center; and waiting with his hands bound outside a medium-security correctional facility, clad in short-sleeved prison browns, in the first week of his prison sentence—a consequence of leading the peaceful protests.

To many in Hong Kong and across the world, Law is synonymous with principled defiance. In 2018, when a bipartisan group of U.S. congressmembers nominated him, along with Wong and their fellow activist Alex Chow, for the Nobel Peace Prize, the lawmakers emphasized that the young men had shown "great courage in the face of harassment, threats, detention, and legal and financial repercussions."

But five years earlier, there had been few signs of that iconic figure when the fresh-faced first-year student decided to run for student government early on in his time at Lingnan University.

That fall campuses across the city were pulsing with debate on the Beijing question. China had promised to allow fifty years of relative self-rule after the British left Hong Kong in 1997. But the Chinese Communist Party kept delaying electoral reforms for universal suffrage and ratcheting up its control over aspects of Hong Kong governance, dimming the territory's hope for autonomy.

When Law arrived on campus, student leaders and other pro-democracy activists across the city were considering the path of civil disobedience, a bold plan to create international pressure on the Chinese government by occupying the city's main commercial district.

In a student government meeting, Law listened carefully as older students explained the mechanics of the occupation, which would be triggered if Beijing failed to deliver its promise to extend universal suffrage. But the end of the meeting gave him pause: A form was passed around, surveying representatives on the level of risk they would be willing to take on in the protests.

There were three boxes to choose from—three levels of risk. At the lowest tier, participants could pass out water to protesters. These students would almost certainly be shielded from any encounters with police. The middle tier involved sitting amid the crowd on the plaza, helping to form a human mass visible for TV cameras. The final box was the riskiest option: sitting in the very front row of the demonstration, likely guaranteeing arrest.

Law's pen hovered over the three options. He'd liked his experience in the student union so far, especially his friendships. But he didn't see activism as his future. "The thought of having a criminal record frightened me," he later recalled in his memoir, *Freedom: How We Lose It and How We Fight Back.*

The son of a father who had escaped from mainland China, Law had been raised in a household where finances were always tight and current affairs were rarely discussed. He was set on taking advantage of the benefits afforded by a university education: making good marks, studying abroad in Europe, and eventually finding a stable job.

He lowered his pen to the questionnaire and checked box number one. Water bottles. No risk at all.

Make It a Big Deal

Signing up to distribute water bottles was enough to bring Law out to the protests and get him closer to the action of a growing movement. In the streets, he saw peaceful activists pepper-sprayed and dragged away by officers. Soon he was sitting among his peers in the demonstration crowds. And within a couple of years, he had become a face and voice of the students of Hong Kong.

"I witnessed more police brutality, more suppression, and more of my friends becoming more committed," he says. "I just had a gradual urge to just do more for my community."

Law's trajectory—from risk-averse novice to professional dissident—isn't as unusual as it seems. According to Breza Race Maksimovic, program director at the Center for Applied Nonviolent Action and Strategies (CANVAS) in Belgrade, Serbia, it can even be by design.

Maksimovic has worked with her home country's student activists, who began protesting government corruption in November 2024 after the canopy over a newly renovated train station collapsed, killing sixteen people. What began as a series of candlelight vigils and demonstrations of public mourning rapidly grew into the country's biggest protest effort in decades, larger even than the movement that deposed Serbian President Slobodan Milošević in 2000.

Maksimovic says the most recent wave of protests benefited early on from conversations between activist students and their classmates who were sympathetic to the cause but not yet ready to participate in overt civil disobedience. Those conversations often began with a simple request of the less involved friends: "Can you bring blankets?"

When the students dropped off the blankets for their shivering peers, they'd witness the camaraderie of the students and faculty huddled in university plazas. Blanket runs would lead to making pancakes for the frontliners, and making pancakes grew into making financial donations. "By the fourth time, they were blocking the universities and going into the streets," Maksimovic says.

Physical risk isn't the be-all and end-all of activism; people who aren't able to put their bodies in harm's way have long played critical roles in social movements. But small, gradual investments help plant the seeds of belonging. Alcoholics Anonymous, the addiction support network, encourages group facilitators to invite newer attendees to help with the setup or cleanup of a meeting. Many AA participants report first feeling "like members" after they took on a small duty, such as setting up chairs or cleaning the coffeepot.

Activists in the United States also use this insight to motivate participation in political organizing. Jake Levin is a community organizer on the staff of Jews for Racial & Economic Justice, a New York City–based grassroots group that leads campaigns on issues like raising wages for home health care workers, reducing police violence, and keeping ICE from operating within the city. Levin says that successful campaigns work to keep people involved by getting them to take on a responsibility, even one that doesn't feel like a big deal. A favorite request of his: asking new members to stop by a corner store on the way to one of their first meetings to pick up snacks.

"That is a powerful, meaningful thing to someone," he says. New people get the message: "I came to a meeting, now there's a role for me. I'm actually helping this happen," Levin says. Then he'll ask them to help facilitate the next meeting.

Making small requests may be the closest thing organizers have to a shortcut. In 2005, sociologists at the University of Arizona found that the single strongest predictor of protest participation wasn't age, education, or political interest—it was whether the person had been asked to take part. "Individuals rarely participate in social movement activities (such as protest) unless they are asked to do so," found Alan Schussman and Sarah A. Soule in their landmark study, which examined the behaviors of over fifteen thousand adults. Their primary takeaway: No factor influences people to take on contentious political activism more than social connection.

Labor unions in the United States have also leveraged this insight in their approach to recruitment, says Jeremy Al-Haj, an organizer who has led campaigns to increase the wages and working conditions of service workers in Illinois, Ohio, Michigan, and Missouri.

A union drive is a numbers game; Al-Haj says that labor strategists will start putting together a campaign for a new union only once they've built an organizing committee that represents 10 percent of a workforce. In the earliest stages, the key is to identify workers who carry some influence inside the worksite, either because of their formal position or their social standing among coworkers. The best way to gauge their sway is to give them tests: "Can you go and sign up ten of your co-workers on a petition?"

How workers respond to these challenges tends to be an early indicator of whether a campaign will succeed, according to Al-Haj, who serves as executive director of the Missouri Workers Center: "If they are the leader, then that means their coworkers will follow them."

Maksimovic, who has trained anti-authoritarian activists from over seventy countries at the earliest stages of their campaigns, says that a small victory can inspire a quiet confidence: "Once they do something small, make it a big deal," she advises. "That's how you actually bring people into the movement."

Get in Small Fights

Bishop Dwayne Royster started small.

"My mom was a community organizer," says Royster, a minister affiliated with the United Church of Christ who today leads the interfaith grassroots group Faith in Action.

Every week, Audrey Royster marched her three children—Deahna, Damon, and Dwayne—out of the house and down the block to the offices of East Mount Airy Neighbors in Philadelphia. There she would set them up at a folding table in the back of the room, and that's where they'd stay as she conducted the business of the neighborhood association. "We sat there and licked envelopes," Royster recalls.

The northwest Philadelphia of the 1970s wasn't immune to the trends that were taking hold across America—White flight, redlining, disinvestment from Black areas. But Mount Airy fought as hard as any community in the nation to resist those forces. Audrey planned campaigns to help keep capital in the neighborhood, maintain racial integration, and pressure local banks to increase their lending to Black residents. And from the table in the back, her son Dwayne was listening.

He was also listening on Sunday mornings from the pews at Zion Baptist Church, whose pastor, Reverend Dr. Leon H. Sullivan, a prominent civil rights activist, was giving voice to a new Christianity—one that blended faith with Black power principles like community ownership and economic boycott. "Don't buy where you can't work," Sullivan would exhort from the pulpit.

All of it left an impression on the young Royster. Today he spends his days persuading fellow clergy to campaign on issues such as public education, affordable housing, and criminal justice reform. "We're not the 'nice faith people.' We're not the ones that you call to do the benediction and the salutation at an event," Royster says. "We're the ones that are going to come in and confront."

A phalanx of religious leaders in their holy garb can be a secret weapon for political efforts, lending an air of moral authority to a political campaign and making things complicated for opponents. No one wants to be on the wrong side of God. But sometimes the spectacle demands numbers, and many clergy—some with congregations of diverse political perspectives—are not nearly as comfortable as Royster is stepping into the activist breach.

He takes a pragmatic approach to recruitment. The key to bringing people into a campaign, he says, is to start slow. "You get them in small fights that you can potentially win," Royster says.

When unemployment was high, he encouraged another Philadelphia pastor to press a nearby frozen food company to commit to hiring locally before recruiting from across the city. The company agreed, Royster recalls, and many members of the pastor's church got jobs. "That meant a lot for their congregation," he says. "To feel like, oh, wow, wait a minute—we can actually have an impact."

To Be Transformed

In July 2016, one week before some fifty thousand people would descend on the city of Philadelphia for the Democratic National Convention, hundreds of workers at Philadelphia International Airport walked off the job.

The workers—employees of American Airlines subcontractors that handled cabin cleaning, baggage, and security—had voted to go on strike after their requests for better working conditions, including a $15 minimum wage and the right to form a union, had gone ignored. The local press had taken notice, but the coverage wasn't enough to protect the striking workers from the consequences: Several of them lost their jobs as a result of the strike.

Some felt that the firings were evidence of why they had sought greater protections in the first place. One of the workers decided to come back to work the next day to ask for her job back. But she wouldn't be arriving alone. When she stepped into the airy portico of Terminal B, she was flanked by ten Philadelphia faith leaders, donning clerical collars and other assorted vestments.

"We were going to say, 'Y'all need to give them their jobs back,'" remembers Royster, who was then leading the Philadelphia interfaith organization POWER (Philadelphians Organized to Witness, Empower, and Rebuild). But the airline wouldn't meet with the worker or with the clergy, Royster recalls. After a few minutes of back and forth, Royster knew that their initial approach was not going to get the group an audience.

So they sat down—right in front of the entrance to the TSA line.

"People would come up the escalator with their suitcase and then find this clump of clergy sitting down and singing hymns," remembers Cecily Harwitt, who was then the organizing director for POWER. "It got to the point where people were lifting their suitcases over groups of clergy."

Reverend Robin Hynicka, lead pastor of Arch Street United Methodist Church in Philadelphia's Center City, sat down near a doorway. "Somebody opened that door and literally ran over me with their suitcase," Hynicka recalls.

The police warnings came: If they didn't move, they would soon be arrested. After the final notice, Royster told the group to scatter. But to escalate the issue, someone would have to walk away in handcuffs. Since it wasn't clear whether charges would be local, state, or federal, Royster wasn't comfortable asking others to take that risk. So he alone would stay.

Hynicka, who is White, turned to his Black colleague. "I'll stay with you."

The huddled clergy glanced around the circle, exchanging nervous eye contact. Then, in a moment of mumbled conversation, the group—many of whom had never before been arrested—decided to remain together.

"Nobody left," recalls Royster. "We stayed in solidarity with one another."

Ten singing clergy in their vestments, hands zip-tied behind their backs, were perp-walked through the Philadelphia airport into a holding area, where the bars clanked shut.

With the Democratic convention just days away, the pressure on the airline continued to mount. The mayor and the governor both stepped in to facilitate negotiations. Prominent officials across the United States began speaking out; the California Democratic Party even encouraged its delegates to consider flying into Newark, New Jersey, instead of Philadelphia.

American Airlines agreed to let the subcontracted workers unionize, and the fired worker got her job back. All of it happened before a single delegate stepped foot on the floor of the Democratic convention. A deal was finalized the next year.

For Naomi Washington-Leapheart, a newly ordained minister who had never been detained by police prior to the airport action, the TSA protest was a revelation.

Washington-Leapheart wasn't used to interacting with police. She had spoken occasionally at demonstrations, and once participated in a "die-in"—lying flat in the street with dozens of others to protest police shootings. But defying officers—that was new. The whole airport ordeal had made her nervous. "I was like, what am I going to tell my wife?" she recalls.

But each of the prior engagements had pushed her to the next one. And as she walked through the terminal that night, the young pastor wanted to do even more. In momentarily disrupting the daily lives of others—travelers, police officers, politicians—she had found herself thinking about her own contradictions. What injustices was *she* ignoring in her daily life? What had *she* allowed to become business as usual?

"I want to be as transformed as we hope to transform the political circumstance," reflects Washington-Leapheart, who says she has since been arrested in multiple civil disobedience actions. "I want to be changed, too."

8

—

Share Your Fate

The Power of Accompaniment

LAUREN MOORE KNEW IT WAS time to leave North Dakota when she no longer felt comfortable leaving home without a gun concealed in her waistband holster. At six feet tall and handy with firearms, she doesn't scare easily. A former weightlifter, she worked construction and mechanic jobs in the state's oil fields for a decade.

But in January 2025, Moore began to fear for her security. Everyday activities started to feel much more daunting. In a pizza shop, she confronted a man who was trying to surreptitiously film her on his phone. Shoppers stared at her and muttered slurs in the aisles of Walmart as a man followed her around the store. "I stopped feeling any semblance of safety," Moore recalls.

The immense difficulty she faced in landing a job finally put her over the edge. "I called one dude at a construction company," she recalls. "I was like 'I'm trans,' and he just hung up on me."

In 2025 alone, 126 laws restricting trans people's access to health care and education were passed in the United States, three by the North Dakota legislature. As the hostility grew, and she became more isolated, Moore was left with the sinking feeling that her life in the place she had long called home was over.

But moving is expensive, and Moore was broke. One evening a friend shared a resource: Nexus Moving Company was offering free relocation services for trans and nonbinary people in the United States. "There's only so long you can stay somewhere where you can't work and you're scared," Moore says. Minnesota had the largest trans community per capita in the nation, and she knew a handful of people in Minneapolis. Perhaps she could crash with them while she figured things out.

Nexus vetted her thoroughly, even calling the Minnesotans she had listed to confirm that she really did have a place to stay. It was one thing to get out of an emergency. But as animus toward trans people spread and inspired new laws across the United States, it was quite another to make sure she wouldn't soon be doing this all over again. "Their big concern was 'we can move you where you need to go, but we want to move you somewhere where you're set up for success,'" Moore recalls.

On the day of the move, Moore opened her front door to

two tired volunteers who had just driven five hours to get to her. In less than an hour they loaded her life into their U-Haul. That evening she was in Minneapolis.

It was a couple of weeks before her nervous system calmed down. But soon Moore had stopped looking over her shoulder as she walked the street. She could finally breathe. "Nobody's going to try to kill me. I'm not being stared at because I'm trans," she says. "It's just because, like, I'm being loud."

Moore is studying to be an EMT in Minneapolis and spends her free time volunteering with the moving company. She lives in an apartment with two roommates. They keep one bedroom vacant, just in case. "If you move here and you don't have anywhere to go for a little bit," she says, "you can stay with us."

Wherever They Go, Walk with Them

Paul Farmer, the famed medical anthropologist, described "accompaniment"—the idea of walking alongside people during their most fearful and difficult moments—as the goal of his public health work with people in poverty around the world. For Farmer, that meant not just treating patients in places like rural Haiti at his clinics but also ensuring that they could travel safely to the clinic and access clean water and food when they were at home.

"The companion, the *accompagnateur*, says: 'I'll go with

you and support you on your journey wherever it leads; I'll share your fate for a while. And by "a while," I don't mean a little while,'" Farmer wrote. "Accompaniment is about sticking with a task until it's deemed completed, not by the *accompagnateur* but by the person being accompanied."

A form of accompaniment called "protective presence" is another technique for supporting people who are being targeted by an oppressive regime. In 1987 the humanitarian group Peace Brigades International began dispatching volunteers to El Salvador, where activists were resisting a regime that was using the military to violently suppress opposition.

Kidnappings, death squads, and other state violence had become common. So the unarmed volunteers from the United States, Canada, and Spain were assigned a partner—a labor leader or a women's rights activist who was at risk of government violence—and given a simple mission: Wherever they go, walk with them.

The goal of the intervention was deterrence, to complicate the calculus of state violence. When a Peace Brigades volunteer was present, any attack on their Salvadoran partner would be an international incident. One Salvadoran labor leader, years later, said that the program sent a clear message to the government: "To kill us together would bring the state a heavy political cost."

Accompaniment can also be homegrown. Women help each other manage medication abortions in hundreds of accompaniment networks in countries around the world where terminating a pregnancy is legally restricted or banned.

The practice began in Brazil, where abortion is illegal and women often suffered trauma from botched underground procedures. In 1986 a new ulcer medication called Cytotec began appearing on pharmacy shelves. Tucked into the box's fine print was a warning: "Can cause birth defects, abortion, or premature birth." Desperate women started experimenting with how many pills would end their unwanted pregnancies.

Whisper networks grew into hotlines that those seeking to terminate their pregnancy could call for firsthand advice. The whisper networks evolved into a more formal practice of women sitting with one another through their self-managed abortions. Soon these grassroots communities had developed protocols and practices to guide others through the process, collecting data about what worked and what could be improved for a safer and less painful experience.

These networks have produced powerful results: A 2022 study in the medical journal *The Lancet* found that, in Argentina and Nigeria, medication abortion with support from an accompaniment group is "highly effective and safe"—and indeed a lifeline for many women in a harrowing moment. Accompaniment also reduces negative emotions, like nervousness, guilt, and shame, that some women experience after an abortion, according to a study of women in Mexico City.

"For many women, it is the first time they are making a decision based on their needs and not their communities' or families' needs," says Oriana López-Uribe, former executive director of Fondo Maria, an abortion fund in Mexico City, who has accompanied many women during medical abortions. "They are regaining their power over their own lives."

In the late 2010s, a feminist movement known as the Marea Verde—the Green Wave—swept through Latin America, aiming to break the stigma of abortion and end violence against women. In Argentina, hundreds of thousands of women took to the streets wearing green scarves, and in 2020 the country finally legalized abortion. The green scarves spread to Mexico in a wave of protests that peaked in 2020. The country's high court decriminalized the procedure in 2023.

Naomi Braine, author of *Abortion Beyond the Law*, a 2023 book studying global accompaniment networks, argues that the movement derives its power not only from mass protest but in the radical acts of women quietly supporting one another—offering care and dignity where the law did not.

"Forcing someone to carry a pregnancy to term is an extraordinary act of state violence, and accompaniment disrupts that," Braine says. "It says, 'We see you, we're here, here's our phone number.'"

A Community of Fate

On the morning that West Virginia's public school teachers went on strike in 2018, seeking a raise and a halt to the rapid rise of their health insurance premiums, Stephanie Johnson wasn't on the picket line. She was at church with more than a dozen teachers, packing sandwiches, granola bars, chips, and drinks into brown paper bags.

"As teachers, we were very aware that students rely on school food to get through," says Johnson, who was working that year in a fifth-grade classroom in the rural Appalachian town of Buckhannon. One-quarter of Buckhannon households are below the poverty line. And because every child in school qualifies for free lunch, she says, each day school wasn't in session would also be a day a child might go hungry.

Johnson had some experience in this area. As a kid in West Virginia's eastern panhandle, with a biological father who was struggling with addiction and often unemployed, she had been accustomed to coming home to an empty fridge. "Even at a young age, I knew that you don't mess around at breakfast and lunchtime at school," she recalls. Sometimes extra food would mysteriously appear in her backpack at the end of the day. It wasn't until she was older that she realized teachers had been quietly slipping it into her bag.

So when the teachers' strike came, even though Johnson was still a trainee working in the classroom to gain clinical training hours, she jumped at the chance to feed the students. "I just knew it was something I needed to do," she says.

Every day, teachers, bus drivers, and cafeteria workers across West Virginia packed and distributed lunches to students in their districts. But the support went both ways: Parents, community members, and labor unions across the country sent pizzas to the striking workers on their picket lines at the capitol and across the state.

"The packing of the lunches was first an act of love but also an act of strategy because it sent a clear message to both the public and the legislators that this was not about leaving our students behind," recalled Jessica Salfia, one of the striking West Virginia teachers, in *Bon Appetit.*

That groups like the teachers and families of West Virginia reject a narrow zero-sum calculus, choosing instead to tie their destinies together, is evidence that rugged individualism is not our civilizational default, argues Margaret Levi, a professor emerita at Stanford University who has studied political communities across the globe. "All sorts of animals, including humans, will pay high individual costs to provide benefits for another perceived as part of their family, herd or tribe," Levi wrote in *Noéma* magazine.

When communities recognize the dangerous gaps that open when decisions are made only according to personal costs and benefits, they often build something sturdier. Levi calls it a "community of fate."

She points to labor unions' long history of leveraging their power to stop human rights abuses in distant lands. In the late 1940s, for example, Australian dockworkers voted to stop work after they learned that the Dutch ships they were loading were carrying arms intended to help Dutch soldiers reoccupy Indonesia. The same happened in the late 1930s, when American longshoremen opposed the occupation of Manchuria. The workers saw their fates—and the fates of others who would never be able to return the favor—as one.

Reorienting as communities of fate is how groups can survive cascading global crises, like climate change and pandemics, authoritarianism and surging poverty, Levi argues. "For societies to survive and thrive, a significant proportion of their members must engage in reciprocal altruism," she writes. And our complex crises require "a form of farsighted reciprocal altruism in which members are willing to make costly sacrifices on behalf of those with whom they believe their fates, and their descendants' fates, are entwined but who may never be able to directly reciprocate."

It worked in West Virginia. "There was that balance of knowing that the strike needed to happen. The things that were happening were not okay," Johnson says of the teachers' working conditions. "But also knowing our students needed to be fed."

After nearly two weeks on strike, the teachers won a 5 percent pay raise, their first in four years, but the deal stopped short of lowering their health care costs, as they had hoped. For Johnson, the episode presented a decision point. Choosing to continue a teaching career would mean a lifetime of scarcity—a new struggle each academic year for her own wages and benefits, and for the basic needs of her students.

She chose it anyway. Today she is a first-grade teacher in

Buckhannon. Every Friday she and her colleagues distribute bags of food for students to take home for the weekend.

"What More Can We Do for Each Other?"

Each July, Remelya Jackalope, a festival operator and events producer, stages a five-day festival for queer and trans people across the San Francisco Bay Area.

Jackalope is proficient at setting up and taking down a small town's worth of infrastructure in a matter of hours. Her crew can quickly assemble tents, kitchens, and bathrooms to serve hundreds of people. But in early 2025, as anti-trans hostility surged in the United States, it occurred to Jackalope that these skills might be needed for another purpose: a trans refugee crisis.

Jackalope, a trans woman, quietly retooled her festival logistics operation into a relocation service for trans people living under increasingly dangerous circumstances across the country. While the Nexus Moving Company's website advertised itself as an events company, careful readers would notice an item at the bottom of the page advertising "free relocation services."

More than five hundred people had clicked the button by late 2025, according to Jackalope. Clients come to the company with different needs. Some, like Lauren Moore, simply can't afford the cost of movers. Others, fearing for their safety, want to be able to check in with someone on their route out of town. In extreme cases, Nexus will find a safe place to which someone can flee—like a church—before the team picks them up. "It's not dissimilar to getting someone out of a domestic abuse situation," Jackalope says.

Her scrappy, bare-bones operation sees a surge in requests whenever another state passes an anti-trans law—a crisis that Jackalope expects will only intensify in coming years, as queer and trans people are likely to be increasingly ostracized, marginalized, and criminalized. "In the U.S. we already see thousands of trans people fleeing," Jackalope says. "We are preparing right now for a potential mass refugee situation."

Jackalope is now spinning the relocation program out of the moving company into its own new nonprofit, the Transcendence Care Network, which will connect trans people to a growing ecosystem of organizations offering relocation. And she is working to build an international coalition that can help develop a disaster relief plan in case they need to start moving people out of the United States.

Jackalope believes that eventually this work will force her to leave the country. But she hopes that sharing information about her work publicly can help others take it over if that day comes.

"Authoritarianism is about how we can do less for each other and still feel okay about it," Jackalope says. "A key piece of fighting against authoritarianism is asking the question, 'What more can we do for each other?'"

III

On Threats and Violence

9

Write Down Your People

You Can't Prepare for Every Threat, but
You Can Improve Your Conditions

CLAIRE ATKIN HAD JUST TOUCHED down on the tarmac in her hometown of Vancouver, British Columbia, when her phone buzzed.

On the screen flashed a series of texts from her neighbor: There was a man outside Atkin's apartment building. He looked to be in his mid-fifties. He was wearing a gray leather trench coat. And he was waiting for Atkin.

Atkin is the chief executive of the digital advertising watchdog Check My Ads Institute. In 2016, working in software marketing, she noticed a strange trend on her social media accounts: bizarre conspiracy theories that claimed "elites" like Hillary Clinton were harvesting the blood of murdered children or that alleged a child sex ring was being run out of a Washington, D.C., pizzeria.

The stories made no sense, but they were traveling at an extraordinary velocity. More disturbing to Atkin was that the online creators spreading these harmful lies seemed to be doing it by using the same digital advertising tools she used to sell software to businesses.

Nandini Jammi, a fellow marketer, harbored the same concerns about digital marketing technologies. In 2017 she had used an anonymous Twitter account to inform brands that their ads were appearing on the far-right news site Breitbart .com. Her campaign proved remarkably successful: The media outlet hemorrhaged 90 percent of its revenue, and the site was eventually blocked by some four thousand advertisers.

Atkin and Jammi began working together. "We started to ask this question: Why is the advertising industry still funding hate speech, even though advertisers have made it so clear that they don't want to be anywhere near it?" Jammi said in a 2022 interview with NPR. The answers they found were complicated. But they all seemed to grow from the same source: advertising technology companies that enabled advertisers to automatically buy placements across thousands of websites without knowing exactly where their ads would appear.

The pair took a big swing in 2022 around the first anniversary of the Capitol insurrection on January 6. Ad tech companies had made a promise to brands that they would never bankroll election disinformation. But as the January date approached, Atkin and Jammi's research showed that intermediaries were still sending money to prominent peddlers of election conspiracies like Dan Bongino and Tucker Carlson. So the organization launched a pressure campaign, calling on ad exchange companies to "defund the insurrectionists."

The campaign worked. Ad tech companies dropped media outlets associated with Steve Bannon, Glenn Beck, and Tim Pool, all of whom had promoted conspiracy theories about the 2020 presidential election. Google, the biggest ad exchange on earth, eventually stopped showing ads for Bongino's website, citing "demonstrably false claims about our elections" and misleading information about COVID-19. Check My Ads estimates that the effort successfully blocked millions of dollars in income to the sites.

But success came at a cost: Atkin and Jammi had made enemies and were now a target for some of the most powerful people in right-wing media.

First came a federal lawsuit. Rumble, the video-sharing platform that hosted content from the podcaster Andrew Tate, the actor Russell Brand, and several January 6 insurrectionists, sued the Check My Ads cofounders after the organization encouraged advertisers to stop advertising on the site. Rumble's CEO staked out a confrontational approach to the lawsuit. "Preserve all your documents," he tweeted.

The influencers hit back, too. The *Bongino Report*, the website of the right-wing firebrand who would eventually serve a brief term as deputy director of the Federal Bureau of Investigation, claimed that Check My Ads was violating tax rules. Seizing on a tweet from Atkin offering to buy books for any teenager who'd had a book banned at school, Bongino called the Check My Ads cofounders "Soros funded perverts" and described them as "savages" seeking to indoctrinate children and censor free speech.

Between September and October 2023, Bongino tweeted about Atkin on at least seven separate occasions. His followers responded with a steady stream of invective, describing Atkin and Jammi in misogynistic and, at times, dehumanizing language.

Then, on a chilly night in December, a man in a trench coat came looking for her.

Fear in Your Body

The level of fear that human beings experience on a day-to-day basis has a lot to do with how far away we think a predator is.

Michael Fanselow, a professor of psychology and psychiatry at the University of California, Los Angeles, has spent his career studying this dynamic. He describes fear as an ancient set of tools that evolved to help protect people against environmental dangers.

"The threat of predation is probably the most powerful evolutionary force that we confront," Fanselow says. Our response evolves as the perceived threat gets closer. He breaks the process down into three distinct stages: anxiety, fear, and panic.

In the first stage—anxiety—a predator is in the distance, but we know it's coming. This is when we have the most flexibility in our thinking. Though we're aware of a looming threat, we're still able to think strategically about our options—the range of possibilities and tools that remain available to us.

When the predator is close at hand, our body activates a set of automatic responses. Adrenaline rises, blood pressure spikes, heart rate changes, palms grow sweaty, breathing becomes more staccato. We also might naturally freeze up or clench our muscles—the body's way of trying to preserve its options. "If you don't move, you're less likely to be detected by your predator," Fanselow says. This is what he calls fear.

The third stage is panic. This is when the predator pounces. Another set of responses take control: We shout, we run, we jump, we fight. We do whatever we can to escape.

———

Sitting on the tarmac, Atkin froze up.

She tried to collect herself. Perhaps there was a rational explanation for the man outside her apartment. She'd been expecting to be served papers in the Rumble lawsuit. Maybe this was just a guy doing his job. But serving papers after business hours seemed unusual. Even an aggressive plaintiff would know that lingering past dark wouldn't go over well in court. It didn't add up.

Atkin replied to her neighbor's message, wondering

whether she should come home. The reply was instant: "I would say don't."

That night Atkin stayed at a friend's place. At daybreak she took an Uber back to her apartment and slipped in through the back entrance. There she remained for two days, blinds drawn and door double-locked. Had the trolls toiling in the darkest tunnels of the internet shown up at her actual doorstep?

Atkin's life as she knew it had changed. This was her new normal.

World Building

The previous year, troubled by the growing belligerence of the internet crowd, Atkin had enrolled in self-defense training in her neighborhood. The threat of violence was a new problem in her life, one she wasn't quite sure how to think about.

The first lessons were more like a philosophy class. The instructor was preoccupied less with physical training and more with ideas like situational awareness, outlining an approach to safety that began long before a physical threat ever arrived.

As the weeks passed, Atkin started to see answers come into focus: As a woman in this line of work, she was going to have to live with the possibility of violence. And if violence did arrive, there wouldn't be a lot she could do. But there were other things in her control to keep the anxiety at a low hum, to make the threats ambient and hold the panic at bay.

"The thing to orient towards is not who wants to hurt me," Atkin began to think. Instead, she would train her energy on another question: "How do I maintain a long-distance vision rather than myopic fear-based decision-making?"

The answer would require building for herself a world where she would be dramatically less likely to encounter daily threats—physical or psychological—and where help was at the ready when she did. Her best resource, Atkin figured, were the people who were closest to her. A mentor suggested she create a map of these people.

One day Atkin grabbed a pen and sat down at her desk. On a white 8½" by 11" sheet of printer paper, she drew three concentric circles, like a dartboard.

Inside the bull's-eye, she wrote the names of close friends and family—the people who loved her unconditionally. In the next ring outward, she jotted down the names of the people who believed in her, like friends and mentors, donors, and board members of Check My Ads. The names of foundation heads and others with resources who had shown their willingness to support the work of her organization went in the outermost ring.

As the days passed, Atkin wrote more names on the page. The new topography located her within a forest of allies. The map was simple, but it struck her as a profound resource, a reminder that she had in her immediate reach deep reserves of wisdom, experience, and help.

"It was much bigger than I thought it was when I first

started," Atkin recalls of the map. If a more immediate threat ever arrived, these were the people she would call.

"I've Got to Talk to Somebody"

If you want to pursue a career as a pastry chef, you're going to encounter flour. If you want to be a surgeon, there's going to be blood. And if you decide to confront the powerful, then personal risk will always be part of the equation. "I run an accountability organization," Atkin says. "People are going to be upset with me."

She has developed a personal philosophy for managing this risk and continuing her work in spite of the fear: Do it with open eyes and do it with others.

The first step is internalizing the logic of threats and understanding what makes them so debilitating. "When you are attacked or threatened, it feels like much more than 'I'm going to take away some money of yours,' or 'I'm going to take away a reputation that you might have,'" Atkin says. "It feels to your body like someone is telling you that your life doesn't matter."

There's a good way to avoid being persuaded by that argument, Atkin says: Surround yourself with a cadre who will testify on your behalf in this internal trial and as character witnesses vouching for your worth, your value, and your cause.

Fanselow, the fear scientist, says there's science behind that intuition. "Even in animals, having your friends and your littermates around will reduce your fear quite a bit," he says. Being around people who feel familiar and supportive can tamp down your fear system and allow other motivations, like core values, to take over.

In a 2016 study, Fanselow and his UCLA colleagues Erica Hornstein and Naomi Eisenberger conditioned participants to fear a neutral image—such as a flower—by pairing it with a mild shock. But later, when the same image appeared alongside a photo of someone the participant relied on for support, like a partner, parent, or friend, the fear response diminished. The images of loved ones softened participants' physiological reactions to fear.

Other approaches, like exposure therapy, physical warmth, and some medications, have also been shown to help. But medication reduces only the symptoms of fear, not the underlying trigger that stimulates it. To develop a resilience to events that generate fear, Fanselow says, surround yourself with familiar people. "Social support is very powerful in reducing fear," he says. "Probably better than meds."

That support can come from neighbors—though such relationships have grown increasingly rare. Fifty years ago, nearly half of Americans spent time with neighbors a few times a month. Today, barely one in four do. That disconnect is a problem in an environment of growing daily stressors, from rising federal law enforcement presence to social welfare cuts that prevent many from meeting basic needs. For those who may be at heightened risk, whether for their activism, their income level, or their identity, an extra set of eyes and ears can be key—people who know their needs, who have a sense of what their life is supposed to look like, and who can spot—and step in—when something is off.

Mentors can do this, too. People who have been at this work longer, or have survived similar ordeals, can help a mentee see around corners. That's what happened to Atkin on the third day after the man in the trench coat came looking for her. She was finding it difficult to focus on work, distracted by a stream of questions. What new threats lurked around the corner? What could she do about it? She picked up her phone and dialed a mentor—someone she had placed in the second circle of her map.

The mentor told her to wait by the phone. A few minutes later, a call came in. It was the leader of a leading human rights group—a man some twenty years Atkin's senior, whom she'd never met, with decades of experience fighting off lawsuits by right-wing governments. He had been in her shoes many times before and lived to tell the tale.

"First time?" the stranger asked. His tone was warm and welcoming. Atkin shared her many causes for concern. The lawsuits. The man in the trench coat. And then, as if moving down a checklist, the voice on the other end drew on his experiences and addressed each one of her fears: the ways he had learned to cope, the legal lessons he wished he'd known earlier, the dos and don'ts of leading an organization in the crosshairs.

"Your first time is always scary," said the caller, no longer sounding like a stranger at all. He stayed on the phone with her and answered her every last question.

"It feels so lonely when you're sitting there in your room being like, what do I do?" Atkin says. "But you have to very quickly pivot to, okay, I've got to call someone. I've got to talk to somebody. I've got to be with somebody."

10

Make a List, Check It Twice

Opposition Research and the New Vigilantism

THE ABORTION CLINIC IN BRISTOL, Virginia, attracts patients from nearly a dozen states. They arrive after long drives—weary and exhausted, and often broke. Many have been unable to access abortion services closer to home, and the town of Bristol, smack on the state line between Virginia and Tennessee, is a place of last resort.

But it isn't always a refuge. Since the U.S. Supreme Court overturned federal abortion protections in 2022, clinics providing reproductive health care have increasingly become targets of trespassing, vandalism, and violence. Death threats and bomb threats are up. Clinic invasions and blockades are growing more common. When patients finally arrive at the clinic, they often must make their way through a sea of seething hostility as they are greeted by demonstrators who feel more emboldened than ever.

But many are also greeted by Barbara Schwartz, a seventy-three-year-old clinic escort who welcomes them and, with her traffic baton, waves them past the noisy crowd and into a parking spot. Schwartz offers the new arrivals gas money for the ride home if they need it, as well as advice on where to get a bite to eat. She gives each one a comfort bag of supplies they might need for after-care, such as socks, ginger ale, and pads. Then she pops open a golf umbrella and plays music on a portable speaker to shield them from the protesters who shout at them as they walk into the clinic.

After five years, Schwartz doesn't agonize too much about the sign-wavers who regularly camp out in front of the clinic. "We know our locals," she says. It's another variety of threat that scares her. "What we are worried about is the randoms," Schwartz says. "Those are the things that just make my nose itch."

In December 2022, Stephanie Rosenwinge was working the front desk when she noticed a different protester outside the window. It was Coleman Boyd. She recognized him from a photo pinned on the corkboard near her desk where the clinic kept pictures and descriptions of known anti-abortion extremists.

"We know what they've done and if they are armed," says Rosenwinge. "We know what each one of them is capable of. That intel is beyond precious."

Boyd had been indicted earlier that year for violating civil rights laws by blocking the entrance to an abortion clinic in

Mount Juliet, Tennessee. He had a history of harassing and intimidating women entering clinics, and he was known to carry a pistol.

Rosenwinge feared what Boyd might be capable of. She dialed the local FBI field office. When they told her there wasn't much they could do, she texted her group chat with other clinic workers and volunteers. They told her to check if he was on probation. She scanned the file pinned to the board. That's when she saw it: The terms of Boyd's federal probation required him to stay in Mississippi and remain at least twenty feet away from abortion clinic buildings.

Rosenwinge asked her colleague to make another call—this time to the U.S. Marshals Service, the federal body charged with enforcing compliance with the terms of federal sentences—and sent an email with photos of Boyd standing near the clinic and breaking the terms of his own probation. He soon left and didn't return for a year.

A Time of Lists

It's not realistic to protect against all possible threats. But it is possible to develop strategies to defend against the most likely ones. Calculating the probabilities, however, requires understanding your opponents and knowing their preferred tactics, behaviors, and vulnerabilities.

Authoritarian leaders use a wide range of threats to suppress dissent—physical, legal, digital, financial. In Russia, Vladimir Putin's political opponents have died in mysterious circumstances. In Hungary, Viktor Orbán defunds and investigates his rivals. In Cambodia—where the Supreme Court acts as an instrument of Prime Minister Hun Sen's repressive regime—justices went so far as to dissolve the opposition party in 2017.

These are all difficult tactics for activists, opposition leaders, and other dissidents to defend against. But among the most formidable challenges for pro-democracy movements are the shadowy threats that appear seemingly out of nowhere—when authoritarians encourage others to commit political violence on their behalf.

The scholars Steven Levitsky and Daniel Ziblatt describe the tolerance or encouragement of political violence as one of the top warning signs of an emerging authoritarian leader. "Partisan violence is very often a precursor of democratic breakdown," they have written. In the twentieth century, such violence has ranged from the Blackshirts, the Italian street fighters who attacked organizations that Benito Mussolini had deemed enemies, to Uruguay's leftist urban guerrilla group, called the Tupamaros, who carried out political kidnappings and assassinated police officers in the late 1960s.

Today such vigilantism can manifest as an online mob incited against political opponents, a "lone wolf" shooter motivated by propaganda, or an armed insurrection that storms a government building seeking to overturn an election on behalf of their preferred candidate. Often the violence is not quite attributable to a political leader but instead happens inside a cloud of plausible deniability.

This type of wink-wink, condoned political violence has a long history even in democracies like the United States, where the government granted American settlers free rein to harass and murder Native Americans in the mid-1800s and failed to punish White Americans who lynched thousands of Black Americans after the Civil War and well into the mid-twentieth century.

Today the United States is enduring another resurgence of state-endorsed vigilantism, which is no longer conducted only by means of violence but also through financial and legal threats.

In 2022, Florida passed a law giving parents the power to sue if their kids are taught about sexual orientation or gender identity in school. In 2021, Tennessee legislators approved a measure allowing parents, students, and employees to sue schools and school districts for allowing transgender people into bathrooms and locker rooms. And in Texas, the Heartbeat Act of 2021 provides financial bounties to citizens who snitch on women having illegal abortions.

Legal scholars Jon Michaels and David Noll argue that without lifting a gun or inciting a mob, these laws transform the everyday threat landscape for regular people. "Vigilantes force the targets of these campaigns of control and terror to conceal their true identities, censor their words and activities, refrain from political and civic engagement, or flee vigilante-friendly jurisdictions for good," Michaels and Noll write in *Vigilante Nation*. "Suffocating democracy is the point."

Today's vigilantes are compiling lists of "deep state" figures to be prosecuted, media outlets to be exiled, and books to be banned. The right-wing group Turning Point USA operates the "Professor Watchlist," a website that tags hundreds of left-wing American professors under labels like "Antifa," "Socialism," "LGBTQ," and "Terror Supporter."

Another nonprofit affiliated with the MAGA movement has built three websites profiling federal government employees—DEIwatchlist.com, DHSWatchlist.com, and DeptofEdWatchlist.com—including their pictures and salaries. The profiles often feature women and people of color. Many have reported leaving their jobs or becoming targets of harassment after appearing on one of these websites.

The website Canary Mission, another watch list, profiles thousands of students, professors, and activists who have expressed support for Palestinian causes. In early 2025, after the White House directed the U.S. Department of Homeland Security to investigate antisemitism on college campuses, agency officials used Canary Mission's list of five thousand names as a starting point. That many on the list were U.S. citizens was likely to make prosecution difficult, given the constitutional protections for free speech. As a workaround, DHS identified two hundred people on the list whom the executive branch could instead target under immigration laws and refer to the U.S. State Department for possible deportation.

One of the students profiled on the site was Rümeysa Öztürk, the PhD student from Turkey whose detention by federal agents on the street in Somerville, Massachusetts, was captured on a neighbor's video and shocked the nation. Öztürk had a valid student visa and was not a leader of protests. She wasn't even an active participant. What landed her on the Canary Mission list was an op-ed she had once coauthored in the Tufts student newspaper asking the university to "meaningfully engage" with the undergraduate student senate's vote to divest from companies with ties to Israel.

A month after her name appeared on the website, plainclothes ICE agents pulled up to a Somerville street and took her away. Two hours after she was arrested, her visa was revoked.

Antisemitism is a longstanding global affliction that persists in American society—stubborn, deep-rooted, and corrosive. For more than a decade, anti-Jewish hate crimes in the United States have been the second most prevalent bias crimes, after anti-Black hate crimes, according to FBI data. The problem has also been exacerbated on social media platforms like X, where between February 2024 and January 2025 antisemitic posts were viewed more than 193 million times. But Öztürk hadn't been accused by the government of a hate crime, nor was there any record of her posting inflammatory content online. In fact, a few days before her arrest a State Department office had determined that there was no evidence that Öztürk had engaged in any antisemitic activity or made public statements supporting a terrorist organization, according to a State Department memo later produced in court.

The arrests of immigrants on the Canary Mission list were part of a larger agenda. The White House was also threatening to withhold millions in federal funding from leading universities, aiming to force them to adopt policies on transgender students, diversity, and campus speech preferred by the administration. The stated reason for the cuts: allegations of antisemitism on campus.

Taken together, the moves mirrored an approach long favored by strongmen who wield accusations of antisemitism as a cudgel to justify authoritarian actions: In 2022, Putin cited the "Nazification" of Ukraine as a pretext for invading Ukraine, a nonsensical claim that conveniently ignored the fact that the country's president, Volodymyr Zelenskyy, is Jewish. Orbán, for his part, has repeatedly linked the fate of Hungary's Jewish community to preventing migration, even as he blames the influx of immigrants on the Hungarian Jewish billionaire George Soros. A slate of anti-migration law passed by the Hungarian parliament in 2018 bore the name "Stop Soros."

Timothy Snyder, a leading historian of authoritarianism, has written that such actions transform the real suffering of Jews "into a bureaucratic tool called 'antisemitism' which is used to suppress education and human rights." In the process, Jews often become both pawns for a regime that needs an excuse for its repressive policies and scapegoats for those who suffer as a result.

The website that has aided the government in this mission appears to be fueled, in part, by students and faculty who submit anonymous tips to the website. One student, who was included on the Canary Mission watch list for her nonviolent activism on her Ivy League campus in 2018, says that some of the information and photos of her on the site could only have come from her fellow university students.

"There are some images of me that are from the back or so blurry that you would only know it was me if you knew who was there," says the activist student, who was let go from two separate jobs by employers who told her they were firing her because she was named on the site. "There is something to me very sick about the idea that your classmates are the ones surveilling you and trying to cause you material harm."

The Show Must Go On

Kat Green was outside a Wichita, Kansas, health clinic, working on a comedy tour to support reproductive rights, when an anti-abortion demonstrator threw a dead baby rabbit at her.

The 2017 tour, organized by the comedian Lizz Winstead, had brought comedians to cities across the United States as a way to fight the stigma of abortion and support providers operating in increasingly dangerous terrain. In the years leading up to the 2022 *Dobbs v. Jackson Women's Health Organization* Supreme Court decision that overturned *Roe v. Wade*, the variety show was an irreverent response to the growing list of repressive state laws.

"Don't be ashamed of having an abortion—maybe be ashamed of how you got pregnant," one comedian told a crowd onstage to uproarious laughter. "I got pregnant the classy way: on the floor. On an Amtrak train. In the handicapped restroom, babeeey!"

For Green, who a few years earlier had suffered two miscarriages while she had an IUD, the tour was also personal. "I was so pissed that my body betrayed me no matter what I did," she recalls. She posted online about her experience. "I hadn't been paying that much attention to abortion stuff until then, and then I was furious."

The post eventually led her to Winstead, a co-creator of *The Daily Show*, who was making satirical online videos about abortion. Winstead enlisted Green to bring her years of experience editing films to the comedian's growing activism.

Green was glad to be able to put her expertise to good use. But once they hit the road for the comedy tour, it wasn't long before she realized that she was only partially prepared. Protesters were showing up at the shows. And then there was the dead rabbit incident. Green understood that she would have to learn more about these people—and how to keep them at bay.

She started a practice: Before each show, she'd call ahead to the staff of the local abortion clinic for information about the local protesters—the regulars. Then she'd put together a "face sheet" for the bouncers at that night's show. It was a helpful resource. She eventually compiled the information into a national database and shared it among all the clinics.

The data, it turned out, told a much bigger story: After the January 6, 2021, insurrection, Green observed that many anti-abortion activists on her list were also members of the Christian nationalist, White nationalist, and militia groups that had attacked the U.S. Capitol. The same people who had been blockading clinics were also storming into drag performer book readings at local libraries. In trying to keep the tour safe, Green had inadvertently begun connecting the dots and mapping the American far-right movement.

"Opposition research is one of the most critical tools we have to protect ourselves," says Green, who has turned her work into a nonprofit, Endora, that investigates far-right groups to help human rights organizations identify and prepare for threats. "Knowing who is coming for you, why they are coming for you, and what their tactics are gives you a huge advantage in terms of planning for it."

Almost always, she says, the best defense is to crowdsource information from your community. For legal threats, that might mean working with allies to assemble a roster of lawyers. To address financial threats, get help from a group of committed donors. And for physical threats, turn to trusted neighbors, family, and friends, who can act as another set of eyes and ears.

Of course, opposition research can also be dangerous. Kristofer Goldsmith, a U.S. Army veteran who has been called the "Neo-Nazi hunter next door" for his infiltration of and reporting on White nationalist movements, knows that his work makes him a target.

"I have a concealed carry permit. I am proficient in firearms training," says Goldsmith. "I have eight cameras running around my house that record twenty-four/seven. I pay for business-quality internet so that everything gets uploaded instantaneously." He even had an escape ladder installed so that he can get out of a second-story window quickly if necessary.

But it's Goldsmith's relationship with the local police that has proven most critical. He has more than once been the victim of "swatting"—when a caller harasses a victim by falsely summoning police to a fake emergency situation, such as a hostage or a bomb threat at the victim's home. Those calls can prompt the police to send out their heavily armed SWAT teams.

It's not exactly in Goldsmith's nature to embrace the police. The website of one of his projects—organizing fellow veterans against MAGA extremism—sells a T-shirt that says: "Cops Don't Stop Nazis, We Do." But when local detectives came over to investigate a hit-and-run of his neighbor's car, Goldsmith decided to enlist them as allies. They bonded over his firearm collection and his ninety-pound pit bull.

Since then, "I've invited the whole department over to come meet my dogs," Goldsmith says. These days, when the police get suspicious calls about him, they don't send the SWAT team.

11

***

Stack Your Defenses

The Swiss Cheese Theory

WHEN ZIMBABWE SHOOK OFF ALMOST forty years of brutal rule by the strongman Robert Mugabe, the transition wasn't nearly as joyous as Nyasha Frank Mpahlo had always imagined.

A longtime pro-democracy activist, Mpahlo had been among the civil society leaders pushing for the country to hold its first free and fair elections after Mugabe's resignation in 2017. But the campaign for a new president was plagued by violence, voter intimidation, and media bias that prompted "deep concerns" from international election observers. In the end, Mugabe's former vice president, Emmerson Mnangagwa, blazed ahead and declared victory.

In Mnangagwa's first days as president, as demonstrators gathered in the center of Harare on Nelson Mandela Avenue to protest the election results, the army opened fire on its own people.

For Mpahlo, the turn of events brought the crushing realization that his years-long advocacy efforts had not meaningfully altered the country's trajectory. Mugabe's rule—marked by rigged elections, arbitrary detentions, and state-sanctioned killings—now seemed set to be replaced by a new era of illiberalism and repression. It was a fate shared by many throughout the continent.

"If you look across Africa, nonviolent movements have been crushed really brutally," says Zachariah Mampilly, a political science professor at the City University of New York who studies African protest movements.

Yet Mampilly is hopeful that a new generation of young people facing aging leaders will find a path to democracy. Though some on the world stage invoke Africa's rapid population growth and relative youth (some six in ten people on the continent are under twenty-five years old) to predict a future of instability and chaos for the continent, he points to twentieth-century movements in India and the United States, as well as African anticolonial struggles of the same period, as proof that sometimes structural reform just takes time.

"It is too early to write off Africa's young democratizers," Mampilly wrote in a 2021 *Foreign Affairs* article about youth protesters. "History shows that it often takes years or even decades for a popular uprising to yield substantive change."

Mpahlo certainly wasn't giving up. In coordination with the Center for Applied Nonviolent Action and Strategies in Serbia, he convened a group of leading activists and planned a strategy retreat to be held in the Maldives, an island country southwest of India.

The Maldives location was a strategic choice. A popular resort spot, the island required no advance visa paperwork of its visitors and was also less likely, as a tourist destination, to cause any suspicion. And it was not a country with close ties to the government of Zimbabwe, where the new president was busy installing facial recognition technology and surveillance cameras.

Because the coterie of seasoned activists making the risky trip suspected they were being watched, they took a number of measures to deflect attention. They booked separate flights, concerned that a group of high-profile reformers traveling together might trigger alarms. Each pledged to buy a new phone for the trip and to communicate only on the encrypted messaging app Signal. And they agreed not to tell anyone where they were going—not their families, and not their fellow activists back home.

The activists arrived in the Maldives. One member of the group—taken by the island's crystal blue waters and white sand beaches—posted a video to Instagram showing herself by the ocean with a heart-shaped filter superimposed over her head. "I can get used to this," she captioned the photo. At the bottom of the frame, she tagged her location: "Indian Ocean."

The post presumably provided enough information to tip off the authorities at home. The activists awoke the next day to a front-page headline in one of Zimbabwe's largest newspapers:

"Plot to unleash violent protests unearthed." The state-run publication breathlessly reported that a "group of shady organisations" was planning to unleash civil unrest in Zimbabwe:

> Currently, there is a group training in the Maldives. . . .
> Eight local activists . . . are attending the programme
> and will be instrumental in training and instigating
> mayhem to be rolled out in June.

Mpahlo was livid. They had done everything right and taken on grave risk to travel to the retreat and restart their efforts toward democracy. Boiling with frustration, he and the group's other members confronted their colleague. Had she outed them intentionally? She insisted it was a mistake.

"We tried not to interrogate why she did it, because we had a mission that we wanted to achieve," Mpahlo recalls. Scared and upset, the activists did their best to refocus on the training and make the best of their limited time away. There was also a sense among the group that this might be their last gathering for quite a while. "We also knew that three or four days later we might be behind bars."

The activists took separate flights back to Zimbabwe. When each one stepped off the plane, their families and friends were waiting for them—but so were the authorities, who took them into custody. "We were taken away, and our lives would never be the same again," Mpahlo recalls. The charges were subversion, counterintelligence, and being trained in the use of small arms. After initially being denied bail and spending more than two months behind bars, the group remained on probation for another year until a judge dismissed the case.

But the damage was done. The new regime had sent a strong message that it wasn't all that different from the old regime. "That incident stopped all the activism around elections in Zimbabwe, because there was so much fear," Mpahlo says. A few years on, the 2023 elections were again marred by intimidation and coercion. He says the government's political repression has had a chilling effect on political opponents, journalists, students, and activists, who are less likely to speak up today.

As Little Dirt as Possible

In his 2024 Pulitzer Prize–winning series, "Annals of Autocracy," *The Washington Post* editorial writer David E. Hoffman chronicled the alarming rise in regimes imprisoning their citizens for content they posted online.

"Social media has made people feel as though they can speak openly, but technological tools also allow autocrats to target individuals," Hoffman wrote. "Protesters are betrayed by the phones in their pockets."

Internet users were arrested for online posts in at least fifty-six countries in 2024, according to a survey conducted by the American nonprofit Freedom House. Thailand sentenced a pro-democracy activist to twenty-five years in prison for eighteen posts about its monarchy on the social media platform X. In Cuba, a woman received a fifteen-year jail term after she posted videos of police attacking protesters. In Pakistan, a seventeen-year-old student was condemned to life in prison for posting images on WhatsApp that allegedly denigrated the Prophet Muhammad.

Breza Race Maksimovic, the Serbian activist trainer who was hosting Mpahlo and the "Zimbabwe Seven"—as the group came to be known—says that people in countries that are sliding into authoritarianism are often taken by surprise when they realize that they must become more judicious in their online behavior.

"Activists from authoritarian countries are more aware of all the threats, including AI, bragging, and everything, because they have learned their lesson," she says. "Activists from the backsliding democracies, or semi-democracies, often don't think their lives will be jeopardized if someone finds out they were in a training."

Maksimovic says that in Serbia, where millions of people took to the streets to oust a dictator in 2000 and a new protest movement is now demanding accountability for government corruption, activism is "deeply in our veins and running in our blood." Serbs have learned from experience that authoritarians will use whatever means they can to discredit an opponent. But for those in backsliding democracies, she says, that change in mindset can take time.

Many Venezuelans, for instance, were caught off guard when President Hugo Chávez, who had been elected in free and fair elections, began suppressing the press, jailing political opponents, and manipulating election laws. Despite these dramatic changes, it took a while for many Venezuelans to realize that the country was sliding out of democracy.

"It creates some tension in your head," says Freddy Guevara, a former member of the Venezuelan National Assembly who is now living in exile in the United States. Guevara recalls a gap between Chávez's early campaigns of repression and his adaptation of his own behavior to meet the rapidly evolving threat landscape. "I posted a lot of things I shouldn't have posted," he reflects.

Guevara was elected to the Assembly after Chávez's death as a member of an opposition party during a brief moment of reform in 2015. But as soon as the president's successor, Nicolás Maduro, took office, the high court dissolved the Assembly, granting Maduro emergency powers. After Maduro threatened Guevara on live TV—"there is already a cell with your name on it"—Guevara sought refuge in the Chilean embassy, where he remained for almost three years.

In 2020, after extended negotiations, Guevara and other opposition politicians were pardoned by the Maduro government. But Guevara was arrested again a year later. He spent a month in prison and then was freed amid the government's efforts to ease American sanctions.

Guevara has been in the United States ever since. But what

he learned during his time in the opposition party was that dissidents must be extremely careful. "You have to be a nun or a saint," Guevara says.

This is a pattern described by dissidents in many countries: Autocrats and their allies use even the most minor personal scandal to discredit activists and weaken their movements. So taking part in activism under a repressive regime requires cleaning up your life—both your digital life and your personal life.

"There's never going to be zero risk," says Ramzi Kassem, a professor of law at the City University of New York and a co-director and founder of the nonprofit and legal clinic CLEAR (Creating Law Enforcement Accountability & Responsibility). Kassem specializes in providing legal support and representation to clients, communities, and movements that have been disproportionately targeted by U.S. law enforcement and security agencies. "You just have to decide how much risk you are willing to carry to continue to do the work you're doing," Kassem says.

Worrying about amorphous dangers can be paralyzing. Instead, dissidents advise writing up a plan for the worst-case scenario—what you'll do if you get fired or audited or find yourself in legal trouble.

It's also worth deleting old social media posts and using only trusted encrypted-messaging apps. Sadly, cleaning up might mean swearing off dating apps—or at least going the extra mile to verify that potential suitors are who they say they are. In the United States, the conservative activist James O'Keefe and his associates have used matchmaking platforms to meet with targets and secretly record them. More than a few have fallen for the tactic and lost their jobs when embarrassing videos of them surfaced.

In Venezuela, Guevara grew into the most cautious version of himself: He was increasingly discerning about the content he posted on social media. He didn't go to clubs. He didn't drive too fast. He always paid his taxes. He didn't write down anything that was sensitive. His general operating principle was to be discreet, even with those he trusted. "Most of the time it's people who rat you out," Guevara says.

"I've seen so many guys bragging, and now they're in jail," he says. "If someone wants to find dirt on you, they will find it. Give them as little dirt as possible."

Beware Your Phone

In February 2020, a thirty-nine-year-old gay man was shopping at a supermarket in Egypt when an undercover police officer appeared, called his name, told him they were going to the police station, and grabbed his phone. "He forcibly took my phone and demanded I open it," the man, who was detained overnight and deported, later told Human Rights Watch.

In Egypt, being gay isn't technically illegal. But that hasn't stopped the country's authoritarian president, Abdel Fattah al-

Sisi, from waging a campaign of terror against its queer community since seizing power in a coup in 2013.

The foot soldiers in Sisi's war are the officers of the General Directorate for Protecting Public Morality, and their preferred tactic is to set up fake profiles on dating apps that entrap victims. Then they seize the phones and use photos, messages, or apps as evidence to gin up charges for such crimes as "debauchery" and "violating family values."

The directorate has arrested some 250 Egyptians on such charges since 2013. Many have gone on to be tortured and beaten. The trend is part of a broader global phenomenon by which governments surveil and punish their citizens by using the inescapable tools of everyday life.

Many modern activists have sought to get around these repressive tactics by using encryption, a technology that allows people to trade messages on apps like Signal and WhatsApp that can't be read by anyone other than the intended recipient. Encryption prevents messages from being read if they are intercepted while they are zipping through internet pipes. It also prevents the app companies from reading their users' messages.

But encryption can't stop someone from physically grabbing an unlocked phone, or forcing a user to unlock their phone and combing through its contents—a threat that looms ever larger for activists around the world. The problem isn't limited to countries without a history of democracy. Federal agents at U.S. airports are permitted to inspect travelers' phones without a search warrant, and courts have ruled that U.S. police officers can forcibly unlock a user's phone by using a person's thumbprint or face ID.

Ana Maria Ramirez, a sexual and reproductive health researcher, realized that phone-grabbing was a top threat when she interviewed people across the United States in 2017 about what they would want from an app that provided reproductive health information for women and for nonbinary and trans people. States had begun to impose legal restrictions on reproductive health care, and some had even started to prosecute pregnant women for taking recreational drugs. Ramirez wanted to understand what it would take for people to feel safe obtaining health information in an increasingly criminalized landscape.

She expected to hear concerns about getting hacked. But what people actually told her was even more alarming. In a series of nationwide focus groups and one-on-one interviews, respondents said that they also feared the "over-the-shoulder" threat—parents or abusive partners physically taking their device and forcing them to open it.

In response, she got creative in deliberately designing an app, called Euki, for users who fear that someone might take their phone or glimpse its contents. The app has its own built-in web browser that retains no information about what users have viewed, so users can search for reproductive health information without leaving any tracks. Euki also prompts users to set two passcodes—one real, one for safety. They can enter the second safety code if someone tries to force them to open the app. It generates a message that blocks the user from opening the app.

Some activists who face similar risks in their public life have developed their own solutions to deal with over-the-shoulder threats. Raphael Mimoun, a longtime human rights activist, grew weary of hearing the oft-repeated advice that people should leave their phones at home when they go to a protest. "It's a good practice if you can," he says. "But realistically, if you are going to a protest, you want to take pictures and share with the world."

In 2019 Mimoun built an app, Tella, that allows users to store video, audio, and text files in an encrypted app that can be accessed only with a passcode. The app comes with its own digital camouflage—it can be disguised as a calculator on some phones—in case the device ends up in the wrong hands. As an extra layer of protection, he advises people who are heading out to a protest to create a Signal group with a few people who won't be attending. "Take all of your photos and your videos directly inside that group," he says. "Then if something bad happens, those people have access to it."

Mimoun calls his approach the "Swiss cheese theory." Each component—the encrypted app, the hidden icon, the Signal chat—has holes. But when stacked together, every layer can cover the gaps in the one below. "Encryption is absolutely central and critical," he says. "It is necessary, but not sufficient."

The Curb Cut Effect

No matter how hard you search, you won't find a photo of Afsaneh Rigot on the internet. She's made sure of that. Maybe you'll find an avatar—a sketch of a woman in dark, stylish shades. But that's not a picture of Afsaneh Rigot. And Afsaneh Rigot isn't her real name.

Rigot uses her legal name only at airports, where she refuses facial recognition when she can. She does not appear in videos or photos. When she speaks at conferences that are filmed or photographed, she wears a mask and sunglasses. She rigorously maintains two separate identities, one professional and one personal, including carrying different phones for each identity. So separate are these two identities that many relatives don't even know what she does for a living.

There's a good reason for the cloak-and-dagger antics. Rigot fled Iran to the United Kingdom with her mother, a former political prisoner, when she was nine years old. Today she is a leading human rights investigator, conducting research on the ways in which phones can betray their users. A queer woman, Rigot knows that her work and her identity, considered subversive by some, could pose dangers for her relatives still living in the country of her birth. So everything stays under wraps.

It's the cost of human rights advocacy. Rigot travels extensively to research how digital evidence from phones is used for repression. Pseudonymity allows her to decouple the person who enters the airport from the person who will author a detailed report on that country's abuses. One of those reports, "Digital Crime Scenes," provided the first comprehensive look at how the governments of Egypt, Lebanon, and Tunisia use the contents of personal cell phones to prosecute LGBT individuals.

"Digital evidence has become a key tool in providing evidence for a crime that is otherwise very difficult to prove," Rigot writes in the report. "Yet, what is deemed too queer to be legal is not defined."

Nearly every case shares one factor in common: A victim's phone was confiscated and searched for "evidence" that they were queer. One government used as court evidence a text message stating "I like you." Another pointed to a phone contact saved as "Honey." A half-dozen defendants Rigot interviewed told her that personal selfies were used against them in court. Many cases were based on WhatsApp chat histories.

For a decade, Rigot has sought to address this human rights crisis through a movement she calls "Design from the Margins," which advocates for tech companies and designers to put the needs of vulnerable people at the forefront of design decisions. That means allowing app icons to be hidden or cloaked, building self-destruct buttons into apps, setting up ways to stop nonconsensual screenshotting, and permitting the use of pseudonyms.

A number of companies have taken up these reforms. In

2023, Meta introduced a feature that allows users to make a WhatsApp chat thread disappear unless the user types a passcode into the search bar, and Signal introduced a feature that lets users change an app's icon to look like another icon, such as a weather app. In 2024, Apple introduced a new feature that lets users lock and hide apps. These are all steps on the road that Rigot ultimately hopes the tech industry will take toward "being able to build deniability into our devices."

This design philosophy is similar to an approach known as the "curb cut effect," after the sidewalk ramps built into street corners in response to advocacy by disabled activists to allow them easier mobility. These curb cuts have proven beneficial for many other people as well—including parents pushing strollers and postal carriers rolling mail carts—and they have become a ubiquitous feature of urban design.

It turns out that when we design for the most vulnerable, everyone benefits.

12

—

Win the War of Persuasion

Nonviolence Is More Convincing than Violence

BY THE TIME ALGERIA LAUNCHED its bid for independence in 1954, the Algerian people had suffered greatly under France's rule for more than a century. The French had repressed the population and murdered an estimated one million Algerians through grotesque means, including suffocating an entire tribe of hundreds of people in a cave by burning fires that choked them with smoke.

So perhaps it was not surprising that the Algerian revolution was bloody. The Front de Libération Nationale fought using every available tactic, including bombings, ambushes, and gruesome massacres. Angry mobs wielding knives, clubs, pitchforks, and axes beheaded and disemboweled French women and children. After nearly eight years of fighting and atrocities committed by both sides, the French signed a peace deal and granted Algeria its freedom.

As a graduate student in political science at the University of Colorado, Erica Chenoweth viewed stories like that of revolutionary Algeria as evidence that violence was a common ingredient in political change. So when Chenoweth signed up for a conference about nonviolent civil resistance in 2006, the future Harvard professor was skeptical but curious.

"I must say I attended the workshop as a cynic," Chenoweth later wrote. When other attendees talked about nonviolent success stories like the People Power Revolution in the Philippines, which bloodlessly toppled the Marcos dictatorship in 1986, Chenoweth countered with stories like China's brutal repression of the Tiananmen Square protests. For every successful nonviolent movement discussed, Chenoweth would raise questions about a counterexample of a failed nonviolent movement.

It wasn't much of a strategy for making friends. Among the participants frustrated with Chenoweth's skepticism was Maria J. Stephan, who had organized the conference and was assigned to be Chenoweth's roommate. Stephan had recently finished her PhD on the role of nonviolent resistance in self-determination struggles.

Stephan challenged her roommate: If Chenoweth was so certain that violence was more successful than nonviolence, why not examine the data and prove it?

Soon the two were collaborating on an unprecedented study: analyzing more than one hundred years of mass movements that sought to topple a national government, obtain territorial independence, or remove an incumbent leader from power. They rated each movement by its success and classified each as violent, nonviolent, or mixed depending on its tactics.

Deciding whether a movement qualified as nonviolent proved tricky. Even movements that have been strongly committed to peaceful means have often included some violent elements—like the Indian villagers in 1922 who set a police station on fire with a policeman locked inside, derailing Gandhi's efforts to lead a nonviolent tax strike against the British. Such stories made for a complicated analysis.

But Chenoweth and Stephan did the best they could, in part by dividing movements into distinct campaigns. For instance, they categorized as nonviolent the First Palestinian Intifada of the late 1980s despite multiple incidents of stone-throwing and the use of explosives that injured Israeli soldiers. But they categorized the string of deadly suicide bombings and other high-casualty attacks targeting Israeli civilians in the early 2000s as a separate violent campaign. Some campaigns were complex to classify on their own—Gandhi's nonviolent Quit India effort of 1942 was unsuccessful in the short term (he was jailed and the movement fell apart), but historians are split as to how much it contributed to the British departure from India several years later. The pair included it as part of India's longer nonviolent struggle against British rule from 1919 to 1945, which they deemed a limited success.

In the end, Chenoweth and Stephan had collected 323

data points and the results were clear: Nonviolent campaigns were twice as likely to be successful as violent campaigns.

Still, the findings were subtler than they appeared. An ideological commitment to nonviolence alone didn't seem to be the winning tactic. It was a means to an end. The most successful movements were the largest ones. And nonviolent efforts were able to attract, on average, eleven times the number of participants recruited by armed insurgencies.

"The bottom-line finding was that the most effective pro-democracy movements were able to build and sustain mass and diverse participation," Stephan said.

Nonviolence, in other words, can be a persuasive marketing tactic for the product that activists are selling: the movement itself.

The War in the Woods

George Alexander was twenty-three years old when his face was slashed nearly in half by a lumber mill saw—the result of a violent resistance tactic of the American environmental movement.

It was 1987 and Alexander was working at a California lumber mill, splitting logs, when the saw made contact with a log that had been spiked with a metal rod. The saw ricocheted away from the log and struck him in the face, slashing his face from eye to chin, cutting his jaw in half and crushing his teeth.

Alexander had become a victim of tree spiking, a controversial gambit adopted by some environmentalists in the 1980s. Aiming to prevent logging of old-growth forests, activists snuck into the woods and inserted metal spikes into tree trunks, creating grave risks for loggers working to cut them down.

The tactic was intended to change the behavior of the logging companies. Activists said they would mark spiked trees and warn firms about areas that were spiked, in the hopes of preventing logging. But in the end, it was sawmill workers like Alexander who bore the violent human toll of the tactic.

"It wasn't nonviolent. We never said it was," says Mike Roselle, one of the cofounders of Earth First!, an organization that promoted tree-spiking. "But we also said it was justified, and I still believe it was."

Roselle and his colleagues had been engaging in nonviolent action for years, blockading the logging roads that led to the old-growth forests in California and Oregon. But after a while, the media stopped paying attention to their protests. "They weren't interested in hippies on the road anymore." Tree-spiking, he says, "was an escalation."

But it was a dangerous strategy. The Alexander incident turned the tide of public opinion against the environmentalists. Lawmakers were outraged. Media columnists railed against the "eco-terrorists." The Sierra Club and other mainstream environmental groups denounced tree-spiking. Eventually, Earth First! reversed course and announced that it would stop using the tactic. The group's core members soon scattered to other causes.

Now in his seventies, Roselle concedes that the movement to stop old-growth logging was a failure by its own terms. "There's less old growth today," he says. "When we started the campaign, there was still quite a bit left—so it was a bad loss, really." The tactics chosen by activists didn't deliver on the one goal they had set out to achieve.

But the controversy "put old growth on the map," Roselle maintains, and spurred on a new generation of activists. "It just made them want to prove that there were other ways to do it," he argues.

He may be right. Consider Meares Island in British Columbia, home to a temperate rainforest with red cedar trees towering as high as 160 feet. In 1985, activists placed 26,000 helix nails in old-growth cedar trees on the island in the hopes of forestalling logging projects. But what actually saved the forest was a four-decade nonviolent campaign by local indigenous groups.

It began with a blockade. Environmentalists joined with members of the First Nations to build wooden huts on the beach to block the logging company helicopters from landing. When the company executives arrived by boat, they were greeted by First Nations elders inviting them for a meal while declaring the land sovereign. Faced with a beach full of peaceful but insistent forest defenders, the loggers decided to leave rather than try to begin logging.

The nonviolent blockades eventually attracted tens of thousands of protesters to what the media dubbed "the War in the Woods." With the attention, the Ahousaht and Tla-o-qui-aht First Nations had bought enough time to bring legal action. They soon won an injunction against the logging company and eventually secured government protections for the old-growth forest.

Authoritarian Nonviolence

In 2018 the Slovakian investigative journalist Ján Kuciak and his fiancée Martina Kušnírová were drinking coffee in their home when someone knocked on the door. A few minutes later, both were dead: Kuciak shot in the chest and Kušnírová in the head.

Kuciak had been investigating why the Slovakian prime minister had hired a twenty-seven-year-old former Miss Universe contestant despite her lack of qualifications. The story had taken a turn when he learned that the contestant was allegedly connected to an Italian organized crime syndicate.

The brutal assassination of Kuciak shocked the nation, prompting massive street protests. The prime minister resigned. The police chief stepped down. The government fell. And a group of journalists who had long been competitors joined forces to publish Kuciak's reporting posthumously and continue further investigations in his name.

This is one of the reasons authoritarian violence often backfires: It can unite a fractious opposition. Beatings of protesters. Soldiers firing into unarmed crowds. State-sponsored assassinations. Masked men kidnapping people off the street. Witnessing these acts of violence can propel people away from the sidelines and into active opposition to a regime.

But of late autocrats are becoming more strategic in their deployment of state violence. In Hungary, prime minister Viktor Orbán has managed to take nearly complete control of the media without a single shot fired. Instead, he funnels money into the outlets that promote his agenda and restricts funding sources for outlets that are adversarial.

"There are no physical threats to journalists," says Tamás Bodoky, cofounder and editor-in-chief of the Hungarian investigative news outlet *Atlatszo*. "It's all about starving out the ecosystem."

In 2024, Hungary's government launched an investigation into *Atlatszo*, alleging that the organization was engaged in intelligence-gathering and disinformation activities in service of a foreign government. Bodoky fought back by suing the government for defamation, and won. Meanwhile, in 2025, the Hungarian government proposed a new law that would designate outlets such as *Atlatszo* threats to the nation's sovereignty and prohibit them from accepting foreign donations. Bodoky believes that the measure, if passed, would effectively kill the last remaining independent media in the country.

A few independent newsrooms, including *Atlatszo*, have formed a consortium to resist the government's quiet assault. But amid the funding setbacks, most member organizations are barely clinging to life. With scarcely any budget to support marketing, outreach, or additional lawsuits, the group amounts to little more than a series of statements opposing the bill.

Where physical violence united the Slovakian media, financial attacks have largely kept Hungarian outlets scattered and disjointed.

"Slovakia is a smaller country, but independent media is much stronger there," Bodoky says. "We are still competing for audience, for funding, for credit, and that makes it pretty hard to do some big solidarity."

"Collective Stubbornness"

Size matters. That's one way to describe Chenoweth and Stephan's findings about the higher success rates of nonviolent movements. After they turned their research into a book, they were inundated with questions about size.

How big did a movement need to be to be successful? Was there a threshold for success? People were desperate for a magic number.

So Chenoweth did the math. The data showed that there was an observable line that nearly all the successful nonviolent campaigns crossed. When at least 3.5 percent of a population participated in nonviolent opposition at peak protests, movements generally prevailed.

The number was an afterthought; the two scholars hadn't even included it in their book. But it has now become an article of faith for political movements across the globe. Chenoweth's 2013 TedX talk about "the 3.5 Percent Rule" has been viewed over half a million times. *The New Yorker* profiled Chenoweth. And the number has been popularized on podcasts and across social media in TikTok, Instagram, and YouTube videos.

For activists living under various states of repression, the 3.5 percent rule has grown into a source of optimism, a concrete reason for hope amid political turmoil. But for the two scholars, it's become a bit of a headache. Chenoweth has published a paper cautioning readers against focusing too much on the number at the expense of the other lessons from the data.

"The 3.5 percent participation metric may be useful as a rule of thumb in most cases," Chenoweth wrote. "However, other factors—momentum, organization, strategic leadership, and sustainability—are likely as important."

Stephan, who trains activists, organizers, and community leaders, believes that focusing on the precise number can be distracting. "I've found that some people interpret that as meaning that if you get lots of people to show up for a mass protest, you win," she says. "When in reality, it takes organizing, strategizing, building unity, growing participation, and powerful tactics like boycotts and strikes."

Getting 3.5 percent of people out onto the streets is often

the culmination of a movement that has built up momentum for years. Rather than the goal itself, the number is best understood as an indicator of what has already succeeded. As veteran Serbian activist Srđja Popović wrote in his book *Blueprint for Revolution*:

> A mass demonstration, as anyone who has ever organized any successful campaign will tell you, is the last step you take, not the first. You urge the masses to march in the streets when you know you have enough of the masses on your side, and only when you've already done all the preparations necessary to bring your campaign to a showdown. The big rally isn't the spark that launches your movement. It's actually the victory lap.

The miles leading up to that victory lap are a grinding series of mass noncooperation actions like strikes, boycotts, sit-ins, refusals to work, and blockades that impede the function of the regime. "I call it collective stubbornness," Stephan says.

Poland's Solidarity movement, which toppled the communist regime in 1989, is considered a gold standard for mass noncooperation. The movement was disciplined in using general strikes to force the government to the negotiating table. After a year of strikes, the Soviets declared martial law and imprisoned the movement's trade unionist leaders.

But Solidarity continued underground, and after nearly

two years, Soviet officials freed its leaders and lifted martial law. The strikes and protests resumed, and by 1988 the Soviets had acceded to the movement's demand for free and fair elections. Voters chose the Solidarity party to lead the country's new parliament.

The movement's success came during the golden years for nonviolent campaigns. Success rates for nonviolent movements soared to as high as 65 percent in 1989, according to Chenoweth's data. Success rates have plummeted since then, to 34 percent for nonviolent campaigns and 8 percent for violent campaigns between 2010 and 2019.

It's not clear exactly why civil resistance is becoming more difficult. Some speculate that autocrats are getting smarter—borrowing techniques from each other and, like Orbán, finding ways to achieve their ends using financial and psychological damage instead of the physical violence that turns the population against them. Others note that the decline may coincide with an overreliance on social media, which allows people to feel like they are doing something without leaving their couch but doesn't always translate into meaningful opposition.

Structural racism can also play a significant role in the success or failure of nonviolent resistance movements. In 2021, scholars Devorah Manekin and Tamar Mitts reanalyzed Chenoweth's data through a racial lens and found that acts of nonviolent resistance led by ethnic minority groups are seen as more violent—and are less successful—than those led by majority groups.

"Minority groups engaged in campaigns for social and political change are often urged to adopt nonviolent tactics or chided for not doing so," Manekin and Mitts write. "Our study shows that such tactics, even when adopted, are often perceived as more violent than they are and as requiring more repression by the state."

But even amid its limitations, civil resistance can still succeed. Consider the Takedown Tesla campaign, among the most effective recent boycott efforts. The protests themselves were often just a few dozen people standing in front of a local Tesla dealership, waving signs that called out Tesla chief executive Elon Musk for his January 2025 Nazi-like salute, his public support for racist, antisemitic and anti-trans ideas, and assaults on the civil service during his tenure at the White House.

But while the in-person protests were small, the number of people who sold their Teslas and declined to buy new ones proved disproportionately large. After just two months of protests, Tesla sales had fallen 13 percent globally, the stock was down 33 percent, and Musk had left his government post under pressure from shareholders to turn the company around.

Most important was the cultural win: The boycott succeeded in denting the auto company's cultural cachet. Tens of thousands of Tesla owners bought stickers to place on their cars apologizing for owning the vehicle and disavowing Musk.

In a war of persuasion, victory is changing the narrative.

IV

On Growing the Ranks

13

—

Seize the Story

The Pleasure of Agency and the Joy in Defiance

ON A WARM CALIFORNIA EVENING in the spring of 1966, the governor of the Golden State rode in a police car, with sirens blaring, past a group of picketing farmworkers. When he stepped out of the car, he was greeted warmly by the head of a large liquor and food conglomerate. The wealthy executive—the employer of the protesting workers—urged the governor to oppose the strike, and for a moment he considered it. But when the governor said no—that he would stand by the farmworkers and support their demands for better wages and working conditions—things went south. The executive physically took hold of the governor and dragged him away, kicking and screaming, from the picket line.

It was a dramatic scene—one that took place not in real life but inside of a theater performance, staged by the labor leader Luis Valdez on the bed of his pickup truck during a twenty-five-day farmworker strike in the middle of the convulsive 1960s.

For weeks, the mostly Mexican and Filipino workers had been walking along a 250-mile route, from the town of Delano in California's farming heartland to the state's capital in Sacramento, demanding higher wages and improved working conditions from the food conglomerates that employed them in their fields.

The United Farm Workers had launched a consumer boycott the previous year, targeting the two largest ranches in Delano. In his 1967 book *Delano*, John Gregory Dunne recounted how the workers picked up people along the route during their 1966 *peregrinación* (pilgrimage): "At each town, the ranks of the marchers swelled as farm workers joined the peregrination for a mile or an hour or even a whole day . . . and their families gave the marchers rosaries, mass cards, fruit, tea, and food."

After each long day of marching, once the union nurse had lanced the blisters on their sore feet, the marchers and others from nearby towns would gather around the pickup truck to watch a theater performance. The plays were often a raucous spectacle. Staged in the stark style of the twentieth-century German playwright Bertolt Brecht, Valdez's *actos* featured abstract caricatures without emotional complexity. Each character—the farm boss, the striking worker, the scab, the governor—acted out the elements of the strike in a didactic manner, with signs draped around their necks to identify their roles.

The cartoonishness was by design. In these oversimplified narratives, an audience could reflect on the political lessons being imparted rather than becoming distracted with the personal dramas of the characters, a tactic that Brecht called the "distancing effect." Valdez's goal was to help workers see power dynamics for what they were, disentangled from the complexities of their day-to-day work.

"To many of you these *actos* may seem to be satire," Valdez said onstage during a 1967 performance in Berkeley after a "farmworker" had just stuffed a "farm boss" dressed as a pig into a barrel to be symbolically cooked. "But, in the eyes of the farmworkers, these are the realities."

———

Activists around the world often rely on storytelling to convey messages on issues that the public otherwise finds irrelevant, uninteresting, or too complicated to merit their limited attention. In 2023 a group of Polish climate activists descended on the building where Poland's biggest state-owned fossil fuel company was holding an investor meeting. The company was reaping windfall profits while the nation was suffering from the costs of an energy crisis.

Critics saw a classic case of greenwashing—promoting renewable energy investments while actually focusing on expanding gas investments. But energy policy is complex, and the country's climate activists needed a way to convey to everyday

Poles—people who didn't know carbon offsets from carbon capture—that the company was not on a serious path to easing their climate problems.

They settled on a plan: As investors arrived at the conference, signs welcomed them to the "multi-energy circus." Circus music honked and whistled from a loudspeaker on the plaza. A demonstrator wearing a head-to-toe clown costume passed out red foam noses to the men in suits shuffling in and out of the building. "Enough clowning around with the transformation" read a poster, framed by the red-and-white stripes of a circus tent.

"From the outside, we looked totally unhinged," recalls Dominika Lasota, one of the activists who planned the spectacle. "But that level of insanity made the people going in deeply uncomfortable. And that was the point."

Lasota and her colleagues are part of a long line of movement leaders who have favored satire as a political tactic. The Serbian youth activists who toppled Slobodan Milošević once painted the authoritarian president's face on a metal barrel that they placed on a busy street. Passersby who donated one dinar could hit the barrel with a stick; those who had no money to spare got to strike the barrel twice. When state police confiscated the barrel, the students put out a press release: Under Milošević, nobody was safe—he had even arrested a barrel.

These activists understood that people who are rarely reached through speeches or marches might hear a message—and even act on it—if it was presented through a stark and simple narrative. This is the same essential insight of movement organizing that Valdez and the farmworkers leveraged in California as they worked to grow their movement for better working conditions in the mid to late 1960s.

By 1969, the farmworkers' *actos*, marches, hunger strikes, and other tactics had captured the nation's attention. But the farming conglomerates still had not agreed to meaningful improvements. So the movement turned its focus toward cashing in on the goodwill it had earned with the public and inflicting economic pain on the growers.

They did it, once again, through simplifying the narrative. "The plan was very simple," recalled Dolores Huerta—who, with Cesar Chavez, led the worker movement—at a fortieth anniversary celebration of the strike. "To take the fight into the cities and have the people help us out with one very easy task of not buying grapes."

Grapes had very little to do with the reality on the ground for farmworkers, and they represented only a fraction of the companies' profits. But they were a luxury food that consumers could boycott easily. Saying no to grapes didn't require extensive study. It didn't mean giving up much in daily life. Instead, it offered regular people the chance to make one small choice. And for people who knew little about the working conditions on California farms, it turned out that choice was a gateway into the fight for justice. The grape boycott was a narrative in which they could place themselves, as well as an opportunity to signal their values and exercise their agency.

Reverend Chris Hartmire, a Presbyterian minister and the director of an interfaith ministry that provided nursing care, Bible study, and other services to migrant farmworkers, took up the baton. He lobbied faith leaders across the nation to join the boycott and dispatched striking workers to churches and synagogues to tell their stories.

"Slowly but surely, hundreds, then thousands, of the best folks said 'yes,'" Hartmire recalled at the fortieth anniversary of the strike. The congregants invited demonstrating farmworkers into their homes for meetings, for meals, and to organize. Soon they joined picket lines, distributed leaflets, and held prayer vigils in supermarket produce sections. They filled shopping carts with grapes and then left them at the checkout counter in protest. The movement grew: 12 percent of Americans eventually said the campaign moved them to stop eating grapes. On July 29, 1970, the grape growers signed union contracts, agreeing to vastly improved conditions for the people who worked in their fields.

It was a historic victory for the farmworkers, who saw their wages rise and their health care benefits increase, and for the first time they enjoyed protections from exposure to toxic pesticides. For the congregants in towns across California who now had their first taste of activism, the win represented another kind of revelation.

"It added goodness and meaning to their lives," Hartmire recalled. People who had known nothing of the farmworker struggle had found purpose, fulfillment, and even delight in participating in small acts of defiance. "If they were here, they would join me in saying, 'Thank you, a thousand times thank you,' to you pioneer strikers and boycotters who challenged us and then led us on the most important and most meaningful ride of our lives."

Far More Exhilarating

In 1979 a bloody civil war broke out in El Salvador between the military dictatorship and a coalition of left-wing guerrilla groups known as the Farabundo Martí National Liberation Front (FMLN). The nation's impoverished tenant farmers—*campesinos*—had been forced to pay higher and higher rents to El Salvador's few wealthy landowners, while not earning enough money to feed their families. At long last, they had a movement fighting for them.

The military junta did all it could to crush popular support for the rebels. They created positive incentives, such as offering new land parcels to peasants who had previously only toiled on large farm estates, but also negative ones: Military death squads roamed the countryside, executing those who were caught supplying the rebels. More than seventy-five thousand Salvadorans were killed during the twelve-year conflict.

And yet an extraordinary number of *campesinos* were undeterred. Despite the intense threats they faced and the tempting inducements of defection, thousands of women, men, and even teenagers smuggled water, food, and weapons to the FMLN fighters. Households took turns sheltering rebel fighters in the countryside or bringing them water and tortillas.

"Each house would send twenty-five tortillas, eight houses at a time. In this, *everyone* contributed," one participant later recounted to scholar Elisabeth Jean Wood. The *campesinos* would sometimes have to pass through army checkpoints. "If they caught us it was death or castration. Or they would cut off your head. We made a lot of sacrifices passing through the army."

Wood, a Yale University professor, interviewed nearly two hundred *campesinos* and found one key reason why they were willing to risk so much during the war: Under conditions of profound fear and repression, supporting insurgent activities "had redrawn the contours of their world." The farmers—long victims of a violent, authoritarian government—were now taking part in the collective project of reimagining their future and experiencing what Wood calls "a pleasure in agency."

Aiding the rebels offered tenant farmers a measure of "dignity in the face of condescension, repression, and indifference," Wood wrote. "Pleasure in agency is the pleasure in together changing unjust social structures through intentional action."

The same basic phenomenon may have motivated many activists during the U.S. civil rights movement more than a decade earlier and half a world away. For many participants in the civil disobedience work of Mississippi Freedom Summer— particularly the White Northern volunteers who traveled

South—there was something special, visceral, even transformative about taking collective risk in the name of a shared value. The sociologist Doug McAdam has called this feeling "cognitive liberation."

"Here was high moral purpose, adventure, and rich community all rolled into one," McAdam wrote in his 1988 chronicle of the movement, *Freedom Summer*. "What many of the volunteers glimpsed in Mississippi was a way of life, a form of community, and a vision of themselves far more exhilarating and engaging than any they had known before."

These outbursts of principled, collective risk-taking—with no guaranteed return on investment—have befuddled some social scientists, who take for granted a certain set of rules of human rationality. Amid the activist convulsions of the late 1960s, the prominent economist Albert O. Hirschman, for example, tried to understand why people would put public interest ahead of their personal benefit. Economists had long attributed these movements to external events that pulled people out of their comfortable private realms. But Hirschman blew up that thesis with his finding that those who participated in public activism—like student uprisings, demonstrations, and strikes—were more often motivated by something internal: the fulfillment of striving toward a common purpose. "The sudden realization (or illusion) that I can act to change society for the better and, moreover, that I can join other like-minded people to this end is in such conditions pleasurable, in fact intoxicating, in itself," he wrote.

The activists of the late 1960s had grown up in a postwar world that felt fixed and set in its ways. But when people came in contact with a social cause—when they could see themselves in a movement's story and as an instrument of its goals—many came to believe that they did have power. The experience, Hirschman wrote, produced "a radical cognitive change, akin to a revelation."

Joy Is a Beachhead for Organizing

In the days after the president of the United States sent the National Guard into the streets of the nation's capital in August 2025, Washington, D.C., residents banded together and reveled in using a joyous tool of defiance: mocking the invasion.

One D.C. local played Darth Vader's theme music from *Star Wars* as he marched behind armed troops patrolling the city's quiet streets. Another became internet-famous after throwing his Subway sandwich at a federal officer. When the former TV host turned federal prosecutor Jeanine Pirro charged him with felony assault, a grand jury refused to indict him for a felony—challenging the maxim that prosecutors could get a grand jury to "indict a ham sandwich." (He was later found not guilty of a misdemeanor in a jury trial.)

If the people of the District seemed almost to be channeling the Serbian students, it might not have been a coincidence. Keya Chatterjee, who leads a Washington self-governance project called Free DC, says that she and fellow organizers have taken inspiration from the youth tactics that helped turn opinion against Milošević.

"It was very important to make fun of him," Chatterjee says. "It is an act of defiance to be joyful."

Turning joy into defiance is at the heart of Free DC's organizing strategy. Ten days after troops arrived in her city, many of the organization's affiliates could be found on the corner of Fourteenth and U Streets, dancing among their fellow D.C. residents to the funky, drum-heavy rhythm of a performance of go-go music, a style that originated in the District in the 1970s.

Another organizer, the local musician Justin "Yaddiya" Johnson, spoke over the beat to the bopping crowd: "Nobody is coming to save us," he said. "Make sure you look out for one another because we are all we got."

The dance party was typical of the Free DC movement, which launched just days before the forty-seventh president's inauguration. The group organizes drum circles, clothing swaps, drag performances, crafting hours, and block parties like the one at Fourteenth and U. The goal is to build a strong and engaged organizing base—with outposts in every part of the city—that can lobby long-term for the district's statehood dreams as well as unite and mobilize residents against a federal takeover.

D.C. has been seeking statehood for generations, but its autonomy gained new relevance as the White House dispatched troops into the city. "You cannot take down an authoritarian without people in the capital rising up," Chatterjee says.

She believes that amid rising authoritarianism, spaces where neighbors can enjoy one another's company are where organizing can begin.

"They want us to be so afraid," she says. "And the only way to counter fear is with joy."

14

Find the Double Thinkers

Bring Others to the Brink of Their
Own Moral Collisions

EVERY WEDNESDAY, JUST BEFORE TWELVE o'clock, Zulema Palavecino prepares to leave her house in the working-class neighborhood of Burzaco, some twenty-seven kilometers south of Buenos Aires. She feeds her two cats and packs a little tote bag with the things she'll need for the day, including goggles (in case of tear gas) and a small carton of milk (which she says helps alleviate the burn). Alberto, her partner of thirty years, gets a kiss, and then it's a short walk to the nearest bus station.

"He is the kindest person I have ever met in my life," Palavecino says. "I love him more every day."

On a good day, the bus comes quickly. But there haven't been many good days in Burzaco lately. The bus has been arriving late, if it arrives at all, and when it doesn't, Palavecino—a retired operator for ENTel, Argentina's state-owned telecom utility—walks another fifteen blocks to a second bus stop. Then it's a bus, to a train, to another bus. It's three o'clock when she finally arrives outside the Congress in downtown Buenos Aires to meet up with a group that calls itself the Jubilados Insurgentes, the "the insurgent retirees."

At seventy-four, Palavecino chalks up her relatively good health to the yoga and tai chi classes she's taken over the years. Perhaps her retirement would look different under different circumstances. But in Argentina, protesting is what pensioners do, and she is among the country's roughly seven million seniors who rely on public pensions.

"We've been protesting for many years," Palavecino, a longtime member of the telephone workers union, says. Argentina's retirees protested in the mid-1990s when President Carlos Menem stopped adjusting pensions for the rising cost of living. They reprised their protests in 2017 when President Mauricio Macri changed the pension formula again. The campaigns have had mixed results, but they proceed apace. As the sun rises and the tides turn, the retirees of Argentina take to the streets.

"The right to a dignified life when a person can no longer work" is the retirees' basic demand, according to Palavecino. "I'm going for all those who would like to be there but can't due to their health," she says.

A polarized politics and a stubborn national debt have turned the pensioners into a national Rorschach test: To some they are folk heroes, to others a drag on an already flagging economy. To Javier Milei, the chainsaw-wielding economist elected president of Argentina in 2023, the retirees are something more sinister: "parasites who live off the state."

When in August 2024 Milei vetoed an 8 percent cost-of-living increase to match soaring inflation rates, the pensioners once again took to the streets. But the government's response this time was different—more violent, more ruthless. Police officers beat elderly protesters with batons and doused them with pepper spray. In the months that followed, police repeatedly blasted older people with high-pressure water cannons mounted on top of police trucks. Some protesters, including opposition lawmakers, required medical attention.

"They must be told we're all terrorists," Palavecino reasons. "Otherwise, how could they be so harsh to elders who would fall over with a puff of wind?"

Since the 1990s, the watchdog organization Freedom House has generally given Argentina high marks on political rights and civil liberties. But doubts are creeping in. The clashes of recent years have unfolded against Milei's broader crackdown on protest rights, including a 2023 measure allowing police to use force "even when [the demonstrators] do not create a situation of danger."

For some Argentinians, the scenes evoke memories of the country's brutal military dictatorship in the 1970s and '80s. Others see in the clashes a government more interested in exerting control than in supporting the needs of its citizens. Even Pope Francis, who served as the archbishop of Buenos Aires before assuming the pontificate, spoke out amid the police violence against protesters in September 2024.

"Workers, people asking for their rights in the street, and the police were pushing them back with the most expensive thing there is: top quality pepper spray," the pope said. "Instead of paying for social justice, they paid for pepper spray."

———

One Wednesday afternoon, Palavecino and her crew of graying, windbreaker-clad grandparents settled into their corner of Plaza de los Dos Congresos. They clutched handmade signs and spoke into bullhorns. Some walked with a limp or a cane. Nearby stood a wall of riot police, two or three rows thick—command staff in the back, rank-and-file in the front, each officer holding a see-through shield in front of his torso emblazoned with the acronym PFA—Policía Federal Argentina.

"The good thing is that they haven't managed to scare us," Palavecino says. "Yes, they can kill us, but they'll kill us anyway by not covering our medicine. If we're going to die anyway, we'd rather die standing."

One of her compatriots must have been feeling especially outraged that day. He approached the police line, settling in front of a young man. "Isn't it your job to protect society?" Palavecino recalls the retiree asking the officer, who didn't flinch. "Instead of fighting cartels, criminals, organized crime—you're here, beating old people who are fighting for a just cause and for what's rightfully theirs."

The protester's voice grew louder, more impassioned. "Do you realize you could be my grandson?" His words were coming faster. "If you were my grandson and you had a grandfather who worked his whole life, and you saw that he wasn't being paid, would it be right to beat him just because he's protesting?"

From behind his riot shield, a tear slipped down the young man's cheek. Then another tear, and then many. He was crying. After a few seconds, Palavecino recalls, a superior officer emerged from the next row to handle the breach in protocol. He tapped the young officer's shoulder. A new policeman stepped forward, filling the gap that had momentarily emerged on the front line.

The young man stepped back, disappearing into the wall of police.

A Shift Along the Spectrum

Natan Sharansky, the famed Soviet dissident who advocated in the 1970s and '80s for the right of Jews to emigrate from the Soviet Union, writes that every totalitarian society is made up of three kinds of people: the true believers, the dissidents, and the double thinkers.

Sharansky's third category—the people who, as he has

written, "no longer believe in the regime but are too scared to say so"—are often the most important in tipping the scales of a successful social movement. They're up for grabs, persuadable, movable. They might even be willing to join the revolution. They're also the toughest to spot.

"The more authoritarian a country becomes, the harder it becomes to gauge what people's true opinions are, and whether they might be willing to shift loyalty or defect in some kind of important way," says Jonathan Pinckney, a political science professor at the University of Texas at Dallas.

"Defect" is the term academics and activists use for switching sides, or abandoning one political group and committing to another. The language is dramatic. It conjures images of Cold War–era spy thrillers and undercover agents swapping their state loyalties.

The truth, of course, is more complicated. When people change their political commitments, they typically do so in subtler ways—more gradually and along a spectrum. "It's really difficult to make a dramatic shift from one group to another," Pinckney says.

That's due, in part, to a fear of how a repressive regime might respond to dissent. But another fear—of social ostracization—can also hold people back. Individuals care intensely about group identity. Belonging to a tribe isn't just a basic human impulse; it can be a matter of survival. We depend on our friends, family, and social or professional communities for a range of needs—spiritual, psychological, and material.

Breaking with our group's dominant views can put those relationships at risk, leaving us alone and vulnerable. That's why speaking out can feel existential, Pinckney explains. "If your strategy depends on saying, 'We need people who are our most vehement opponents to become our most vehement supporters or else we're not interested,' that's unlikely to work."

A better goal, strategists say, is provoking smaller shifts among the targets of a campaign. As Nadine Bloch, the strategic nonviolent action trainer, writes, "Movements and campaigns are won not by overpowering one's active opposition." Bloch, who has worked on a range of issues, from banning dangerous chemicals in schools to fighting nuclear proliferation, says that most of the activists she works with don't have enough time or money to focus on flipping particularly entrenched opponents.

Bloch believes there's a time and place for more aggressive tactics. "Extreme opposition folks need to be isolated, made to look bad, exposed as evil, ridiculed," she says. But when it comes to moving those who might be persuadable, the best path to victory is focusing on who is needed to win and "shifting each group one notch along the spectrum."

Activists during the U.S. civil rights movement tapped into a similar logic when they aimed to make allies of sympathetic White Northerners. In 1964 organizers with the Student Nonviolent Coordinating Committee realized that thousands of White students receptive to the cause of civil rights had no easy point of entry into organizing efforts.

SNCC began recruiting White students, many from Northern campuses, for a summerlong campaign to register Black voters in Mississippi.

The idea had set off intense internal debate: Members of SNCC's national staff had believed that White students could undermine the leadership of local Mississippi activists. But many on the ground supported the proposal. They had seen that their struggles tended to receive more attention from both the media and the federal government when White allies were around. Fannie Lou Hamer, a local civil rights activist, argued that there was great value in expanding the movement's ranks: "If we're trying to break down segregation, we can't segregate ourselves," she said as SNCC deliberated.

In the end, the scenes the students witnessed on the ground—the violence endured by Black Southerners simply trying to exercise their constitutional rights—turned many from passive supporters to active members of the civil rights struggle. The organizers of Freedom Summer identified people who were getting close to their own moral breaking point and ushered them over the edge and into the arms of a waiting movement.

The Connected Critic

In the early 2000s, Mikhael Manekin—a religious Jewish Israeli—was completing his mandatory service as an infantry officer in the Israeli army when his unit deployed to a Palestinian village in the northern West Bank.

It was the early days of the Second Intifada, and deadly roadside attacks targeting Israeli civilians were becoming more frequent. One day orders came down to Manekin's unit: They were to stop any Palestinians from crossing a road designated for the exclusive use of Jewish settlers. The soldiers found a building near the road that could serve as a lookout point. They commandeered the building, evicting the Palestinian family for whom the building was home. With nowhere else to go, the family moved into the house next door.

Because the building had no functional toilet, the soldiers used the yard. One day when Manekin stepped into the yard to relieve himself, he locked eyes with someone staring at him from the window of the neighboring house. It was one of the women whose home he and his soldiers had seized. Under the woman's defiant gaze, Manekin's embarrassment quickly turned to shame. In an instant the young officer felt alienated from the *middot*, the Jewish values of humility and compassion with which he had been inculcated by his Orthodox Jewish parents. It seemed to him that now he stood somewhere else, somewhere far away from those values and the world of traditional Judaism in which he had grown up.

"I would not have understood the significance of this moment without my traditional Jewish upbringing," he later reflected. He suddenly became aware of the *kippah*—the skullcap that Jewish men traditionally wear—sitting on top of his head, underneath his helmet. The dissonance was unbearable. "If there was one moment in my life at which I knew in a single instance, as clear as day, that I was desecrating God's name, it was then," Manekin later wrote. "I barely recognized myself."

The moment helped propel him to action. At the end of his army service, Manekin began working with a group of fellow veterans to share with Israelis the realities of military service in the occupied Palestinian territories—the everyday acts of humiliation and violence the soldiers had witnessed or committed against Palestinians, often to carry out government policy. That many members of the group—known as Breaking the Silence—had also been brought up Orthodox, wasn't surprising, Manekin says.

"There's actually quite a bit of work and knowledge [in the Jewish tradition] on how to create a space for thinking on your own, caring about the suffering of others, creating a different narrative, which doesn't feed into the narrative that the regime is telling you," he says.

Manekin is drawing on that tradition and trying to embolden Israelis, religious and secular alike, to recognize and work to prevent Palestinian suffering. Today he is one of the most prominent Jewish religious voices in Israel's anti-occupation movement, a somewhat lonely perch in a country where Orthodox Judaism has become virtually synonymous with right-wing politics. In early 2023, after influential Israeli politicians invoked Jewish teachings to justify violence against

Palestinians, Manekin cofounded Smol Emuni (the Faithful Left), a small but growing movement of religious Israeli Jews who reject interpretations of the Jewish tradition that sanction violence or promote the dehumanization of Palestinians.

One tool he has developed, in collaboration with the activist Dvir Warshavsky, is *Preservation of the Soul*, a small booklet of Jewish ethics. Published and distributed by Smol Emuni to enlisted soldiers, the compendium draws together short readings from classical and rabbinic Jewish texts that emphasize traditional Jewish virtues like caution and vigilance, compassion, and fear of divine judgment.

The booklet is intended to start a conversation with and among soldiers who might be having quiet doubts about the orders they are receiving or the behaviors of the people around them. "I think there's a deep, subversive element of telling somebody, 'You can actually think for yourself,'" Manekin says. Some readers have remained in the military, while others have transferred units or decided to refuse military service altogether. Rather than asking Israelis to abandon their community—a demand he views as unrealistic and unlikely to succeed—Manekin's effort, he says, "is about responding from within to the rhetoric of violence, vengeance, erasure, and transfer."

The work puts into practice what the political philosopher Michael Walzer calls "connected criticism": the idea that people are more likely to take in difficult truths, change their minds, and eventually shift their behavior if the call comes from within their own community or from someone they perceive as sharing their own values and interests.

"This critic is one of us," Walzer writes. Though he may rebuke his people in harsh, even blistering terms, the connected critic "is not intellectually detached. Nor is he emotionally detached . . . he seeks the success of their common enterprise."

This is the tradition of Martin Luther King Jr., who located his aspiration for racial justice as "deeply rooted in the American dream," and the author George Orwell, who, despite his socialist proclivities, never scolded his fellow Britons for their materialism. Manekin's advocacy sits within this tradition as well: He is not a disconnected stranger casting judgment on his community from the outside, but a "local prophet," as Walzer calls it, who criticizes his people out of a deep concern for the moral and spiritual character of the country he loves and whose future he seeks to ensure.

Breaking through to Israelis has only become harder since the Hamas terror attack of October 7, 2023. In 2024, as the world took in graphic reports from Gaza—razed hospitals, mass displacement and starvation, tens of thousands of Palestinians injured or killed, many of them children—much of this news was suppressed in the Israeli media. The country's military censor blocked or altered nearly eight thousand news reports inside the country, an average of twenty-one stories per day. Fostering ignorance or denialism is a policy choice, a state-sanctioned strategy that encourages Israelis to look the other way.

Yet Manekin, who says he would refuse if he were called up for reserve duty in Gaza, theorizes that Israelis would soften their stance toward Palestinians if they honestly confronted the daily costs and injustices endured by those living under Israeli occupation. "I am confident that if we understood the price that millions of people must pay for our freedom, we would not be able to continue our lives as usual," Manekin wrote in 2023, adding:

> We would not be able to function if we internalized our responsibility for hunger in Gaza or the fact that there are people in the South Hebron Hills without water . . . if we understood the pain of tens of thousands of families divided by different residency statuses or the many thousands of people whose parents or children have been jailed for years in administrative detention.

It isn't an accident that Manekin invokes the word "we." "I want to talk with them in our language," he says of his fellow Jewish Israelis. Advocating in the first-person plural is a choice, one intended to establish an emotional bond with an audience that is instinctively hostile to his message and largely rejects his vision for the future of a country in which two distinct national groups—Israelis and Palestinians—have an equal right to self-determination and dignity in the land they share.

"This is actually what politics is about. It's about having

deep, serious, meaningful engagement with people who make different decisions than you, and trying to meet them where they are," Manekin says. "If I don't have the ability to engage with them, then I don't understand what I'm doing as a political activist."

The Lily Pad Theory

Committing to this sort of difficult engagement is one thing. Identifying someone who might be ready or willing to make a shift is quite another. Amid social, financial, and physical risks, the costs of dissent provide a strong set of incentives for many to keep their true views close. But Rich Logis, founder of Leaving MAGA—a community of people who have walked away from the U.S. president's far-right movement—is trying anyway.

"I think that there are more people across the country than we know of who are having doubts right now," says Logis, who owns a small business in Florida that sells tech products. "We need to be able to get to people who are going through maybe an inner turmoil about the choices they've made in supporting MAGA."

Logis is a credible narrator. In 2016, after becoming disillusioned with the status quo in U.S. politics, he began volunteering on the insurgent presidential campaign of a former reality TV star. Soon MAGA had become his home. He started his own MAGA podcast, and the movement rank-and-file became his inner circle. "We would talk every single day," Logis says of his friends during that period. They'd meet up for holiday parties and birthdays. "MAGA was our identity. It was our being. It was our personhood."

But Logis's faith in the movement began to falter in the fall of 2021 when Florida Governor Ron DeSantis held a press conference at which multiple speakers shared false claims about the COVID vaccine. The display left Logis feeling disoriented. He had seen the images of desperate parents in ICUs. He thought of his two daughters, then ages two and five. "It really shocked me, especially because kids were getting sick," Logis says.

A small internal voice began expressing quiet doubts. He began to diversify his news diet, reading outside the Breitbart universe. "I started to slowly realize that a lot of what I had believed was false," he says.

His doubts kept growing. And then, in May 2022, a teenage gunman murdered nineteen children and two teachers at an elementary school in Uvalde, Texas. Watching the horror unfold, Logis could already predict the GOP apologia: Second Amendment rights, arming teachers, thoughts and prayers. It was too much. "I knew that it was all bullshit," Logis recalls. "It felt as if my morals were in combat with my dignity."

Since then, he's tried a bit of everything to help others see that there is life after MAGA. He's active on social media and has gathered and published testimonials from people in at least fifteen U.S. states who have left the movement. Occasionally, he drives a digital billboard with a giant QR code around his home state: "Having doubts about MAGA?," it reads. "You are not alone. We are here to help." Plans are in the works to fly an airplane banner in the skies above West Palm Beach. "Anyone who's at Mar-a-Lago will see it," he says with a grin.

But no technique is more effective in breaking through to the movement's devotees, Logis contends, than hearing from someone they love. "There's a relatability factor," he says. He is building a support group of friends and family of the MAGA-affiliated, and one autumn evening nearly fifty of them gathered on a Zoom call. An upbeat social worker facilitating the meeting asked for a show of hands: "How many people are grieving the loss of a relationship?" A hand went up in nearly every box. An older woman hadn't heard from her brother since the inauguration. Another, in her thirties, wiped her eyes and spoke about her dad. "If there's something scary happening in the world—and there are fifteen things right now—I can't even talk to him as a parent."

There's a lot of heartbreak. But at least one member of Leaving MAGA has made some inroads. Stephania Messina, a respiratory therapist and former charismatic Christian nationalist, broke with the church and the MAGA movement after watching her community in Michigan ignore the devastation caused by the coronavirus.

"We were Christians and supposedly loving people, striving to protect those around us. But people were dying," Messina wrote in her testimonial on the Leaving MAGA website.

"I saw it was a convoluted position that was neither Christian nor patriotic." As with Logis, it was a new information diet—books about trauma and psychology, news reports on NPR, and videos from ex-evangelicals on TikTok—that helped the mother of five make sense of the constrictive world she had fallen into, and finally break out.

In the summer of 2024, Messina's eldest son was diagnosed with Hodgkin's lymphoma. On long drives every week for chemo, he would tell his mom about his favorite podcast host, Andrew Tate, the bombastic conservative commentator known for his misogynistic views. So Messina began subscribing to Tate's email newsletter. Every week, as they drove together, she asked her son about items she found particularly objectionable. The questions opened a regular exchange of information between mother and son.

As she sent him new Instagram videos, his social media feeds changed, and so did the tenor of their conversations. "The more he came back, the more he'd ask me questions," she says. Messina tried a similar approach with her brother, a single dad and tattoo artist also enthralled by the podcast manosphere. Soon his algorithm was showing videos of ICE raids—images he'd never seen that reminded him of the police who used to harass him and his friends in high school. She says both have disavowed MAGA.

It matters, in Messina's view, that the new content comes from her. "They know me. They know I'm not some crazed lunatic," says Messina, who is still a practicing Christian.

"When they talk about 'radical leftists,' I'm like, 'Look at me. I'm talking about feeding our neighbors.'"

Her approach to persuasion operates on a kind of lily pad theory: Even if people want to jump, no one wants to drown, so they must have something to jump to. "I don't want to make people a project," she says. "They just need another place where they can go." She continues to speak the familiar language of scripture. She's toyed with calling herself a Christian social-ist. It all adds up to someone in whom her loved ones can see themselves—not a caricature but a living, breathing, relatable model for a life on the other side.

"Any inroads I've made have only been because I can em-pathize and they can tell that I'm not just trying to change their mind," Messina says. "There *has* to be a softness coming in—which I have, because I've been there."

15

———

Start a Belief Cascade

It's Scary to Be First, but No
One Wants to Be Last

THE YOUNG ACTIVISTS HUDDLED OVER a table inside of a Cairo coffeehouse on a warm night in August 2010 had told almost no one of their plans.

All summer a rumor had been swirling in the smoky cafés of the capital: It appeared that the aging president, Hosni Mubarak, was preparing to hand the reins of leadership to his son Gamal.

Mubarak had ruled Egypt since 1981, a tenure marked by political repression and widespread corruption. Under his reign, the country's social safety net shrunk as those close to the president got rich. Mubarak hand-selected editors for Egypt's major newspapers. The country's security police tortured political prisoners. Those held arbitrarily and without charges numbered in the tens of thousands.

But amid growing domestic disillusionment and pressure from the West, Mubarak had begun allowing a handful of liberalizing measures, including opening elections to other candidates and privatizing some markets. Gamal, a former investment banker, had helped implement new incentives to attract private foreign investment. The son's expanding responsibilities were widely seen as a prelude to succeeding his father in power.

But in the eyes of the country's young activists, a dynastic handover threatened to reverse the country's progress. "La lil tawrith" (no to inheritance) had become a rallying cry at anti-Mubarak demonstrations across Egypt. The powerful military apparatus—long allied to Mubarak—also seemed to be against the father-son handover. Every president of Egypt since the 1950s had been a military man. That the country's leader would emerge from their ranks was an article of faith, especially among officers. Gamal Mubarak, however, had never served a day in uniform.

But the sweeping sense of opposition to *tawrith* didn't make much of a difference. The younger Mubarak was quickly growing more visible in Egyptian media, and news outlets across the world ran stories speculating about his likely rise.

One morning in late August, posters bearing Gamal's face mysteriously appeared in Cairo's working-class neighborhoods. "The hope of the poor," the banners read. The event seemed to confirm what many Egyptians had suspected. *Tawrith* now seemed a sure thing, freighted with the weight of inevitability.

The young men in the coffeehouse had been waiting for a moment like this. Months earlier, they had hatched a plot: They would stage a campaign of their own to disrupt the succession plans. But instead of promoting an opposition figure who was sure to be disqualified by the regime outright, they would promote someone from the military establishment. They settled on Omar Suleiman, the nation's longtime intelligence chief, a Mubarak loyalist rumored to be dissatisfied with the succession plans.

"Our idea was: There is something happening in the regime, so let's try to enhance that division," recalls Amr Salah, a cofounder of "The Constitution," a center-left opposition party, and one of the activists at the table. The hope was that exposing tensions among establishment power brokers might help to destabilize the country's leadership and push the succession plans off course. "There could be a political opportunity for democratization if there is a division within the ruling elites," he says.

Shady ElGhazaly Harb, a surgeon and fellow party activist, had heard about the army's complaints from people in his social circle. "I had some insights about what was happening and I sensed that there was a disconnect," ElGhazaly Harb says. "I saw this as an opportunity to widen the gap."

The activists had already set up a blog promoting Suleiman that they circulated on social media. Under pseudonyms, they published articles on the blog, such as one headlined "Suleiman Is Capable of Leading the Transitional Transformation in

Egypt." Now that Gamal's campaign had spilled into the streets, they would move their countercampaign into its next stage.

The operation would have to be a secret, including from Suleiman himself. Posters bearing the spy chief's face would go up under the cover of night. Come morning, Cairo would wake up to a political earthquake—the specter of a Mubarak loyalist challenging the succession and, by extension, the president himself.

All that was missing was the manpower to put up the posters. That could come courtesy of the April 6th Youth Movement—a reformist group named for a labor strike that had broken out on that date in 2008. The movement's leaders had worked with Salah and ElGhazaly Harb before, as part of a broader coalition of groups pressing for democratic reform in Egypt. The youth movement organizers had at their disposal an army of volunteers with years of experience plastering city walls.

Since there was no precedent for a stunt like this, it was difficult to predict the consequences. So the coffeehouse activists made a pact: If things went south, they alone would take the blame and they would refuse to name anyone else.

The plan was set. If the rumors had been overblown, nothing much would come of the stunt. But if there were divisions in the ranks and Mubarak was losing support from his military, the action could draw the government further into infighting and instability.

"Everyone was waiting for evidence that there was a rift in the regime," recalls Salah.

———

The digital clock on Salah's dashboard glowed against the deep black Cairo sky. It was not yet 4:00 a.m. He breathed anxiously. Soon the streets would wake with worshipers leaving their homes and heading toward mosques for the early morning Fajr prayer. He pulled the car quietly up to a curb and kept the engine running as the rear doors swung open and two twentysomethings from the April 6th movement jumped out into the muggy late summer air.

Across the city, similar late-night maneuvers were unfolding. One hour was what they had settled on for getting the posters up—taking any longer would be pushing their luck. Every team had three members: one person to hoist the posters to the wall, another to glue them up, and a driver to keep watch, monitoring the area for any police officers who might be making predawn rounds. After putting up ten posters, they'd drive off to the next destination.

"We identified points where Gamal Mubarak's posters were placed," ElGhazaly Harb remembers. "We wanted to surround them by Omar Suleiman's posters to make it look like a challenge."

There were two kinds of locations on the target list. Some teams hit major public thoroughfares, like the Giza neighborhood and the streets around Tahrir Square, where thousands of ordinary people would happen upon the posters on their morning commute. Salah's group was responsible for the city's ritzier neighborhoods. The idea was to plaster Suleiman's face near the homes of government ministers, members of parliament, and military officers who lived there. "The first thing you'd see in the morning if you're leaving your compound is these posters," Salah recalls.

The poster's design was simple: a waving Suleiman, in a suit and tie and dark aviator sunglasses, framed by the black and red streaks of the Egyptian flag. A snappy slogan hovered just above the spy chief's head: "The real alternative."

"We knew the police would take them down immediately," ElGhazaly Harb remembers. But by then it would be too late.

It wasn't quite 4:30 a.m. when Salah stumbled back into his place in Giza. Splayed out on his mattress, he composed a text message on a burner phone and cued up a list of recipients: foreign correspondents from *The New York Times* and *The Washington Post*, Egyptian government officials, writers, economists, and civil society leaders. At 7:00 a.m., he hit send. "Every intellectual living in Cairo that morning got a message that the campaign had started," Salah recalls.

Footsteps in the Train Station

In 1989, a few months after communism fell in East Germany, a market research institute polled residents of the former Soviet bloc country to solicit their views about the extraordinary political change that had just unfolded across Eastern Europe.

A year ago, residents were asked, *did you see a peaceful revolution coming?* Just 5 percent of those surveyed said they had expected the collapse. More than three-quarters of the respondents said that they had not anticipated the fall of East Germany at all.

How could an upheaval as consequential as the fall of a regime come as such a shock, even to the people living inside its borders?

One explanation came from Timur Kuran, a Duke University political scientist and economist, in his 1991 study "Now Out of Never": "People alienated from the communist regime did not know how widely their alienation was shared."

In the Eastern Bloc countries of the 1980s, people were less likely to speak out if they believed the regime was going to stay in power for the foreseeable future. But if they thought the regime was headed toward collapse, there was a much higher chance that they would make their opposition known.

The study presents a social paradox: Lots of people might be ready to join your movement. They just need to see that others have already signed on.

All of us have preferences that we choose to make public and others that we opt to keep to ourselves. But in a repressive society, the costs of expressing vocal opposition to the regime can be high. "We are able to falsify our preferences," Kuran explained about his findings in a 2024 interview on *The Good*

Fight podcast. "We are able to project a preference that is different from our private preference."

Jonathan Pinckney, the University of Texas at Dallas political science professor, says there's an important lesson for activists in Kuran's research: A small critical mass of dissent can be enough to move many people from hiding their private opposition to a regime to expressing it publicly.

"If people think that dissent is only being done and engaged in by a small handful of radicals, that's unlikely to continue to cascade throughout the rest of society. If people think that there is groundswell of opposition that is growing throughout society . . . people could be more likely to shift loyalty," explains Pinckney, whose work focuses on nonviolent resistance and democracy. "Communicating how widespread dissent actually is" becomes essential.

Hearing dissent in a repressive society is like standing in a train station when someone suddenly starts running. Then another person. Then everyone is running. And though you never heard an announcement, you start running too. That's how dissent spreads; by showing people they're not alone, that the train is already leaving. Nobody wants to miss the train.

"A society can come to the brink of a revolution without anyone knowing this, not even those with the power to unleash it," Kuran wrote.

He issued a prediction: Political revolutions, he wrote, will "inevitably continue to catch the world by surprise."

A Chain Reaction

Gamal Mubarak did not become the president of Egypt. Neither did Omar Suleiman. But six months after the provocation of the coffeehouse activists, a spark burst into a blaze. On January 17, 2011, amid a wave of protests across the Arab world, a man screaming anti-government slogans lit himself on fire outside the parliament building in Cairo and set off the demonstrations that would bring about the end of the Mubarak regime.

After days of gatherings in Tahrir Square—where shouts of "get out . . . we want you out" echoed morning to night—the military declared its support for "the freedom of expression . . . guaranteed for everyone" and said the army would not put down the protests. Mubarak had lost the military. He resigned on February 11.

Now a lecturer in conflict resolution at George Mason University, Salah believes the Suleiman stunt he helped plan was one factor among many that set off a kind of chemical reaction, leading to Mubarak's resignation.

"Part of the chain reaction is newspapers writing about different things. Labor movements are protesting, activists protesting, seminars, the U.S. pressure," Salah says. The combination of factors meant it was "more likely you'll have the opportunity for social movements to influence the democratization process."

In the hours after the posters went up, the Egyptian authorities ordered a media blackout on the story, and all newspapers carrying the news were destroyed. The BBC said the blackout appeared to "derive from a fear that news of a campaign in favour of the General could refuel speculation that there is a power struggle within various wings of the ruling elite." Reuters reported the posters had "rattled the establishment."

Salah and ElGhazaly Harb were both arrested, along with a third activist. They were blindfolded, handcuffed, and interrogated by the secret police. They stuck to the plan and took full responsibility and were released after a few days. But the damage to the regime's credibility was irreversible. "It reverberated around the whole world," ElGhazaly Harb recalls with a smile.

Margaret Levi, professor emerita of political science at Stanford University, says that movements often require a first actor—a committed person or group who can take the first steps and demonstrate that it's safe to join. "You're never sure you know what others believe until enough others do what you think should be done," she says. As the crowd of dissenters grows it sweeps greater numbers into a sense of comfort with participating in acts of defiance. Levi calls this phenomenon igniting a "belief cascade."

Democracy never quite arrived in Egypt. The military seized control after Mubarak's resignation, ushering in a bloody period of insurgent violence, government infighting, and political repression. ElGhazaly Harb was later imprisoned for his activism under a subsequent Egyptian president and held under brutal conditions, including being denied a bed for over two weeks and restricted to solitary confinement for twenty-one months.

But the maneuver did succeed in deepening the rift between the elder Mubarak and his army. A few months after the president stepped down, ElGhazaly Harb was invited to tea with a high-ranking Egyptian general. The revolution had made the coffeehouse activists well-known figures in Egypt, and the military had begun to make overtures to the leaders of the movement that had proven a formidable force.

With the uprising in the rearview mirror, ElGhazaly Harb asked the general about the stunt. How had it actually played out behind the scenes?

The general spoke frankly: "'It changed our calculus. We figured out that the people didn't want Gamal Mubarak to come to power,'" ElGhazaly Harb recalls him saying. "'What you did had a huge effect on all of us.'"

16

———

"Get the Jeep Out of the Mud"

The Art of Imperfect Coalitions

FRED BAUMA HAS SEEN MORE than his share of violence and political repression. For much of his childhood and teenage years, his hometown of Goma in equatorial Africa had been controlled by rebel forces fighting against the Congolese government. Kidnappings, disappearances, rape, and extortion were commonplace. Bauma hoped things would get better when in 2003 a negotiated peace allowed the city to be controlled by the new transitional government of President Joseph Kabila in the Democratic Republic of the Congo.

But the arrival of democratic elections in 2005 wasn't the end of Goma's problems. The city of about one million, located on the eastern border between DRC and Rwanda, was still ravaged by violence and poverty. The Congolese army and rebel groups continued to skirmish and kill civilians. The Rwandan genocide in 1994 had driven nearly a million refugees to camps in and around Goma. A nearby volcano erupted in 2002, displacing tens of thousands of residents, destroying fourteen thousand homes, and damaging the roads.

In 2012, then a college student, Bauma joined a loosely organized group of young people in Goma bound by their dissatisfaction with the conditions in the city. The group advocated for clean drinking water. They brought attention to the high rates of unemployment among Goma's youth. They focused on basic needs like electricity access, unemployment, and the rapidly deteriorating roads.

The group called itself Lutte pour le Changement (Struggle for Change), or Lucha. They had no leader, and no formal mandate, a structure that allowed the activists maximum independence over their agenda and a modicum of safety from the eyes of a snooping government. Every Sunday the group gathered at a local school, where they debated their priorities and voted on all decisions. "It's a really good experience of democracy because it forces the group to find a consensus to move," Bauma reflects. The intense focus on local issues and self-governance also kept the group relatively small and regional, never bigger than a few thousand people. "It's very heavy to sustain," he says of their organizing structure.

Goma's problems were made worse by the ineffectiveness of the Congolese government. "If you are campaigning on water, on access to water, we would go to the water company, and then listen to them, and they will tell us it's an electricity problem. And then we go to the electricity, they tell us it's the problem of the governor. You go to the governor, he tells us that we never received funds from the central government," Bauma recalls.

But there was hardly a door to knock on in the DRC's central government. By 2015, it was becoming clear that Kabila had no intention of stepping down when his constitutionally mandated term came to an end. "What was seen as a democracy was turning very quickly into a dictatorship," Bauma later recalled in a speech at a human rights forum. The young activists in Goma became convinced that their basic services problem was really a political problem, and that these needs could be met only by elected leaders who were accountable to the people. Such a government—responsive and democratic—would never be achieved by a movement that remained small. Lucha would have to grow.

Across the region, activists were forging new models for empowering more people to fight dictatorship. Senegal's youth movement Y'en A Marre (We're Fed Up!) and the grassroots opposition group in Burkina Faso, Balai Citoyen (Citizen Broom), had made major inroads in organizing young voters. These movements were making noise and, in some cases, winning, and Bauma and his Lucha colleagues began to wonder what it could look like to join forces.

"We started thinking about the need to build a pan-African coalition," Bauma recalls. More voices would mean a bigger platform. A bigger platform would translate to greater attention and hopefully a certain material change that wouldn't be possible with Lucha's relatively tiny megaphone and narrow, local coalition.

Easier said than done; the idea faced a few fundamental obstacles. Some were merely cosmetic: Both the Senegalese and Burkinabe efforts, for instance, had been ignited by popular hip-hop artists and spread their pro-democracy message through music, in sharp contrast to Lucha's modest volunteer road cleanup efforts.

Deeper philosophical differences also stood in the way of building a broader movement. The Senegalese and Burkinabe groups were darlings of international media and Western donors. But Bauma and his Congolese colleagues had grown deeply skeptical of international aid, wary of promises from global institutions for infrastructure projects that had never actually materialized. People on the ground, Bauma and his colleagues believed, were better off setting their own priorities and avoiding dependence on outside actors—even if that meant a slower pace of progress.

But the groups shared a common problem: leaders who would not leave office. The Senegalese had recently helped block their nation's president from winning a third term despite a constitutional limit of two terms. The Burkinabe were in the midst of a fight to stop their leader from staying in power beyond his mandated time in office. The fight to prevent strongmen from entrenching themselves in office and to protect fragile democracies was the activists' best bet at a shared movement.

On March 15, 2015, the three groups held a joint press conference at a music studio in the DRC's sprawling capital city of Kinshasa. The activists had spent the previous day recording a song promoting free and fair elections across the continent, which they hoped would mobilize the Congolese youth vote. But the stage hadn't even gone up when military officers appeared and began arresting everyone in sight. More than twenty-six activists, musicians, journalists, and bystanders were shoved into unmarked white pickup trucks, accused by Kabila's government of promoting violence. The authorities imprisoned Bauma on charges of "plotting a conspiracy against the head of state," which carried the penalty of death.

The raid might have been enough to sink an earlier iteration of Lucha. But for a coalition that had become deeply integrated with other African freedom struggles, the raid instead was a catalytic event: Those arrested became a cause célèbre for pro-democracy activists across the continent who heard in Bauma's plight haunting echoes of their own struggles with autocracy.

While activists from across the DRC made a weekly pilgrimage to arrive during visiting hours at the prison where Bauma was being held, their counterparts in Senegal and Burkina Faso held protests on his behalf, attracting international attention to the case. Human Rights Watch called for his release, and the United Nations Working Group on Arbitrary Detention declared his detention illegal. Amnesty International awarded him "prisoner of conscience" status and generated more than 170,000 messages of support sent to Congolese authorities.

Rather than sink the movement, the arrests revealed its strength, its powerful network of international allies, and its power to mobilize ordinary people in the DRC and across the continent.

When Bauma emerged after eighteen months in prison, he understood that the ground had shifted and the cause of democracy in the DRC had taken on new life. Within days of his release, he was appealing directly to the global community to keep up the pressure on Kabila to step down in speeches before international audiences, from the Oslo Freedom Forum to the U.S. House of Representatives. He joined those lobbying faith leaders in the DRC to take a stand, and ultimately dozens of Congolese Catholic church bishops and archbishops issued a statement insisting that the president honor his commitment to retire.

In 2018, under intense international pressure and amid organizing from a newly energized domestic movement, Kabila agreed to hold elections and step down. The DRC experienced its first peaceful transfer of power the following year. For a country that had known so much political violence, "it signaled that if people organize," Bauma says, "they could be more powerful than a government with guns."

"A No and a Yes"

In the early 2000s, Debra Javeline, a political scientist at the University of Notre Dame, examined a puzzling phenomenon in Russia: Despite going unpaid for months at a time, workers across the country were not taking to the streets.

The crisis had been brewing for some time. Throughout the 1990s, as the country's economy transitioned from communism to capitalism, wage delays had become more common. In several polls, Russians even listed the delays as the most urgent national challenge. Yet the crisis triggered only a limited organized response, mobilizing no more than 2 percent of the country's workforce.

Javeline assessed data from over two thousand Russian workers and discovered a fairly straightforward explanation: relatively few workers were taking to the streets because they couldn't figure out whom to blame.

"The vast majority of Russians do not attribute blame specifically and have not been asked to protest. They have therefore not taken collective action," Javeline wrote. "The greater the specificity of blame attribution, the greater the probability of protest."

In showing that an effective campaign can emerge not around a fine-grained set of policy goals or government reforms but around defeating a shared foe, Javeline's conclusions can help organizers seeking to mobilize broad coalitions. Some researchers call such a formation a "negative" coalition. "I like to think of negative coalitions as being instances in which different groups have settled on a common target of who is to blame," said Peter Cummings, a researcher also at the University of Notre Dame who has studied democratic movements in Latin America, in a 2025 lecture. Negative coalitions consolidate support from groups that may otherwise have little in common around a basic message: "no." The simplicity of this message makes for a relatively low threshold for participation—and it has worked to help reverse democratic backsliding around the world.

In Zambia, clergy from multiple Christian denominations joined together with a lawyers' association to stop President Frederick Chiluba from changing the constitution and seizing a third term in office. After far-right leader Jair Bolsonaro mobilized supporters in a violent attempt to overturn the results of a presidential election, he was denounced in a public letter by over one hundred leading Brazilian institutions—from unions and businesses to universities and faith leaders. And following efforts by the Polish government to intimidate and sideline the country's independent judiciary, judges who rarely participated in political activism stepped up to collaborate with veteran activists from the country's civil society groups to mobilize protests and beat back the far-right efforts.

And yet people living in backsliding democracies and authoritarian societies know that while a common enemy can be helpful, it isn't always enough to mobilize massive coalitions. "Grounding this work in an affirmative vision of the kind of inclusive democracy that prioritizes human dignity" is key, says movement scholar Maria J. Stephan. "You're saying no to something and saying yes to something else."

Erica Chenoweth, the Harvard political scientist, likens a backsliding democracy to a Jeep that's stuck in the mud. "You're trying to gather as many 'small-d democrats' as possible to pull the Jeep out," Chenoweth says. It doesn't matter who pushes, or why they push, or how they push, as long as they're willing to push. "You need to have multiple different narrative strategies to bring civil society to the back of the same Jeep."

The key phrase in Chenoweth's formulation is "the *same* Jeep." If what you're after is a democracy where all people have equal rights, dignity, and opportunity, it might not make sense to make common cause with those who believe some should be excluded. Not everyone actually wants to pull the same jeep out of the mud. People of good faith can get played—and movement goals can suffer—by what researchers Duncan McCargo and Rendy Wadipalapa call "toxic alliances."

"While superficially compelling, calls for unity may be wide open to manipulation and abuse by the politically unscrupulous," McCargo and Wadipalapa wrote in 2024 in the *Journal of Democracy*. If democrats are joining together with authoritarians, reformers in league with those accused of corruption, sketchy figures cuddling up with those who might cleanse their image—all these are warning signs that you may not be aiming to save the same Jeep.

The Rubber Band Theory

Hong Kong independence is among the most divisive concepts among pro-democracy reformers in the former British colony.

Since the United Kingdom handed control of the territory to China in 1997, residents have been fighting for their autonomy. Some advocate for full independence—reconfiguring Hong Kong as a sovereign city-state entirely separate from China. Other activists, believing independence to be an unrealistic demand for a tiny peninsula on China's southern coast, push instead for a lower threshold that they call self-determination, which could include a range of measures, from a law preventing interference from China to giving citizens the power to directly elect their leader.

Nathan Law knew he would have to navigate between factions when he was elected as the youngest ever member of the Hong Kong legislature in 2016. Having emerged as a leader of the 2014 student protests demanding the right to vote for the leader of Hong Kong, Law entered politics hoping to find a legislative solution to the problems that the street protests had failed to solve.

But not long after he took office, a local pro-independence group began advocating for the removal of all mainland Chinese people from Hong Kong. For Law, the campaign presented a problem. On the one hand, he knew that winning autonomy required the widest possible coalition and that refusing to support the proposal risked alienating a cohort that might otherwise help push that cause forward.

But the policy made him deeply uncomfortable. "Hong Kong should be free from malign influence from the Chinese regime, but we should not target people, and it should remain diverse," Law reflects. "It wasn't my values. It was different, even contradictory to my fundamental values. It touched the very core of things, and I felt it wasn't going to work."

Law's approach as a legislator may have helped him shake the image of a rash, strident student protester that many Hong Kongers associated with his leadership of a seventy-nine-day occupation of a public plaza in 2014. "Once more radical ideas emerged, my ideas sounded fairly reasonable," Law says.

Holding all the parts of a democratic movement together requires that leaders adopt what Law calls a "rubber band theory"—a coalitional strategy in which movement leaders aim to move the general public toward a set of ambitious political goals without pushing so hard as to sever their connection with the people. "If your rhetoric goes too far, it will naturally lose influence because people just feel like you are not the same species as them," he reflects. "The best spot is if you move a bit and test the boundary and generate enough momentum to move together."

Law's position in the legislature didn't last. In 2017, he was disqualified along with several other pro-democracy lawmakers under a technicality imposed by China. By 2019, as China continued to ratchet up its control over Hong Kong, tensions began to boil over.

The flash point came when China moved to exert more control over Hong Kong's independent legal system, demanding the power to extradite to the mainland anyone deemed a criminal. Pro-democracy activists saw the proposal as yet another incursion on Hong Kong's limited autonomy.

Once again, hundreds of thousands of Hong Kong residents took to the streets in a largely leaderless mobilization. The protesters coordinated logistics on encrypted messaging apps and voted through a Reddit-style portal on which actions they would take to push forward their five demands. Among the demands were the withdrawal of the extradition bill and the right of Hong Kongers to pick their own leaders without China vetting candidates first. Though independence wasn't on the list, the demands appealed to a group of activists broad enough to mobilize a coalition.

The pro-independence and pro-self-determination activists stood shoulder to shoulder in protests that stretched on for months. The government dropped the extradition measure, but activists held out for other demands—universal suffrage, amnesty for arrested protesters, and inquiries into alleged police brutality. But when the COVID-19 pandemic forced the protesters indoors in early 2020, the Chinese government used the shutdown to ram through a draconian national security law that functionally criminalized all dissent.

Law managed to flee Hong Kong. In late June 2020, he slipped quietly onto a plane bound for the United Kingdom, where he was granted political asylum. Some of his collaborators, like Joshua Wong—with whom Law had been nominated for the Nobel Peace Prize—remain in prison. Other friends from the movement have completed jail sentences and now struggle to find work in Hong Kong.

From his London flat, Law is still trying to make meaning of it all. In 2025, he launched a program to bring fellow dissidents to share their stories in high school classrooms in the United Kingdom, where trends show that some students are souring on democracy. The project has allowed him to reflect on his own experience, including the strengths and weaknesses of the movement he helped to spark.

"My belief is that we actually have to continue to find common ground," Law says. He concedes that it's hard to motivate people to keep fighting when all they have faced so far is defeat. But he likes to remember that the story isn't over. Every once in a while, he poses a question to himself:

"What if we're in the middle of history?"

Conclusion

For the Long Run

THE PEOPLE HUDDLED IN THE hotel conference room near Washington, D.C., in the summer of 2024 had good reason to be alarmed, and perhaps even afraid. During their short simulation exercise modeling the actions of an authoritarian leader, the group had glimpsed an unsettling future that their fellow Americans would encounter soon enough. They saw that when a president is unconstrained by democratic norms and unconcerned with adhering to the Constitution, the experience can feel disorienting, like being transported to a dark and unfamiliar place.

One can hardly begrudge the participant who drew the grim conclusion that these events were new and that we lacked the tools to confront them. But during our year of interviewing dissidents, activists, and theorists across five continents, we found that he was wrong. The counterpoint is found in these pages, within the stories of people who confronted the risks of dissenting in their workplace, their community, or their country—and did it anyway.

The courage of the dissidents in this book forms the basis of a much more hopeful truth: Amid political repression, countless tools are available to us. Our task as people who desire a more just society is to learn how to use them.

1. We can begin by listening intently to the internal voice that is uncomfortable with what's going on around us. This doesn't require that we ignore our fears, but rather that we manage them with careful planning and a sharp focus on what is in our control. In an authoritarian environment designed to make us feel as if we have less and less room to maneuver, holding closely to our deepest values helps open space for dissent. Though authoritarian conditions can cast us in oppositional terms—defining us by who and what we are not—effective dissent emerges from being clear about who we *are* and about our fundamental vision for the world. Beginning with small acts like showing up, telling the truth, searching for our options, and bearing witness to injustice can embolden us to do more.

2. Dissent becomes easier, and more effective, when we do it with others. Under authoritarian conditions, a political home—a place where we regularly gather,

process, and strategize with people who share our political values—is an essential part of our social safety net. Many of us don't yet have these kinds of explicitly political communities, but we don't have to grow them from scratch; their seeds can almost certainly be found within our existing networks. People whom we never imagined would engage in the work of dissent might well join us if we simply ask them to show up, give them a bit of responsibility, and then the opportunity to do even more. Still, power doesn't only come from organizing with those in our lives; it also emerges from tying our fate to that of people who haven't historically been in our circles and expanding the scope of who we mean by "we."

3. Community is our best chance for staying safe amid the physical, psychological, and digital risks that come with dissent under authoritarian conditions. Though it's not realistic to protect against all possible threats, there are countless ways to defend against the most likely ones. By building relationships with neighbors and cultivating mentors, we can keep fear to a low hum and ensure that help is available if threats do arrive. We can also study our opponents, learn their preferred tactics, behaviors, and vulnerabilities, and share information with oth-

ers facing similar threats. We can get more cautious online, use technology that helps protect us against dangers, and avoid giving opponents opportunities to distract from and discredit our movements. And we can commit to responding to threats and violence with strict nonviolence, knowing that it is nearly always more persuasive than its alternative.

4. A society in which everyone has equal rights, dignity, and opportunity demands that we bring more and more people into the work of achieving it. Though our work might begin in a political home big enough to house a committed few who share our commitments, we will succeed only when that home grows to fit a far broader range of ideas and identities. This basic arithmetic problem means sometimes living with contradictions, even embracing them, and drawing on a range of tools to persuade new people to join our ranks. Growing our circle and our movement is one long argument, one that can be made not only in the stories we tell but through the pressure we create, the strategic bridges we build, and the posture we take toward people on the fence. We can use every single tool. Indeed, we must.

———

Make no mistake: defeating political repression demands a stubborn patience. But on this score, we have models, too.

In 2025, Benjamin Nathans was awarded the Pulitzer Prize for General Nonfiction for his intimate portrait of the lives of the people who made up the Soviet Union's dissident movement in the latter half of the twentieth century. In over eight hundred vivid pages, the University of Pennsylvania history professor unearthed new details about well-known activists and illuminated the remarkable stories of many Soviet dissidents whose voices had otherwise been lost to history.

The end of a repressive government cannot be attributed to any single cause. Long before the regime collapsed, the Soviet Union had been beset by a slow accumulation of problems—internal corruption, economic fragility, and pressure from the West. But Nathans explains that the dissidents' unrelenting efforts to expose internal contradictions—the Kremlin's refusal or inability to abide by its own laws and constitution—played a pivotal role in draining the government of its legitimacy, both inside and outside the Soviet Union.

These figures—poets and writers, mathematicians, scientists, and many students—sustained a culture of dissent through an emotional balancing act: "It was the ability to harbor feelings of hopelessness and perseverance, despair and boldness, at the same time," Nathans says. "To be able to keep both of those in mind at the same time, which is another way of saying—being in it for the long run."

In the late 1970s, when the secret police had banished

many Soviet dissidents to forced labor camps and psychiatric institutions and others had fled the country for freedom, the activists continued writing their books, making their art, and bearing witness to the crimes of the state.

Nathans titled his book after a toast favored by the dissidents even in their darkest hours:

"To the success of our hopeless cause."

A decade after all seemed lost, the Berlin Wall came down.

Acknowledgments

MORE THAN 120 PEOPLE ON five continents spoke to us for this book. We owe a debt to each of them for sharing their stories and trusting us to tell them faithfully.

Our agent, Laurie Liss, was this book's earliest champion and most passionate cheerleader—and we are grateful to Pearl Cadigan and the rest of the wonderful team at Sterling Lord Literistic Inc.

Our exceptional editor, Peter Hubbard, understood intuitively what we were trying to accomplish with *On Courage* and gave us the space and the feedback to help usher it into existence. Peter's collaborative spirit and sharp editorial instincts were a great gift, as were the talents of the entire team at Mariner and HarperCollins, including Olivia Kane, Alana Bonfiglio, Ben Steinberg, Hope Breeman, and Maureen Cole.

An outstanding team made it possible for us to dig into a diverse range of topics, histories, and geographies—and ensured that no detail was missed: Atul Dev and Andrea Vega Yudico provided diligent research assistance on very tight timelines. Rosemarie Ho ably led our source verification process. And Ben Kalin delivered a thorough fact-check of these pages. This book owes a great deal to each of them.

Rachel Kadish, Evelyn Larrubia, Margaret Levi, and Lilly Sandberg read early drafts of the full manuscript and provided invaluable feedback. Their comments were incisive and thoughtful, and improved this work beyond measure. We are also indebted to Levi, as well as to Erica Chenoweth, Maria J. Stephan, Benjamin Nathans, and Jonathan Pinckney, for patiently helping us navigate the scholarship on social change.

We benefited from the research resources of Harvard University and its libraries through our respective affiliations with the Kennedy School. At the Shorenstein Center on Media, Politics and Public Policy, Nancy Gibbs and Laura Manley were key advocates, providing space for our early whiteboarding sessions while the Shorenstein Center's A.M. Rosenthal Writer-in-Residence program supported Julia's work. And at the Allen Lab for Democracy Renovation and the Ash Center for Democratic Governance and Innovation, Danielle Allen and Darshan Goux were deeply supportive of Ami's pursuing this project.

Yehuda Kurtzer and Sam Balogh generously opened up workspace for us at the Shalom Hartman Institute, Adam Goldstein took a field trip to the Moakley Courthouse to confirm details about the building's lobby, and Lily Kravetz gave critical feedback on the cover. We are also grateful to *The New Yorker*—with special thanks to executive editor Michael Luo and senior editor Carla Blumenkranz—for the opportunity to publish our original essay, "So You Want to Be a Dissident?" as that publication's "Weekend Essay" on April 12, 2025.

IN 1989, IN THE MIDST of the uprisings that helped topple communism in Czechoslovakia, Václav Havel wrote a poem whose last lines reverberate in my head: "Whether all is really lost / or not depends entirely on / whether or not I am lost."

This project took me back to my roots as a high school organizer for Amnesty International, spending my lunchtime hours writing letters seeking to free Havel's fellow prisoner of conscience, Jiří Wolf. It was deeply liberating—and a bit uncomfortable—to return to a declared pro-democracy, pro-nonviolence, pro-civil-resistance point of view after years of writing from a traditional media "view from nowhere." Amid our country's descent into authoritarianism, the exercise left me feeling more grounded and hopeful than ever before.

I am so grateful for the constellation of friends, mentors, and allies who accompanied me on this journey, including Lisa Friedman, Allen Gunn, Janet Haven, Rachel Kadish, Evelyn Larrubia, Margaret Levi, Geoffrey MacDougall, Rina Palta, Motoko Rich, Lisa Tharpe, Madeleine Varner, and Meredith Whittaker. My excellent collaborator, Ami Fields-Meyer, inspired me with his deep generosity of spirit and dogged pursuit of the absolute best words.

To my family, I offer endless thanks not only for their patience but also for inspiring me with their fierce commitments to justice. My late great-aunt Blanche Stein, who fought to protect consumers as the first female attorney in a Federal Trade Commission field office. My mother, Meredith Angwin, still blogging in her eighties as the Electric Grandma in her quest to shore up our electric grid. My father, George Angwin, with his total devotion to our family and to a better popular understanding of mathematics. My husband, Vijay Modi, battling to bring better infrastructure to rural communities in Africa. My daughter, Mira, with her kindness, wisdom, and passion to reduce greenhouse gases. My son, Avi, and his relentless quest for knowledge. My brother, Ilan, and his wife, Mari, with their fierce commitment to their girls.

I also owe a debt to places that nurtured me along the way, including the Bellagio Center Residency Program at the Rockefeller Foundation, the Brown Institute's Entrepreneurs-in-Residence program at the Columbia Journalism School, and the Walter Shorenstein Media and Democracy Fellowship at the Harvard Kennedy School.

But more than anything, I am grateful for every person who is taking brave actions today, who conquered their fear yesterday, or who is planning to take their first courageous step tomorrow. Telling a small sampling of their stories has been the privilege of a lifetime. There are so many more stories we couldn't tell—ones that are unfolding every day.

Knowing what we are called to do is a gift. And with it in hand, all is not lost.

—Julia Angwin

THE HASIDIC MASTER RABBI NACHMAN of Breslov taught: "Know that a person needs to cross a very, very narrow bridge, and the rule—the essence—is to not give in to fear at all." As we've been writing *On Courage*, I have reached for those words and for the people who have shown me what it can look like to live by them.

Some of those people are at the Harvard Kennedy School. This book would not exist had Danielle Allen not invited me to join the Allen Lab at the Ash Center. It was there that I connected with "the Backsliders," a small, informal study group on anti-authoritarian resistance that included Naomi Beyth-Zoran, Shady ElGhazaly Harb, Freddy Guevara, Patrycja Horodyska, Maria Kuznetsova, Eylam Leshem, Kris Li, Isabella Pícon, and Dana Schleifer.

This work was strengthened by a community of dear friends who gave of their time to read and comment on section drafts, facilitate connections, or otherwise offer their wisdom and expertise, including Andrew Belinfante, Miranda Bogen, Adam Braun, Aviv Gilboa, Adam Goldstein, Emily Grant, Micah Hendler, Jonathan Jacoby, Ben Kassoy, Reba Lichtenstein, Alex Pascal, Ellen Qualls, Zev Rose, Yoav Schaefer, Jonah Schatz, and Amy Spitalnick.

My professional life can be broken into two stages: before and after I went to work at the White House for Alondra

Nelson, a once-in-a-generation visionary on matters of justice and conscience. I owe much to her transformative mentorship, along with other role models, including David Myers, Greg Good, Sharon Brous, and Josh Marshall—as well as my Emory University professors Hank Klibanoff, Carol Anderson, and Brett Gadsden, who seeded a reverence for civil and human rights.

Nasrina Bargzie, Aryeh Cohen, Farrah Fazal, Mikaela Gerwin, Aziza Hasan, Andrea Hodos, Ramzi Kassem, Elad Nehorai, Isa Qasim, Dana Shubat, Kirkpatrick Tyler, and Brooke Wirtschafter have each modeled for me the kind of solidarity politics that is required in a true multiracial democracy. Miles Taylor, Daniel Sokatch, Jonathan Eig, Barbara Demick, and Alondra Nelson all offered invaluable advice about book writing—as did Julia Angwin, my outstanding collaborator.

During the constant motion of writing and reporting, I often relied on the generosity of friends and family for a place to work or even to stay, including Becca, Aaron, and Lavi Karas, Ilana Sandberg and Adam Goldstein, Lily Kravetz and Jonah Schatz, Sherry and Steve Ebrahimi, and Nora Feinstein and Yoav Schaefer.

I owe a special debt to Lance Leener, Jamie Nicholson, and Jesse Leener, who not only provided me with a roof over my head for many months as we completed this book but were also a wellspring of encouragement, wisdom, and nourishing late-night conversation after long writing days.

To my Savta Sandey, who is my model of civic virtue; Papa Del, who passed down his deep appreciation for Leonard Cohen; Bubbe Lora, who is a constant source of love and support; and my late Grandpa Jim, who showed all of his grandchildren that history isn't a faraway abstraction but something that belongs to us.

To my siblings, Ezra Fields-Meyer, Noam Fields-Meyer Gould, and Kelly Fields-Meyer Gould, who enrich my life every day with art and music, laughter and joy, belonging and love.

Finally, I dedicate this book to my parents, Shawn and Tom Fields-Meyer, who are the quiet voice in my head and the foundational blessing from which all else in my life flows. For their love and their values, for our family, and for their constant reminder to try to be a mensch—my gratitude is endless.

—Ami Fields-Meyer

A Note on Sources

This book is an exploration of the inner life of dissidents—what it takes for them to do their work, what motivates them, what scares them, and how they navigate risk. As such, it is heavily reliant on our interviews with more than one hundred dissidents, activists, and theorists around the world.

When recounting dissidents' stories, we have sought to support their account as much as possible with contemporaneous news reports, court documents, academic research, and materials they provided us, such as photographs, screenshots, and email records. Their dialogue and inner thoughts are generally reconstructed from their interviews with us, but we note in the text where we are pulling from outside sources. Some quotes from our interviews have been edited for clarity. We also try to note in-text when characters are remembering the words of other people from whom we have not obtained confirmation.

In cases where we are telling historical stories of people who are deceased or otherwise unavailable for comment, we rely whenever possible on descriptions from people who witnessed the events and from the accounts of professional journalists and historians. Essential sources, both first and third person, are listed in the notes for each section. We do not include every source we consulted to confirm widely reported events.

We have not sought to obtain comment from the targets of the dissidents' actions, whether a repressive regime or a prison guard. Our goal in this book is not to adjudicate the legitimacy of the causes for which dissidents fight, but rather to bring readers into their minds and hearts as they attempt to surmount obstacles in their work.

In the vast majority of cases, those interviewed for this book chose to share their real names, but a few dissidents chose to remain anonymous or to use an alias to protect themselves. These cases are noted in the notes for each section.

Notes

Prologue: A Stress Test for Democracy

To reconstruct the series of democracy stress-testing exercises conducted during the summer of 2024, we interviewed two of its organizers: Barton Gellman, a senior adviser at the Brennan Center for Justice at the New York University School of Law, and Nils Gilman, a senior adviser to the Berggruen Institute, a nonprofit based in Los Angeles.

As events unfolded in 2025, Gilman told us that the simulations had foreshadowed for him the anemic American pushback to an authoritarian president. "Participant actions (and more importantly, inactions) revealed that small-l liberals' commitments to institutional continuity, legality, and norms of political decency crippled their ability to imagine effective strategies for resisting an authoritarian president with focus and drive to execute his vision," Gilman wrote to us. "They remained committed to fighting with their butter knives even when staring down the barrel of a gun."

Our engagements with the organizers were supplemented by details from Barton Gellman's August 1, 2024, report on the event for the Brennan Center, "How to Harden Our Defenses Against an Authoritarian President," and an April 4, 2025, blog post describing the simulations written by a participant, Daniel Hunter, on the website Waging Nonviolence titled "What to Do if the Insurrection Act Is Invoked in Minnesota." We also interviewed Hunter, a direct action organizer and cofounder of Choose Democracy, who recounted to us the story of the frustrated fellow participant who said, "This is new, we don't have any tools for this." Hunter told us that he responded: "Actually, we actually do have a technology for this—it's called nonviolent civil resistance."

Introduction: Forget Your Perfect Offering

Democracies are collapsing and repressive regimes are rising. There are many ways to characterize this global trend: Some call it a surge in authoritarianism, while others invoke words like "autocratic," "fascist," or "totalitarian." In this book, we have mostly used "authoritarianism," even though the word is imprecise and doesn't quite roll off the tongue, because it is broad enough to encompass many varieties of governments that consolidate power in the hands of a few and restrict the rights of many.

To illustrate the scale of the global backslide of democracy, we relied on the authoritative data collected annually by the V-Dem Institute, based at the Department of Political Science at the University of Gothenburg in Sweden. The V-Dem Project tracks democratic qualities such as free and fair elections, civil liberties, judicial independence, executive constraints, gender equality, media freedom, and civil society to create a granular ranking of how countries are faring on different measures of democracy.

The institute's Democracy Report 2025, "25 Years of Autocratization—Democracy Trumped?," is a sobering analysis of the global wave of autocratization that has brought liberal democracy to its lowest point in nearly fifty years. "The global democratic decline deepens, regardless of how we slice the data and whichever measure we use," the report's authors wrote. "The unchanged direction of decline across the world makes the situation undeniable, maybe even to previously skeptical observers."

There is a vast literature on how and why this trend has taken hold. We do not dive deeply into this body of work except to cite a few highlights, such as Steven Levitsky and Daniel Ziblatt's book *How Democracies Die* (Crown, 2018) and Timothy Snyder's book *On Tyranny: Twenty Lessons from the Twentieth Century* (Penguin Random House, 2017). We also appreciated the work of Vesla M. Weaver and Gwen Prowse, who remind us in their September 4, 2020, *Science* article "Racial Authoritarianism in U.S. Democracy" that members of racial minority groups have experienced a form of authoritarianism in the United States since long before our current episode of democratic backsliding. "When police engage in excessive surveillance, incursions on civil liberties, and arbitrary force as a matter of routine patrol many scholars of American politics are reluctant to consider it a violation of democracy and instead deem them aberrations in an otherwise functioning democracy," Weaver and Prowse write.

A touchstone in our reporting on pro-democracy movements was the seminal work of Erica Chenoweth and Maria J. Stephan, *Why Civil Resistance Works: The Strategic Logic of Nonviolent Conflict* (Columbia University Press, 2011). We also reviewed some of the classic field manuals for nonviolent resistance, from Gene Sharp's *Power and Struggle: The Politics of Nonviolent Action* (Porter Sargent Publishers, 1973) to Saul Alinsky's *Rules for Radicals: A Pragmatic Primer for Realistic Radicals* (Penguin Random House, 1989).

Readers may take a measure of comfort, as we did, in Jonathan Pinckney and

Claire Trilling's analysis of how civil resistance can improve the odds of reversing authoritarian trends, "Breaking Down Pillars of Support for Democratic Backsliding," published in the October 2024 issue of *Mobilization: An International Quarterly*, as well as in Maria J. Stephan's explanation of the paper's findings in the June 3, 2025, *Just Security* post "Big Tents and Collective Action Can Defeat Authoritarianism." But note that the Pinckney and Trilling study is based on thirty-five episodes of democratic backsliding in twenty-six countries—a small sample whose results, the authors write, "should be interpreted only as suggestive correlations."

Howard Thurman was a spiritual guide for us as we were writing this book, as he has been to generations of civil rights leaders; Martin Luther King Jr., whose father was friendly with Thurman, is said to have carried a copy of the theologian's seminal work, *Jesus and the Disinherited* (Beacon Press, 1949), during the civil rights movement. The works of two experts on Thurman were especially helpful in situating his ideas within our narrative: Peter Eisenstadt, who wrote the Thurman biography *Against the Hounds of Hell* (University of Virginia Press, 2021); and Luther Smith Jr., who has written several books on Thurman, including *Howard Thurman: The Mystic as Prophet* (The University of America, 1981), and whose comments from our interview with him are quoted in the chapter. The 1976 Thurman University of Redlands lecture from which we quote is "America in Search of a Soul."

Thurman believed in the power of community to overcome fear, but he also felt that communal interests shouldn't sublimate the needs or will of the individual. He wrote and preached about a kind of universal truth, a default setting for the natural world that would come to pass sooner or later. To illustrate how philosophy manifests in other global freedom struggles, Smith recalled to us in an interview an oft-told story about Desmond Tutu, the South African archbishop. At the height of apartheid, Tutu was leading a service in a Cape Town church when storm troopers came in to break up the gathering. The archbishop told the troopers that he served a power greater than them, and then he invited them to join the gathered masses: "Since you have already lost, I invite you today to come and join the winning side!"

1. A Moral Collision

Paul Osadebe's story of deciding to come forward about the dismantling of the U.S. Department of Housing and Urban Development's fair housing office comes from multiple interviews with Osadebe, as well as from an interview with his supervisor, Erik Heins, who was also terminated for his advocacy.

We supplemented their stories with the August 27, 2025, whistleblower report sent by Paul Osadebe and Palmer Heenan to Senator Elizabeth Warren, as well as with contemporaneous reporting on the firings and disruptions at HUD. Most notable among these were Jesse Coburn's March 25, 2025, ProPublica article, "Federal Investigators Were Preparing Two Texas Housing Discrimination Cases—Until Trump Took Over"; Debra Kamin's September 22, 2025, *New York Times* article, "Trump Appointees Roll Back Enforcement of Fair Housing Laws"; and Tami Luhby, Rene Marsh, Matt Egan, and Sean Lyngaas's reporting, "Thousands of Probationary Employees Fired as Trump Administration Directs Agencies to Carry Out Widespread Layoffs," for CNN on February 14, 2025.

We reviewed the allegations in the legal complaint filed by Palmer Heenan, Paul Osadebe, Julia Dykstra, Ashley Vazquez, and Hannah Gordon against the U.S. Department of Housing and Urban Development in United States District Court of the District of Columbia on September 22, 2025, and we watched Osadebe's appearance on MSNBC's *The Saturday/Sunday Show* with Jonathan Capehart on February 15, 2025, and his appearance on BreakThrough News on September 30, 2025.

The history of the Fair Housing Act and Martin Luther King's efforts around it are well documented. We pulled primarily from official sources, including the U.S. House of Representatives Archives and President Lyndon B. Johnson's remarks on signing the law as chronicled in the American Presidency Project archives at the University of California, Santa Barbara.

Adriana Gomez is an alias. Her narrative is based on our interview and other correspondences with her, including voice notes and written answers to questions as well as her testimony in past interviews about her work. We also conducted multiple interviews with another Venezuelan activist who is familiar with the details of Gomez's story and background and engaged another person who has worked directly with her on the ground.

Andrei Sinyavsky's story and words are drawn primarily from his essay "Dissent as a Personal Experience," published in the collection *In Late and Post-Soviet Russian Literature: A Reader*, edited by Mark Lipovetsky and Lisa Ryoko Wakamiya (Academic Studies Press, 2015); and from Benjamin Nathans's epic Pulitzer Prize–winning history, *To the Success of Our Hopeless Cause: The Many Lives of the Soviet Dissident Movement* (Princeton University Press, 2024).

Nathans's work has been a profound resource for us in our reporting. In one of our interviews, he used the term "moral collisions" to describe how Soviet dissidents came to their dissent. Though in his own book Nathans uses Sinyavsky's phrase "stumbling blocks" to describe these moments of friction and revelation, we felt that the language of "collision" resonated deeply with what we were hearing in our dissident interviews. We have adopted it, with great homage to Nathans.

In a 2024 interview with the Andrei Sakharov Foundation, Nathans expanded on these collisions:

> My impression, based on dozens of dissident accounts, is that a person's response to a potentially morally compromising situation—being pressured by the KGB to inform on one's peers, for example—was the most common point of departure for dissenting activity. The writer Andrei Sinyavsky called these situations "stumbling blocks," and millions of Soviet citizens encountered them over the course of their lives. Those who became dissidents typically reacted to such situations from a position of high, uncompromising moral principle—and in many cases, those principles were inculcated as part of their Soviet education.
>
> People of high intelligence who understood the nature of the Soviet system could always find reasons not to protest—by telling themselves that nothing would ever change, by devoting themselves exclusively to their chosen profession, by assuming that politics was by nature a dirty business. Intellectuals are very good at coming up with reasons to justify their actions—or inaction.

2. Bear Witness

Our reporting at the Delaney Hall ICE detention center took place over multiple visits in August and September 2025. During these visits, we observed the lack of signage about visiting hours and the arbitrary decisions made by the guard about which visitors he would allow inside. We interviewed multiple "Eyes on ICE" volunteers, such as Sister Susan Francois, about their experiences and followed up with more in-depth phone and Zoom interviews with Kathy O'Leary and Stephanie Campos, who are both quoted in the chapter. We chose not to identify the visitors to protect them from retaliation.

Since our reporting trips, the visiting hours have changed and are now sometimes posted at the gate, but they are not always the correct hours. We chose to limit our reporting to a snapshot in time when we were on the scene, knowing that conditions continue to evolve at Delaney Hall and at ICE detention facilities across the nation.

Our reporting on transitional justice after authoritarian regimes relied heavily on Priscilla B. Hayner's important book, *Unspeakable Truths: Confronting State Terror and Atrocity* (Routledge, 2001). We also interviewed Patrick Ball, director of research of the Human Rights Data Analysis Group, and read his testimony in the retrial of Guatemalan dictator Ríos Montt. Our descriptions of the Guatemalan truth commission drew from contemporaneous news reports and the 2013 Report of the Commission for Historical Clarification, "Guatemala Memory of Silence."

Two sources we quote from in this chapter are worthy of further exploration by interested readers. Paul Farmer offers a more detailed explanation of "fighting the long defeat" in Tracy Kidder's excellent book, *Mountain Beyond Mountains: The Quest of Dr. Paul Farmer, a Man Who Would Cure the World* (Random House, 2003). And Václav Havel's 1978 essay "The Power of the Powerless" examines in gorgeous prose the nature of dissent in what he calls a "post-totalitarian" regime, describing the inner work that individuals must take on to see a brighter future.

Havel ends his essay with a challenge to his reader: "For the real question is whether the brighter future is really always so distant. What if, on the contrary, it has been here for a long time already, and only our own blindness and weakness has prevented us from seeing it around us and within us, and kept us from developing it?"

3. Look for Your Options

We relied on our interviews with Maria Kuznetsova to tell her story, as well as contemporaneous reports of the background events she recounts, such as coverage of the FSB raids of the Open Russia offices by Radio Free Europe/Radio Liberty. The narrative about Andrei Pivovarov's arrest, prison time, and release weaves together details from media reports with firsthand memories that Pivovarov recounted in our interviews and correspondence with him.

In addition to mainstream publications, several human rights organizations and activists helped to keep Pivovarov's story in the spotlight while he was incarcerated, including his partner Tatiana Usmanova, a public relations professional; Mikhail Khodorkovsky, an exiled businessman and founder of Open Russia; and Human Rights Watch. We also turned to their contemporaneous reports and dispatches in reconstructing the Pivovarov narrative.

While in pretrial detention prior to his sentencing, Pivovarov was held in a special cell block in the southern city of Krasnodar. As Pivovarov tells it, in the cell to his right was the longtime boss of the crime syndicate for Russia's southern region. To his left was a convicted murderer who was already serving life in prison. From the cell between them, Pivovarov launched the campaign he had planned before his arrest with the help of his partner and lawyers. He told us that he was the first Russian citizen since the Russian Revolution to run a full campaign from inside a prison. "This campaign was about showing that I am not broken," he told us. "It was such a spit in the system."

In addition to the firsthand accounts of Pivovarov and Kuznetsova, our snapshot of how the Russian government keeps its population in fear drew on a composite of NGO reports and academic scholarship. We reviewed research from OVD-Info, an independent human rights NGO founded by Russian journalist Grigory Okhotin and programmer Daniel Beilinson, with particular attention to the data the organization has collected on denunciations in higher education, the government's prosecution of the antiwar movement, and the full sweep of repressive legislation that the government has passed since the start of the Ukraine War.

The probabilities combine country-level political prisoner counts and per-capita rankings from the World Population Review with Russia's total population figures from Macrotrends to derive the per-capita estimate. We compare that likelihood to Russia's 2023 transport fatality, as reported by the Ministry of Transport in Russia in 2024, published in March 2025.

Most instructive in drawing the broader contours of this dynamic was the political scientist Vladimir Gel'man's paper "The Politics of Fear: How Russia's Rulers Counter Their Rivals," published March 8, 2016, in *Russian Politics*. The paper offers a thorough yet accessible explanation of concepts such as "selective persecution" and lays out how Russian leaders have moved from defaulting to what was familiar (the costly, energy-intensive work of maintaining an information regime modeled on the late Soviet years) to a set of lower-cost, high-leverage actions to maintain the implied threat of violence.

4. Practice and Prepare

Mike Mathis's account of discovering that he had videotaped the shocking detention of Tufts University graduate student Rümeysa Öztürk is derived from interviewing Mathis directly and from his court testimony in the *AAUP v. Rubio* case in the United States District Court in the District of Massachusetts.

We attended courtroom proceedings at the John Joseph Moakley Courthouse of the U.S. District Court in Boston on July 7, 2025, the day on which Nadje Al-Ali gave most of her testimony in the *AAUP v. Rubio* case. Our reporting on her story and background relies on notes from that day, reporting from live virtual testimony on other days of the trial, and the official trial transcript, as well as multiple follow-up interviews with Al-Ali that we conducted both before and after the judge ruled in the case. Our interview with Ramya Krishnan, the Knight Institute lead counsel, further painted the picture of the plaintiffs' preparatory sessions.

Fatality and kidnapping numbers resulting from the October 7, 2023, Hamas attack on Israel are from Mary Kekatos's October 7, 2025, article for *ABCNews*,

"The Israel-Hamas War's Devastating Human Toll After 2 Years, by the Numbers." Gaza fatality numbers are from Wafaa Shurafa and Samy Magdy's AP article of November 29, 2025, "Palestinian Death Toll Has Surpassed 70,000 Since the Israel-Hamas War Began, Gaza Ministry Says."

In reconstructing the timeline and atmospherics around these events, we relied on a variety of sources, including the March 25, 2025, press release announcing that MESA, AAUP, and the Knight Institute had filed suit against the Trump administration; Olivia Ebertz's November 11, 2023, article "Brown University Faculty Push for Charges Against Student Protesters to Be Dropped" for Rhode Island PBS/The Public's Radio; the White House press release of January 30, 2025, "Fact Sheet: President Donald J. Trump Takes Forceful and Unprecedented Steps to Combat Anti-Semitism"; and the ruling of Judge William Young in the *AAUP* case. That last document is a rollicking read, at times reading more like a manifesto for liberalism and democracy than a sober legal analysis.

Historians and activists in the U.S. civil rights movement have done extraordinary work to preserve the memory of how young activists prepared to commit courageous acts of nonviolent civil disobedience. For the section on Reverend James Lawson's training workshops, we drew on a wide array of sources, including oral history interviews with John Lewis and C. T. Vivian in the Civil Rights Movement Archive, the SNCC Digital Gateway's profile of the Nashville Student Movement, and obituaries of Lawson published by both Stanford's Martin Luther King, Jr. Research and Education Institute and *The New York Times*.

Barry Everett Lee's 2010 University of Georgia PhD dissertation, "The Nashville Civil Rights Movement: A Study of the Phenomenon of Intentional Leadership Development and Its Consequences for Local Movements and the National Civil Rights Movement," offered rich details from workshops as well as recollections from young activists who went on to become legendary movement leaders, including Bernard Lafayette, who offered the pithy description of Lawson's sessions as "a nonviolent academy equivalent to West Point." Brian Martin and Patrick G. Coy's "Skills, Training, and Activism," published in the August 2017 issue of *Reflective Practice*, provided context for Lawson's experience in India and how he had been influenced by Gandhian nonviolence.

We situate the Lawson workshops as a "movement halfway house," a term coined and explained by Aldon D. Morris, an emeritus professor of sociology at Northwestern University, in his book *The Origins of the Civil Rights Movement: Black Communities Organizing for Change* (Free Press, 1984). Morris defines a movement halfway house as "an established group or organization that is only partially integrated into the larger society because its participants are actively involved in efforts to bring about a desired change in society." Such spaces are where many civil rights activists trained for nonviolent action.

5. Make a Minyan

The narrative about Patrice Lawrence comes from multiple interviews with her as well as public interviews she has given about her work and personal experiences. Some details came from photos she provided to us and from contemporaneous reporting on the efforts of UndocuBlack where relevant, including the October 31, 2021, article in *Politico*, "The Supreme Court Case That Created the 'Dreamer' Narrative" by Jesús A. Rodríguez. We drew additional information about the 2019 organizing efforts in support of Liberian refugees from a number of sources, including contemporaneous reporting, the *Congressional Record*, the website of the U.S. Citizenship and Immigration Services, and a November 26, 2019, press release from the Office of Minnesota Attorney General Keith Ellison.

The argument of the subsection "Small Circles" grew out of "Find a Political Home," an essay that Ami authored the week after the November 2024 election, published on Substack. In building out the section on Soviet-era dissident circles, two papers from *The Oxford Handbook of Soviet Underground Culture*, edited by Mark Lipovetsky et al. (2021), were especially instructive: "The Ukrainian Underground: Aesthetics, Resistance, and Performance" by Tamara Hundorova lays out in colorful detail the formal and informal ways in which these circles formed and functioned, and we quote Tatsiana Astrouskaya's insights on the development of social trust in these circles from "Belarusian Underground Culture." Benjamin Nathans explains the Soviet dissident movement's relatively small size in his 2024 book *To the Success of Our Hopeless Cause*, as well as in our interviews with him. Félix Maradiaga's story of community resilience came from our interview with him and was originally reported in our April 12, 2025, *New Yorker* essay, "So You Want to Be a Dissident? A Practical Guide to Courage in Trump's Age of Fear."

The Islamic custom requiring three local male residents for the *Jummah* derives from a *hadith* in Sunan Abi Dawud (one of the six major Sunni collections of the Prophet Muhammad's actions, words, and directives): "The Friday prayer in congregation is a necessary duty for every Muslim, with four exceptions; a slave, a woman, a boy, and a sick person." The full text of the Christian verse referenced is from chapter 18, verse 20, in the Book of Matthew: "For where two or three are gathered together in my name, there am I in the midst of them." Rabbis Aaron Alexander and Aryeh Cohen explained in our interviews with them that the Talmud—a record of legal debates among Jewish sages on countless practical and philosophical topics, compiled between around 200 and 500 CE—cites as the source of the requirement of ten men (or people of any gender in modern liberal denominations) for communal prayer a verse in the Book of Numbers, which refers to the ten spies who spoke poorly of the Holy Land as a "wicked community."

Perhaps it is a coincidence that many of the dissidents we interviewed and studied speak of small groups of eight, ten, or twelve that often formed the nucleus for their early efforts. American rabbi Sharon Brous argues regularly that "our deepest spiritual work is finding our way to one other—in celebration, sorrow, and solidarity," both in her sermons and in her 2024 book *The Amen Effect: Ancient Wisdom to Mend Our Broken Hearts and World* (Avery, 2024), from which we quote her comments on mourning and community. IKAR, the Jewish community that Brous cofounded with Melissa Balaban in 2004, has long called the group of congregants who lead its social justice community organizing efforts "Minyan Tzedek," which translates in Hebrew to "Minyan of Justice."

M. Gessen writes about "moment(s) of recognition" in "The Chilling Consequences of Going Along with Trump," published on February 8, 2025, in *The New York Times*. The phrase emerges from a story about the first time Gessen's Soviet-born parents traveled outside the Soviet Union and saw the film *Cabaret*, set in prewar Germany. In the scene, a teenager wearing a Hitler Youth uniform stands up in a quiet biergarten and begins to sing a Nazi ballad. Soon nearly everyone in the courtyard has joined in, and the boy raises his hand in a Hitler salute. Gessen's parents, who had only ever known the repression of the Soviet Union, recognized what it looked like for a country to fall into lockstep behind a strongman. "It was, apparently, possible to maintain a sense of facts and values," Gessen writes. "If that was possible in the Soviet Union half a century ago, then it is certainly possible in the United States today."

6. Don't Start from Scratch

The story of how faculty at the Big Ten universities developed a Mutual Academic Defense Compact to defend against government pressure is informed by an interview and correspondence with David Salas–de la Cruz and news reporting, including the April 30, 2025, *New York Times* article, "This State University Has a Plan to Take on Trump," by Tracey Tully. Context for the dwindling faculty power in the shared governance model between university faculties and administrators comes from a 2020 article by Robert A. Scott, "Leadership Threats to Shared Governance in Higher Education," in the American Association of University Professors' *Journal of Academic Freedom*.

Columbia University's submission to government demands was extensively covered in 2025 reports, including a March 21 Reuters article, "Columbia University Caves to Demands to Restore $400m from Trump Administration," in *The Guardian* and the analysis of Jameel Jaffer et al., "What the Columbia Settlement Really Means," published on August 4 by the Knight First Amendment Institute at Columbia University. Information on the size of Columbia's endowment as of June 30, 2025, is taken from an October 2025 disclosure by the Columbia Investment Management Company. The Rutgers Resolution—a "Resolution to Establish a Mutual Defense Compact for the Universities of the Big Ten Academic Alliance in Defense of Academic Freedom, Institutional Integrity, and the Research Enterprise"—has inspired dozens of institutions to adopt similar language. The University of Massachusetts Amherst has set up a mutual defense compact tracker, and the nonprofit Stand Together for Higher Ed is working to organize faculty across the nation.

The response to the October 2025 White House letters to universities was chronicled in news reports, including Alan Blinder's October 20, 2025, article, "All but 2 Universities Decline a Trump Offer of Preferential Funding" in *The New York Times*, and the responses of the last two universities were documented in an article by Paul Leech, "University of Arizona, Vanderbilt Decline to Sign Trump Administration's Higher-Education Compact," published October 21, 2025, in *Jurist News*.

"On Stage with the Velvet Revolution," Petr Oslzlý's first-person account in a 1990 issue of *TDR* of the role played by playwrights, actors, and theaters in Czechoslovakia's Velvet Revolution, supported our work to develop that section, along with the recollections of former student activist Monika MacDonagh-Pajerová in a 2017 interview in *Radio Prague International*. A report in a 2019 episode of *Current Time TV* by Aleksandr Kasatkin and Yulia Maslova, "Performing for Change: How Theater Professionals Helped Stage the Velvet Revolution," was helpful, and *The Guardian*'s archive of its coverage of the Velvet Revolution, republished in 2019, also helped paint a picture of the moment.

Václav Havel's 1990 New Year's address to the nation, like everything he wrote, is a pleasure to read. In it, he urges people to look within to find the best in themselves and others: "Our main enemy today is our own bad traits: indifference to the common good, vanity, personal ambition, selfishness, and rivalry."

Details on the Black Panthers' free breakfast program of the late 1960s came from the 2017 article "'Children Can't Learn on an Empty Stomach': The Black Panther Party's Free Breakfast Program" by Husain Lateef and David Androff in the December 2017 issue of the *Journal of Sociology and Social Welfare*, and the 2016 book *Black Against Empire: The History and Politics of the Black Panther Party* (University of California Press, 2016) by Joshua Bloom and Waldo E. Martin. To understand how the breakfast initiative fit into the party's broader efforts to build a social safety net for Black people, we turned to Alondra Nelson's book *Body and Soul: The Black Panther Party and the Fight Against Medical Discrimination* (University of Minnesota Press, 2011), as well as Robert O. Self's *American Babylon: Race and Struggle for Postwar Oakland* (Princeton University Press, 2003). Elaine Brown explained the broader political philosophy of these programs ("maybe they would ultimately want some abstract thing called freedom") in an interview for the 1988 Academy Award–nominated documentary series *Eyes on the Prize* produced by the filmmaker Henry Hampton.

Our portrait of Bushwick Ayuda Mutua drew on several interviews and follow-up conversations with five members of the BAM community who have participated in organizing efforts with the group, including Maria Herron. We included supplemental details from additional correspondence, including voice notes and messages exchanged with these sources, as well as a group interview of several people involved in broader mutual aid efforts in Brooklyn. In addition to our interviews with Herron, whose comments on solidarity and the structure of the organization are quoted in the chapter, we reviewed the May 31, 2019, Remezcla profile by Cecilia Nowell, "With Mil Mundos, María Herron Has Built a Bookstore for the Black & Brown Bushwick Community," as well as BAM's "Community Agreements" document.

Data from the Deportation Data Project shows that ICE arrests in New York City spiked significantly during the summer of 2025, with 1,364 in June and 1,333 in July, up from 570 in May. Our timeline of the community response to the ICE incident in Bushwick that summer was re-created with the help of sources familiar with the events, who spoke on the condition of anonymity. We also reviewed the "know your rights" materials used during that mobilization. The reference to armed agents removing a neighbor off the street is corroborated by a video posted on September 25, 2025, by Immigration Coalition on Instagram. Our reporting on Bushwick Ayuda Mutua revealed an extraordinary model of solidarity in practice; if true multiracial democracy ever arrives in America, it will probably look something like BAM.

For the section on *tatreez* in the West Bank, we reviewed Israel Defense Forces Order No. 101 "Order Regarding Prohibition of Incitement and Hostile Propaganda Actions," issued in August 1967 and translated by the Israeli human rights organization B'Tselem, as well as a March 3, 1981, report from the *Christian Science Monitor* on the banning of the flag's colors by Israel Shahak, then-chairperson of the Israeli League for Human and Civil Rights, "Banning the 'Terrible' White, Black, Green, and Red." The June 2022 *Jewish Currents* article "Israel Moves to Ban the

Palestinian Flag" by Isaac Scher also offered helpful details on specific incidents, as did "The Palestinian Arts Movement Gets a Beirut Spotlight," published in May 2019 by *Al Bawaba*. On the broader issues of legal supremacy, civil inequality, and land dispossession in the West Bank, we relied on the December 17, 2019, Human Rights Watch report "Born Without Civil Rights: Israel's Use of Draconian Military Orders to Repress Palestinians in the West Bank" and the 2002 B'Tselem report "Land Grab: Israel's Settlement Policy in the West Bank."

There was no single cause that led to the wave of Palestinian activism, protest, and violence known as the First Intifada; Israel's 1982 invasion of Lebanon and a 1987 traffic accident that killed four Palestinians both contributed to an increasingly tense environment. But the encroachment by the Israeli government onto Palestinian land and the trampling on rights are accepted as the fundamental conditions that eventually sparked the uprising. Our description of the Palestinian-led nonviolence civil disobedience campaigns during this period draws on "When Pickles Become a Weapon: Economy of the First Intifada"—a write-up on the website of the Palestinian Museum in the West Bank—as well as a March 2019 summary of these actions, "What You Need to Know About the 1987 Intifada," by Peace Is Loud, posted on the PBS website.

Most instructive in our effort to illustrate the politics of Palestinian embroidery was the work of Rachel Dedman, whose writing and curatorial work is a deep repository of information on *tatreez* and its social significance. Her chapter "The Politicisation of Palestinian Embroidery Since 1948" in the book *Dangerous Bodies: New Global Perspectives on Fashion and Transgression*, edited by Royce Mahawatte and Jacki Wilson (Palgrave Macmillan, 2023), informed our historical summary of the art form's political evolution. We drew additional details about the embroidery designs used during the demonstrations of the late 1980s from Dedman's reflections published by *The Oxford Student* in June 2025, as well as those from Dalia Al-Dujaili in an April 2025 *British Journal of Photography* piece, and from Niveen Mosleh.

Katherine Pangonis wrote about Mosleh in her essay on *tatreez* in the book *Daybreak in Gaza: Stories of Palestinian Lives and Culture* (Saqi Books, 2024), a collection edited by Mahmoud Muna and Matthew Teller. The quotes from Mosleh that appear in this chapter are drawn from both that essay and from Pangonis's original notes from her spring 2024 correspondence with Mosleh, which Pangonis generously shared with us. A June 1, 2025, piece in *Garland* magazine by Amer Shomali, Sunbula, and Rachel Dedman, "Three Dresses Rescued from Rafah: Palestinian Culture Hangs by a Thread," reported that the building housing the Sulafa Embroidery Centre, which Mosleh directs, had been destroyed in the bombing. Our characterization of *sumud* was enriched by our interview with Bshara Nassar, founder and director of the Museum of the Palestinian People in Washington, D.C. For more on the history of *tatreez*, readers may appreciate Wafa Ghnaim's *Tatreez and Tea: Embroidery and Storytelling in the Palestinian Diaspora* (self, 2018) and *Thobna: Reclaiming Palestinian Dresses in the Diaspora* (self, 2023), Shelagh Weir's *Palestinian Embroidery* (British Museum, 1970) and *Palestinian Costume* (University of Texas Press, 1989), and Widad Kamel Kawar's *Threads of Identity: Preserving Palestinian Costume and Heritage* (Rimal Publications, 2011).

7. Bring the Blankets

The story of Nathan Law's gradual evolution from reluctant activist into international fugitive comes from our multiple interviews with Law, with some narrative details drawn from his 2021 memoir *Freedom: How We Lose It and How We Fight Back*, with Evan Fowler (The Experiment, 2021), and the 2024 POV documentary on PBS *Who's Afraid of Nathan Law?* by filmmakers Joe Piscatella, Matthew Torne, and Mark Rinehart. We supplemented these sources with information from the July 14, 2015, *New York Times* article "Student Leaders Charged over Hong Kong Protest" by Alan Wong; the August 2015 *Sur Journal* paper "Occupying Hong Kong" by Kin-man Chan; and the Council on Foreign Relations' regularly updated white paper "Hong Kong's Freedoms: What China Promised and How It's Cracking Down" (last updated December 15, 2025).

The photograph of Law toward the start of his prison sentence, standing handcuffed and in a prison uniform—referenced early in the chapter—won the 2017 "Focus at the Frontline" award jointly given by the Department of Journalism of HKBU's School of Communication and the Hong Kong Press Photographers Association. The letter from twelve members of the U.S. Congress nominating Law, Joshua Wong, Alex Chow, and their pro-democracy movement for the Nobel Peace Prize was dated January 31, 2018. The letter noted China's "authoritarianism and deep disregard for universally-recognized human rights"; the first signature was that of then-Senator Marco Rubio, who is now the U.S. secretary of state.

Breza Race Maksimovic, Jake Levin, and Jeremy Al-Haj's insights on using small tasks and investments to bring people into activism—sometimes referred to by organizers as the "leadership ladder"—come from our interviews with each of them. In summarizing the protests that swept Serbia after November 2024, we drew on the November 21, 2024, Associated Press article "Why People Are Protesting over a Deadly Roof Collapse in Serbia" by Dusan Stojanovic and "How Serbian Students Created the Largest Protest Movement in Decades," a rich analysis of the dynamics of the campaign by Race Maksimovic and CANVAS founder Srđja Popović in the *Journal of Democracy*. Al-Haj's work on wage increases and working conditions is profiled in the February 23, 2023, post "Spotlight On: Growing a Multiracial Worker Movement Across Missouri!" on the website of PowerSwitch Action.

The paper that emphasizes the importance of asking someone to participate in activism is "Process and Protest: Accounting for Individual Protest Participation" by Alan Schussman and Sarah A. Soule, published in *Social Forces* in December 2005. A 2018 facilitator guide titled "The A.A. Group . . . Where It All Begins," published by Alcoholics Anonymous World Services, includes the insight on the power of participating in setup or cleaning in order to feel "like members."

The story of the groundbreaking efforts to achieve racial and economic equity in northwest Philadelphia led by Black grassroots leaders during the 1960s, '70s, and '80s is worthy of its own book. A detailed timeline featured on the website of East Mount Airy Neighbors (EMAN)—the community organization that helped inspire Dwayne Royster as a child—is a scorecard full of victories: campaigns to collect accounts of real estate discrimination that over time turned into successful zoning battles; renovation of community facilities; defeat of redlining practices; and construction of new affordable housing owned by members of the community.

We relied on the EMAN timeline to paint a picture of this historical moment, as well as two interviews with Dwayne Royster; the "Church History" page on the website of Zion Baptist Church of Philadelphia; and OIC Philadelphia's February 1, 2021, article "The Lion of Zion: Reverend Dr. Leon Sullivan's Unyielding Quest for Equality and Empowerment." The phrase "don't buy where you can't work"— which Sullivan exhorted from the pulpit—was also the name of a series of protests organized in 1936 by Samuel London Evans, a prominent Philadelphia civil rights leader. Evans mobilized Black youth in the city to picket outside of stores that refused to employ African Americans.

Our reporting on the July 2016 clergy action at the Philadelphia airport relied heavily on our interviews with Royster, Cecily Harwitt, Robin Hynicka, and Naomi Washington-Leapheart, all of whom were present during the action. In reconstructing the timeline, we also turned to contemporaneous reporting, including the July 18, 2016, press release from 32BJ SEIU "Philadelphia Airport Workers Vote to Strike During DNC, Demand $15 and a Union"; the July 19, 2016, WPVI-TV story "Hundreds Protest at Airport as DNC Nears"; the July 22, 2016, WHYY story "Police Cite Clergy Staging Sit In to Stand Up for Fired Philly Airport Worker"; the July 22, 2016, 32BJ SEIU press release "32BJ SEIU Statement on Airport Strike Averted"; the Associated Press's July 23, 2016, story "Mayor: Deal to Avert Airport Worker Strike During Convention"; and the July 27, 2016, *The American Prospect* article "How the DNC Avoided a Philly Airport Worker Strike" by Justin Miller.

8. Share Your Fate

A wave of hostility against trans people in the United States was accelerating while we were reporting this book. It intensified with an executive order on January 20, 2025, declaring that the U.S. government would recognize only two sexes, male and female, which the White House declared are "not changeable and are grounded in fundamental and incontrovertible reality." A flurry of federal actions and state laws followed over the following year: At the state level, 126 anti-trans laws passed and 1,022 were proposed in 2025, according to the Trans Legislation Tracker. In December 2025, U.S. Attorney General Pam Bondi issued a memo designating people with "radical gender ideologies" as domestic terrorists.

Amid this fast-evolving and increasingly dangerous situation, which *The New York Times* columnist M. Gessen has likened to a "denationalization project" that could ultimately deny citizenry to trans and nonbinary people, we offered pseudonymity to the trans individuals who agreed to share their stories with us.

Lauren Moore is an alias. We reconstructed her story through interviews and correspondence with her, as well as with the moving company that helped her relocate. The founder of the trans moving company is in the process of legally changing her name to Remelya Jackalope and told us that by the time the book comes out this will be her legal name. We interviewed Jackalope multiple times and also spoke to two of her colleagues at the company in order to establish further details of their work.

When noting why Moore wanted to move to Minnesota, with its large trans community, we relied on statistics from an August 2025 report "How Many Adults and Youth Identify as Transgender in the United States?" by the Williams Institute at the University of California Los Angeles School of Law.

The concept of accompanying people through difficult and dangerous situations has a storied history in the fields of public health and human rights. Among the most eloquent narrators of the idea of accompaniment was the Harvard medical anthropologist Paul Farmer, whose article "Partners in Help: Assisting the Poor over the Long Term" (*Foreign Affairs*, July 29, 2011) we quote from. Another type of accompaniment we explore—the human rights work of "protective presence" as practiced in El Salvador by Peace Brigades International—is described in Swarthmore College's Global Nonviolent Action Database, an invaluable resource that catalogs cases of nonviolent action.

Our descriptions of global abortion accompaniment networks were informed by the wealth of research that has emerged documenting the practice. Some notable contributions include R. M. Barbosa and M. Arilha, "The Brazilian Experience with Cytotec," *Studies in Family Planning* (July/August 1993); and the landmark study published in the January 2022 *Lancet*, Heidi Moseson et al., "Effectiveness of Self-Managed Medication Abortion with Accompaniment Support in Argentina and Nigeria (SAFE): A Prospective, Observational Cohort Study and Non-inferiority Analysis with Historical Controls." We also interviewed many activists and researchers within the movement, including one of the authors of the *Lancet* study, Caitlin Gerdts, vice president for research at Ibis Reproductive Health; Naomi Braine, author of *Abortion Beyond the Law: Building a Global Feminist Movement for Self-Managed Abortion* (Verso, 2023); and Oriana López-Uribe, former executive director of the Fondo Maria abortion fund in Mexico City, whom we quote in the chapter. López-Uribe is a coauthor of the study "The Influence of Feminist Abortion Accompaniment on Emotions Related to Abortion: A Longitudinal Observational Study in Mexico," published in *SSM—Population Health* in September 2022, which we cite.

The narrative of the West Virginia teachers who packed lunches for students during the strike of 2018 was shaped by interviews with Stephanie Johnson, who participated in the action, and Emily Hilliard, a folklorist at Berea College in Kentucky, who coauthored a colorful account of the strike, *55 Strong: Inside the West Virginia Teacher's Strike*, edited by Elizabeth Catte, Emily Hilliard, and Jessica Salfia (Belt Publishing, 2018). We also reviewed contemporaneous reporting on these events in *The New York Times*, *Bon Appetit*, and WJLA, the ABC television affiliate in Arlington, Virginia.

John S. Ahlquist and Margaret Levi articulated the concept of a "community of fate" in their study of global labor union solidarity, *In the Interest of Others: Organizations and Social Activism* (Princeton University Press, 2013), and Levi elaborated on the idea in the context of the global COVID-19 pandemic in a July 7, 2020, article in *Noéma*, "An Expanded Community of Fate." "Economies are the result of moral and political choices, which can be made and remade," Levi writes in the *Noéma* piece. In proposing that ours be remade with greater attention to the value of reciprocal altruism, she invokes a labor slogan: "An injury to one is an injury to all."

9. Write Down Your People

Claire Atkin's story of facing the threats that emerged as she led boycotts against online mis- and disinformation purveyors comes from multiple interviews with her, with many details supplemented by the media coverage of the campaigns she has led with her former business partner Nandini Jammi. Atkin and Jammi discussed their strategy in a June 9, 2022, NPR interview with Steve Inskeep, and the Check My

Ads Institute website offers a fairly comprehensive account of its campaigns. For context on the lawsuit, we also relied on Rumble's 2023 complaint against Atkin and Jammi in U.S. District Court, as well as the company's initial press release announcing the lawsuit and CEO Chris Pavlovski's tweet warning them to preserve their documents. The case was dismissed by the United States District Court, Middle District of Florida, Tampa Division, in 2025.

A 2021 study by *The Economist* Intelligence Unit shows that more than eight in ten women who spend time on the internet have witnessed online violence, while nearly four in ten report personal experiences as the target of such violence. The leading threat tactic, according to the report, is mis- and disinformation, defined as "spreading rumors and slander to discredit or damage a woman's character." This describes many of the tweets posted by Dan Bongino about Atkin that we reviewed. We chose not to publish the specific text of the Twitter replies posted by Bongino's followers, many of which were misogynistic and dehumanizing.

We didn't want this book to be only about profiling courageous people; that book, though interesting, would offer little agency to the reader. Instead, our intention was to break courageous actions into their component parts—behaviors, practices, patterns—and place the individual at the center so that anyone could do something with the insights we present. By the time we interviewed Michael Fanselow, the UCLA professor who specializes in the science of fear, we had spoken with dozens of dissidents around the world. In one way or another, many of them had described being more fearful of abandoning their values than of facing the immediate consequences of their dissent (a phenomenon we describe in "A Moral Collision").

We went into the conversation with Fanselow especially curious about how this happens: Are some people just naturally more motivated by these bigger-picture fears? Or was something else going on? Fanselow, who primarily works with rats, showed us that what's more common—and scientifically proven—is that we are more capable of acting on our values if our fear is diminished. "[A rat] who is less afraid is more likely to go [grab some food] if there's a cat out there," he told us. "For those other motivations to take precedence, they have to be individuals who are not going to be as reactive to the immediate threats." His 2016 study with Erica Hornstein and Naomi Eisenberger is "A Safe Haven: Investigating Social-Support Figures as Prepared Safety Stimuli," published in *Psychological Science*.

As we note, Atkin—who refers to the mapping exercise as creating one's "community of care"—has come to similar conclusions. In one interview, she told us that a security consultant she once hired, in laying out a range of strategies for managing online threats, ranked one strategy high above the rest: The people in your neighborhood, the consultant said, will keep you safe. Two major studies—the annual General Social Survey by NORC at the University of Chicago and Pew Research Center's 2025 survey of how connected Americans feel to their neighbors—show that strong neighborhood bonds are increasingly uncommon. But Atkins's investment in her community paid off for her. "My neighbors protected me," Atkin told us.

10. Make a List, Check It Twice

The 2022 Supreme Court decision in *Dobbs v. Jackson Women's Health Organization* that overturned federal abortion protections darkened the climate at abortion clinics across the nation. Harassment and threats against clinics, providers, and patients became more prevalent, according to reports such as Cassie Miller's June 13, 2024, piece for the Southern Poverty Law Center, "Abortion Clinics Face Increased Harassment Post-Roe," and statistics compiled by the National Abortion Federation.

The story of how Barbara Schwartz and Stephanie Rosenwinge navigated one of those threats—the arrival of anti-abortion activist Coleman Boyd at the Bristol, West Virginia, abortion clinic—comes from interviews with Schwartz and Rosenwinge, as well as from the photos and documents of the incident that they provided to us. We also reviewed court documents and news coverage of Boyd's earlier federal indictment, as well as the terms of his pretrial release. (Boyd was sentenced in 2024 but granted a presidential pardon on January 23, 2025.) In 2023, Schwartz and Rosenwinge cofounded a nonprofit organization, State Line Abortion Access Partners, to expand their work beyond clinic defense to providing free reproductive health supplies and services throughout Appalachia.

We only scratched the surface of the literature on the growth of politically motivated violence and its links to authoritarianism, with references to Steven Levitsky and Daniel Ziblatt's book *How Democracies Die* (Crown, 2018) and Jon Michaels and David Noll's *Vigilante Nation: How State-Sponsored Terror Threatens Our Democracy* (Atria/One Signal Publishers, 2024).

The Reuters investigation reported August 7, 2025, in "Pro-Trump Group Wages Campaign to Purge 'Subversive' Federal Workers" by Linda So, Peter Eisler, and Ned Parker is a deep-dive into how MAGA movement watch lists were eventually used by the federal government to punish people included on them. The Reuters reporting revealed that at least half those on the American Accountability Foundation's government employee watch lists had left the government or been forced to take administrative leave.

Our description of how the U.S. government targeted people on the Canary

Mission watch list for their pro-Palestinian activism is derived mainly from testimony and evidence presented in the *AAUP v. Rubio* lawsuit that is the focus of the earlier chapter "Practice and Prepare." The watch list website describes the group's mission as documenting "people and groups that promote hatred of the USA, Israel and Jews." A detailed summary of how it is alleged that a Department of Homeland Security "Tiger Team" used the Canary Mission website to compile its own list of targets for ideological deportations can be found in the plaintiffs' "Proposed Findings of Fact and Requested Rulings of Law" filed in that case, and in Judge William G. Young's subsequent ruling in favor of the plaintiffs.

During the trial, Peter Hatch, assistant director of Homeland Security Investigations, testified that he was instructed to search the Canary Mission website for international students to investigate for possible deportation, according to court documents and reporting in *The New York Times* (Zach Montague, "Immigration Officials Used Shadowy Pro-Israel Group to Target Student Activists," July 9, 2025). A memo from Deputy Assistant Secretary of State Stuart Wilson that was introduced as evidence in court stated: "While Öztürk has been involved with actions protesting Tufts' relationship with Israel, DHS/ICE/HSI has not, however, provided any evidence showing that Öztürk has engaged in any antisemitic activity or made any public statements indicating support for a terrorist organization or antisemitism generally."

During the trial, Patrick Cunningham, the ICE investigations agent in Boston who oversaw Öztürk's arrest, testified that officials at the agency's central offices in Washington, D.C., headquarters were unusually interested in the Öztürk arrest. But when he saw that the allegations against her centered only on an op-ed, he consulted the in-house lawyers before proceeding. "When you receive information from headquarters, at this level, top down, um, it—you make the assumption that it's legally sufficient," Cunningham testified.

The plaintiffs in *AAUP v. Rubio* showed in a filing to the court that the State Department had determined there was no evidence Rümeysa Öztürk had committed antisemitic actions. In a memo cited by Judge Young in his opinion, Stuart Wilson had written: "While Öztürk has been involved with actions protesting Tufts' relationship with Israel, DHS/ICE/HSI has not, however, provided any evidence showing that Öztürk has engaged in any antisemitic activity or made any public statements indicating support for a terrorist organization or antisemitism generally."

Our statistics on antisemitism in America come from FBI data on hate crimes and a study by the Center for Countering Digital Hate and the Jewish Council for Public Affairs, "A Home for Hate: How Anti-Semitism Is Reaching Millions on X," that identified 679,584 antisemitic posts on the social media platform X between February 1, 2024, and January 31, 2025.

Descriptions of how Russian President Vladimir Putin and Hungarian President Viktor Orbán used accusations of antisemitism to justify authoritarian actions are built from news reports and analysis of their regimes, including Jeffrey Veidlinger, "Analysis: Putin's Claim That War on Ukraine Is to Target Nazis Is Absurd. Here's Why," *PBS News*, February 28, 2022; and Ira Forman, "Viktor Orbán Is Exploiting Anti-Semitism," *Atlantic*, December 14, 2018. A March 14, 2025, post on historian Timothy Snyder's "Thinking About" newsletter, "'Antisemitism' and Antisemitism," compares the ways in which the Russian and U.S. governments have used antisemitism as a tool toward other illiberal ends and explains that "Jews in the United States are being instrumentalized in an effort to build a more authoritarian American system."

The story of the student who was told by two separate employers that she was losing her job owing to her inclusion on the Canary Mission website comes from interviews with that student. We granted anonymity to protect the student from any further retaliation for pro-Palestinian activism.

Kat Green's story is drawn from interviews with Green, as well as news reporting about the comedian Lizz Winstead's comedy tour, including an article by Melena Ryzik, "Using Comedy to Push for Abortion Rights," *New York Times*, July 15, 2022. The narrative of Kristofer Goldsmith's opposition research comes from interviews with Goldsmith as well as reporting about him, including "The Neo-Nazi Hunter," episode 2 of *Exploring Hope*, 2023, PBS; and Tim Dickinson, "The Neo-Nazi Hunter Next Door," *Rolling Stone*, February 2, 2023.

11. Stack Your Defenses

The story of Nyasha Frank Mpahlo's struggle to maintain operational security for himself and fellow Zimbabwean activists who attended a training session in the Maldives comes from interviews with Mpahlo as well as from supporting documentation of the Instagram post in question; news articles about the activists in the Zimbabwean media outlets the *Herald*, *Pindula News*, and *ZimLive*; and an interview with an organizer of the session, Breza Race Maksimovic of the Center for Applied Nonviolent Action and Strategies in Serbia.

In illustrating the political climate in Zimbabwe surrounding the 2018 election, we drew on contemporaneous news reports, including *The Washington Post*'s August 22, 2018, article by Vasabjit Banerjee, "Even After Mugabe, Zimbabwe's Elections Do Not Appear Free or Fair," and from election observer reports such as a January 8, 2018, pre-election assessment from the Diplomatic Service of the European Union titled "Improved Political Climate, but Un-level Playing Field and Lack of Trust in the Process" and a 2019 post-election report from the International Republican Institute and the National Democratic Institute. The joint analysis concludes that "Zimbabwe has not yet established a process that treats all political parties equitably and allows citizens to be confident that they can cast their vote and express their political opinion free from fear of retribution."

Reports about more recent political repression in Zimbabwe come from a Human Rights Foundation article of June 26, 2024, "Eight Ways Zimbabwe's Regime Hijacked the 2023 Vote," and Human Rights Watch's 2025 country report on Zimbabwe. Details on the brutal human rights record of Robert Mugabe's nearly forty-year rule can be found in several 2019 obituaries of the former president, such as "Robert Mugabe, Strongman Who Cried 'Zimbabwe Is Mine' Dies at 95," September 6, 2019, *New York Times*, and "Robert Mugabe: From Liberator to Tyrant," *BBC News*, September 6, 2019. Our interview with Zachariah Mampilly, a political science professor at the City University of New York, and his writings, including "The Promise of Africa's 'Youth Bulge'" (*Foreign Affairs*, July 7, 2021), helped to ground our understanding of the rising generation of African pro-democracy activists.

To explain the global phenomenon of autocratic regimes retaliating against citizens for content posted online, we reviewed the 2024 Pulitzer Prize–winning series "Annals of Autocracy" in *The Washington Post*, as well as "Freedom on the Net 2024: The Struggle for Trust Online," a report from Freedom House, and local news reports supporting some of the stories recounted in that report. Freddy Guevara described adjusting to the fast-changing political climate in Venezuela in our interviews with him; other details are taken from published accounts of his struggle, including Stephen Gibbs, "Maduro Critic Freddy Guevara Flees to Chilean Embassy," *The Times* (UK), November 7, 2017, and "Freddy Guevara MC/MPA 2024 Is Not Giving Up on the Global Struggle for Democracy," published May 20, 2024, by the Ash Center for Democratic Governance and Innovation at the Harvard Kennedy School.

In "Learn How to Become an American Swiper," which he posts on Facebook, X, and Instagram, conservative activist James O'Keefe has publicly described how he recruits people to secretly record embarrassing videos of dates. There have been numerous reports of people being fired as a result of these recordings, including an Associated Press article about a Pentagon contractor who lost his job. One victim of a covert recording, a former employee of the Department of Justice, sued the agency after his firing.

Ramzi Kassem was one of the first people we interviewed in our reporting for this book. A professor of law at the City University of New York and a codirector and founder of the nonprofit legal clinic CLEAR (Creating Law Enforcement Accountability & Responsibility), Kassem has long provided legal support for Muslims and other people in New York City who have been "targeted by the government under the guise of national security and counterterrorism," according to the CLEAR website.

Not long after our interview, Kassem began representing Mahmoud Khalil, a former Columbia University graduate student and leader of pro-Palestinian protests on the campus who in March 2025 was seized by plainclothes ICE agents for alleged immigration violations. Khalil was released from detention after more than three months by the U.S. District Court in the District of New Jersey. As of this writing, his case is ongoing. On January 1, 2026, Kassem was appointed chief counsel to New York City Mayor Zohran Mamdani.

The story of the Egyptian gay man whose phone was grabbed by the country's morality police was recounted in the February 21, 2023, Human Rights Watch report "'All This Terror Because of a Photo': Digital Targeting and Its Offline Consequences for LGBT People in the Middle East and North Africa." Additional context about Egypt's practices can be found in "The Trap: Punishing Sexual Difference in Egypt," a November 22, 2017, report from the Egyptian Initiative for Personal Rights; Ayça Alemdaroğlu, "The Politics of Sexuality and the LGBTQ Crackdown in Egypt," *Georgetown Journal of International Affairs*, February 16, 2018; and Rasha Younes, "Egypt's Denial of Sexual Orientation and Gender Identity," Human Rights Watch, March 20, 2020. In its "2022 Country Report on Human Rights Practices," the U.S. State Department included an estimate that more than 250 people in Egypt had been arrested since 2013 based on sexual orientation or gender identity. Victim descriptions of torture were recounted in the 2023 Human Rights Watch report.

U.S. Customs and Border Patrol notes on its website that the federal agency searches electronic devices on "rare occasions." In 2024, the Ninth Circuit Court of Appeals ruled that the California Highway Patrol did not violate the Fourth Amendment when officers forced Jeremy Travis Payne to unlock his cell phone with his thumb during a traffic stop.

Ana Maria Ramirez told us about her work to develop the privacy-protecting reproductive health app Euki in our interviews and correspondence with her. We also reviewed the underlying research that she and her colleagues at Ibis Reproductive Health conducted, including the 2019 publication "Testing a Sexual and Reproductive Health mHealth Prototype in the United States." Human rights activist Raphael Mimoun also spoke to us about his encrypted video app, Tella, which has been downloaded more than one hundred thousand times, and his very helpful "Swiss cheese theory" of layering security defenses.

Afsaneh Rigot's research on how states, corporations, and other power holders use technology to facilitate human rights abuses was foundational to our thinking on digital defenses. Rigot, whom we interviewed and corresponded with about her work and the steps she takes to protect her identity, is the founder and principal researcher at The De|Center, a nonprofit organization researching "technology design interventions that work to reduce the mass-scale harms of existing and emerging technologies."

Rigot's 2022 report "Digital Crime Scenes: The Role of Digital Evidence in the Persecution of LGBTQ People in Egypt, Lebanon, and Tunisia" (March 4, 2022) documents the evidence used in twenty-nine cases against queer people in Egypt, Lebanon, and Tunisia and provides a unique insight into how states are using digital evidence to prosecute identity or thought. In May 2022, she published with the Harvard Belfer Center a paper outlining her methodology for how to "Design from the Margins: Centering the Most Marginalized and Impacted in Design Processes—From Ideation to Production."

The De|Center collaborated with the human rights group Article 19 on the July 2024 report, "Protecting MENA's Queer Communities: Recommendations for Tech Companies," which suggests design changes such as hidden app icons and self-destruct buttons in apps. Some of those changes have been adopted by leading tech companies, and others Rigot is still advocating for. "Building based on those with the least power and who are the most affected makes better tech and futureproofs for resilience against abuse and authoritarianism," she told us.

12. Win the War of Persuasion

The brutality that France inflicted on Algeria during its colonial rule has been well documented by scholars such as William Gallois, a professor at the University of Exeter, who recounted the suffocation of a tribe in a cave in the chapter "Dahra and the History of Violence in Early Colonial Algeria," in *Violence, Military Encounters, and Colonialism*, vol. 2 of *The French Colonial Mind*, edited by Martin Thomas (University of Nebraska Press, 2011). In his book *A History of Violence in the Early Algerian Colony* (Palgrave Macmillan, 2013), Gallois describes the French attempt to exterminate the local population and writes that although the exact death toll is debated, "what is generally accepted is that the French empire induced an Algerian demographic catastrophe." Some deaths, Gallois wrote, came from "hunger, misery, drought, cold and disease," which the French used as tools of war.

In the early days of what would be known as the Algerian War of Independence, the Front de Libération Nationale, along with its supporters, attempted to limit its ambushes and assassinations against the colonial government. Martin Thomas details the escalation in retaliatory violence between rebel and security forces, including the former's turn toward mass civilian massacres, in his chapter "Repression, Reprisals, and Rhetorics of Massacre in Algeria's War," in *Rhetorics of Empire: Languages of Colonial Conflict After 1900*, edited by Martin Thomas and Richard Toye (Manchester University Press, 2017). In *Uncivil War: Intellectuals and Identity Politics During the Decolonization of Algeria* (University of Nebraska Press, 2006), University of Nebraska history professor James D. Le Sueur summarizes Algeria's bloody revolution, describing the Front de Libération Nationale's massacre in Philippesville as a turning point in the conflict. "The overzealous French military reactions to Philippeville destroyed the last chances of political moderation," Le Sueur wrote.

An interesting perspective on the FLN's terrorist tactics can be found in "Algiers—1957: An Approach to Urban Counterinsurgency," by U.S. Army Major Robert J. Kee in the April 1974 issue of *Military Review*. Kee analyzes—and ultimately condemns—the interrogation, torture, and population control with which the French responded to the FLN. Kee wrote that if the U.S. Army was called upon in the future to address a similar insurgency, he hoped that "it will reject those methods of expediency which disregard the basic dignity of man. To fail to do so would be to dishonor our heritage and to prove ourselves unworthy of the great responsibility entrusted to us by our nation."

The story of how Erica Chenoweth changed their view on political violence comes from interviews and correspondence with Chenoweth, as well as their 2013 TEDx talk, "The Success of Nonviolent Civil Resistance," and "The Origins of the NAVCO Data Project (or: How I Learned to Stop Worrying and Take Nonviolent Conflict Seriously)," posted May 7, 2014, on their blog, the *Rational Insurgent*.

Multiple interviews with Chenoweth's collaborator Maria J. Stephan were also crucial to our reporting. Like Chenoweth, Stephan is a scholar of civil resistance, as well as the co-lead and chief organizer at the Horizons Project, which supports social change movements. When she met Chenoweth, she had just completed her PhD thesis, "Fighting for Statehood: The Role of Civilian-Based Resistance in the East Timorese, Palestinian, and Kosovo Albanian Self-Determination Movements."

Stephan guided us not only through the story of her work with Chenoweth, but also through the field of nonviolent civil resistance movements. Readers interested in a deeper dive into the mechanics of these movements should consider reading

Chenoweth and Stephan's book, *Why Civil Resistance Works: The Strategic Logic of Nonviolent Conflict* (Columbia University Press, 2011).

Data nerds may also be interested in examining the dataset that emerged from their collaboration. The Nonviolent and Violent Campaigns and Outcomes (NAVCO) data project began in 2013 as an analysis of 323 campaigns "with the objectives of expelling foreign occupations, regime change (i.e. removing dictatorships or military juntas), self-determination or separatism, and in some cases, other major types of social change (i.e. anti-apartheid campaigns)."

Chenoweth and Stephan coded the First Palestinian Intifada as nonviolent with a violent flank. A 1990 Human Rights Watch report explains, "According to IDF figures, only five percent of violent activity by Palestinians during the intifada involves the use of clearly lethal weapons: guns, knives and gasoline bombs. Eighty-five percent is stone-throwing, 60 percent of which is carried out by children 13 years of age or younger. (Stone-throwing ranges in severity from the tossing of pebbles at far-away soldiers to the hurling of small boulders from rooftops or at the windshields of moving cars.)"

From the initial dataset, NAVCO has expanded to include 670 campaigns, Chenoweth told us, collected with additional researchers. The success rate for nonviolent movements has continued to decline, even as the number of nonviolent movements has increased. In an article in the July 2020 issue of the *Journal of Democracy*, "The Future of Nonviolent Resistance," Chenoweth speculated on some possible reasons—such as autocrats getting smarter about tactics, but they also noted that "the most compelling explanations for the declining effectiveness of nonviolent campaigns lie in the changing nature of the campaigns themselves."

One challenge Chenoweth notes in that article is an overreliance on "mass demonstrations while neglecting other techniques—such as general strikes and mass civil disobedience—that can more forcefully disrupt a regime's stability." In *Blueprint for Revolution* (Penguin Random House, 2015), veteran Serbian activist Srđja Popović and coauthor Matthew Miller also call for mass demonstrations to be "the last step you take, not the first."

In 2020, Chenoweth published "Questions, Answers, and Some Cautionary Updates Regarding the 3.5% Rule," noting that the 3.5 percent participation metric is more a rule of thumb than a prescription for success. Chenoweth also noted in the updated data that there have been exceptions to the rule, such as Bahrain's nonviolent movement of 2011–2014, which failed despite achieving over 6 percent participation at its peak.

Our account of the rise and fall of tree-spiking as a tactic of the environmental movement comes from an interview with Mike Roselle, one of the cofounders of

Earth First!, in addition to contemporaneous news coverage, such as a May 15, 1987, *Los Angeles Times* article by Larry B. Stammer, "Environment Radicals Target of Probe into Lumber Mill Accident," and a March 5, 1990, article in *The Washington Post*, "Tree Spiking an 'Eco-Terrorist' Tactic." The debate among environmentalists about the tactic was well covered in a November 4, 1990, *New York Times* article profiling the activists who put their bodies on the line to try to save old-growth forests, "If a Tree Falls in the Forest, They Hear It," by Trip Gabriel.

A particularly eloquent manifesto against tree-spiking comes from former Earth First! organizer Judi Bari—who was severely injured in a never-solved car bombing in 1990—in her book *Timber Wars* (Common Courage Press, 1994). Bari calls tree-spiking a "failed tactic by any standard" and recounts the story of the failure of tree-spiking on Meares Island in British Columbia, followed by the success of other nonviolent tactics. We found additional details about the Meares Island campaign on the website accompanying a Canadian documentary film *British Columbia: An Untold History*; the site contains original photos of the "First Logging Blockade" in 1984 and of peaceful demonstrators at the "War in the Woods" in 1994. Photos of the forest protecters waiting to greet logging executives on the beach appeared in the *Meares Island News* in 1985. The Ahousaht and Tla-o-qui-aht First Nations finally secured rights to establish nature conservancies on the island in 2024, with the support of $40 million raised by the Canadian nonprofit Nature United.

The journalistic community's response to the assassination of Slovakian investigative journalist Ján Kuciak and his fiancée Martina Kušnírová was swift solidarity. In 2018, colleagues at competing outlets banded together to publish Kuciak's final investigation and established a new nonprofit in his name to continue investigating organized crime in Slovakia. Journalists have continued to write about his legacy, including "'They Can't Kill Us All': Slovakian Journalists Defiant After Murders," published in *The Guardian* in 2018, and "Four Years After Journalist's Murder, Slovakia Has Changed," published by the Organized Crime and Corruption Reporting Project in 2022.

The story of how Hungarian Prime Minister Viktor Orbán has managed to take control of the media comes from international news reports, such as the Associated Press's July 31, 2024, analysis, "How Hungary's Orban Uses Control of the Media to Escape Scrutiny and Keep the Public in the Dark" by Justin Spike, and also from interviews with Hungarian journalists, including Tamás Bodoky, founder of the Hungarian investigative news outlet *Atlatszo*, and Éva Bognár, president of the MédiaFórum Association. In December 2025, *Atlatszo* won the first round of its lawsuit against the Hungarian Sovereignty Protection Office when the judge ruled that the news outlet was not engaged in intelligence gathering, as had been alleged by the government.

A significant finding about the role of structural racism in nonviolent movements comes from scholars Devorah Manekin and Tamar Mitts in their September 2021 article "Effective for Whom? Ethnic Identity and Nonviolent Resistance," published in the *American Political Science Review*. Manekin and Mitts analyzed Chenoweth's data through a racial lens and found that acts of nonviolent resistance led by ethnic minority groups are seen as more violent—and are less successful—than those led by majority groups. This is one reason that "multiracial and multiethnic coalitions are very important in ensuring the success of nonviolent resistance," Chenoweth told us.

An example of a successful nonviolent boycott campaign has been the Takedown Tesla movement, a story well told by Aarian Marshall and David Gilbert in "The Definitive Story of Tesla Takedown," *Wired*, June 16, 2025. According to a May 2025 Axios Harris Poll 100 survey, Tesla's reputation plummeted from eighth highest among one hundred U.S. companies in 2021 to ninety-fifth in 2025.

13. Seize the Story

The story of Cesar Chavez and the Delano grape strike is well documented. For our focus on the elements of the movement related to narrative, joy, and agency, we relied on John Gregory Dunne's *Delano: The Story of the California Grape Strike* (Farrar, Straus and Giroux, 1967), as well as the stories recounted by many of the strikers at the United Farm Workers' fortieth anniversary reunion in 2005. We also referenced the extensive collection of photos and documentation of the movement—including performances of El Teatro Campesino—that are stored at the Farmworker Movement Collection at the California State University Northridge university library. Luis Valdez still leads El Teatro Campesino, a theater ensemble company that promotes social change and is based in San Juan Batista, California.

Our account of Polish climate activists staging a "multi-energy circus" outside of an oil company's investor conference comes from interviews and correspondence with one of the organizers, Dominika Lasota, as well as photos and video of the event. For background on the company, Orlen, and the political dynamics surrounding the action, we reviewed Tadeusz Michrowski, "Tracking the 'Green Eagle': Unpacking CEE's Biggest Oil Company's Promises to 'Go Green,'" published in *VSquare* (October 2024), an independent news outlet that covers the Visegrád Four country group, which includes Poland, Hungary, Slovakia, and the Czech Republic.

The Serbian student activist group Otpor! is renowned for its use of humor during the successful movement to oust Slobodan Milošević in the late 1990s and early 2000s. Otpor! cofounder Srdja Popović has often told the stories of Milošević-in-a-barrel and other antics. Some may enjoy his essay, coauthored by Mladen Joksic, "Why Dictators Don't Like Jokes," published in *Foreign Policy*, April 5, 2013, and his January 2013 TedX talk on "The Power of Laughtivism." Popović now leads the Center for Applied Nonviolent Action and Strategies (CANVAS), which trains nonviolent activists across the globe.

Sources for details of the conflict between El Salvador's landowners and the insurgency include T. David Mason et al., "Land Reform Versus Repression in Counterinsurgency: Evidence from El Salvador," *Journal of Conflict Resolution* (February/March 2025), and Paul Heath Hoeffel, "Eclipse of the Oligarchs," *New York Times*, September 6, 1981. An accounting of the death squads, the death toll, and the brutal tactics employed by the regime during the civil war is found in the United Nations Report of the Commission on the Truth for El Salvador, *From Madness to Hope: The 12-Year War in El Salvador*, published in 1993.

The concept of the "pleasure of agency" comes from Yale political science professor Elisabeth Wood, who offers a detailed examination of the experiences of El Salvador's *campesinos* in her book *Insurgent Collective Action and Civil War in El Salvador* (Cambridge University Press, 2003). Wood cites Douglas McAdam's concept of "cognitive liberation," experienced by the civil rights activists whose struggle he chronicles in his book *Freedom Summer* (Oxford University Press, 1988). Wood also references the work of Albert O. Hirschman, who examines this phenomenon from an economic standpoint in his book *Shifting Involvements: Private Interest and Public Action* (Princeton University Press, 1982).

Accounts of the centrality of joy in the Free DC movement's organizing are drawn from interviews with the organization's founder, Keya Chatterjee, as well as from Instagram posts profiling Free DC actions, including the "Defend the District" go-go dance party hosted by Justin "Yaddiya" Johnson. Chatterjee believes so strongly in joy as an organizing principle that she published a futuristic romance novel, *The Revolution Will Not Be Rated G* (Green Writers Press, 2025), set during a revolution.

14. Find the Double Thinkers

As many scholars of civil resistance argue, a nation's capacity to withdraw support for a regime and sustain long patterns of noncooperation is what ultimately brings down authoritarians. The work of Erica Chenoweth and Maria J. Stephan, for example, understands authoritarian regimes as being held up by "pillars" of society, such as private businesses, religious institutions, unions, and the military. Successful campaigns weaken popular support for an authoritarian leader by encouraging different pillars to withdraw their support from a corrupt or unjust regime. One by one, the sectors defect, and eventually the leader may weaken and their government may fall.

People do not exist in the aggregate, however, and societies do not "move" of their own accord. They move as the result of many coordinated actions of individuals. This chapter tries to understand more about defection at the level of the individual. What does it take for people to change their minds, or to walk away from long-standing political and ideological commitments, even at great potential cost? What are the relative powers and limits of shame, proximity, and social connection as tools of persuasion? Why does a person who hears in their head a voice raising objections—that is, who arrives at a moral collision—choose to follow the voice?

Our interview and correspondence with Jonathan Pinckney, Assistant Professor of Political Science in the School of Economic, Political, and Policy Sciences at the University of Texas at Dallas, provided a strong theoretical foundation for the literature on defection. Another helpful academic resource was the 2017 paper "Motivated Numeracy and Enlightened Self-Government" by Dan M. Kahan et al., published in the journal *Behavioural Public Policy*. These authors describe their "identity-protective cognition thesis," defined as "a psychic self-defense mechanism that steers individuals away from beliefs that could alienate them from others on whose support they depend in myriad domains of everyday life."

Activists past and present illustrated for us the utility of provoking small shifts among targets of a campaign to get around the problem of identity-protective cognition. Nadine Bloch's comments on "shifting each group one notch along the spectrum" is a reference to an organizing tool called the "Spectrum of Allies" and developed by the sociologists George Lakey and Martin Oppenheimer. Bloch's explanation of this tool and how it can be used is available on the website of the Commons Social Change Library. We pieced together the story of SNCC's work with Northern students during Freedom Summer from multiple accounts, including the June 23, 2014, "Fresh Air" piece on NPR, "50 Years Ago, Students Fought for Black Rights During 'Freedom Summer,'" and the profile of Fannie Lou Hamer on the SNCC Digital Gateway.

Our profile of Zulema Palavecino began with an interview we conducted with Mariela Belski, the executive director of Amnistía Internacional Argentina, who described to us the experience of leading a human rights NGO amid attacks on civil liberties and civil society from the insurgent right-wing government. Belski also spoke about the struggle of the retirees who were the tip of the spear of resistance to Javier Milei's government. The story of Palavecino—one leader in these efforts—

emerged from an initial interview and extensive written and voice-note correspondence with her. Reporting from the independent Argentinian news agency Agencia de Noticias RedAcción offered helpful context for the Jubilados Insurgentes, Palavecino's "insurgent retirees" group. One word of caution for readers who aspire to follow in Palavecino's intrepid footsteps: Milk is not sterile, and the American Academy of Ophthalmology does not recommend its use to mitigate the effects of tear gas. Instead, the organization says, flush eyes out with clean water or eyewash, blink frequently to cause tearing, and seek immediate medical assistance.

Milei's austerity efforts have been well documented. Particularly instructive for our writing was the December 2, 2024, *New Yorker* profile, "Javier Milei Wages War on Argentina's Government" by Jon Lee Anderson. The Argentinian president's remarks about "parasites who live off the state" comes from his speech at the World Economic Forum in Davos in January 2024. Our brief history of the pensioner protests prior to Milei's tenure was aided by a December 19, 2017, BBC article, "Argentina Passes Pension Reform Despite Violent Protests," and Pablo Meriguet, "Argentinian Retirees Continue Their Fight for Dignity," *Peoples Dispatch*, May 16, 2025.

To capture the texture of the violence during the ongoing protests—beyond what we gleaned from our interviews with Belski and Palavecino and the photos furnished by Palavecino—we combed frontline reports, including an article published June 13, 2024, in *The Guardian*, "Argentina: Violent Protests as Senators Back Austerity Measures of President Milei"; the April 3, 2025, Human Rights Watch report "Argentina: Abusive Response to Protest"; footage from the Associated Press archive from March 12, 2025; and the Argentina Security Ministry's Resolution 943/2023, "Protocol for the Maintenance of Public Order in the Event of Road and Transit Blockades," issued in December 2023. Pope Francis made his "pepper spray" comments in a September 20, 2024, speech at the Vatican.

Our section on Mikhael Manekin is drawn from an initial interview and written and voice-note correspondence with him, and supplemented by the extensive reporting on his organizing efforts with Smol Emuni and Breaking the Silence. Details on the violence of the Second Intifada come from the Council on Foreign Relations' regularly updated "Israeli-Palestinian Conflict" briefing webpage, and information on the early days of Breaking the Silence is taken from Steven Erlanger, "Israeli Soldiers Stand Firm, but Duty Wears on the Soul," *New York Times*, March 23, 2007.

Statistics on the devastation in Gaza and the media censorship within Israel after October 7, 2023, come from Wafaa Shurafa, Sam Magdy, and Sam Metz, "Israel Strikes a Gaza Hospital Twice, Killing at Least 20, Including Journalists and Rescuers," Associated Press, August 25, 2025; Sam Mednick, "Experts Warned That

Gaza Was at Risk of Famine. Here's Why They Confirmed It for Gaza City," Associated Press, August 22, 2025; and Haggai Matar, "Breaking New Records, Israel Sees Unprecedented Spike in Media Censorship," *+972 Magazine*, May 2, 2025. Manekin writes in much greater detail of his moment of revelation in the Palestinian village in his book *End of Days: Ethics, Tradition, and Power in Israel* (Academic Studies Press, 2023), which is also the source of the later quote from his argument that witnessing the suffering of Palestinians could break through to Israelis. Michael Walzer's theory of connected criticism is articulated in his seminal work, *Interpretation and Social Criticism* (Harvard University Press, 1987).

Many polls show that Jewish Israelis broadly oppose Manekin's vision for a country in which Israelis and Palestinians have an equal right to self-determination and dignity in a shared land. An October 2025 survey by Israel's Institute for National Security Studies found that 68 percent of Jewish Israelis oppose the establishment of a Palestinian state under any circumstances. Another 2025 survey, commissioned by Pennsylvania State University and conducted by the Israeli research institute Geocartography Knowledge Group, showed that 82 percent of Israeli Jews support the forced expulsion ("transfer") of Palestinians from Gaza and 56 percent support expelling Palestinian citizens of Israel.

We arrived at the "lily pad theory"—the idea that even if people want to jump, no one wants to drown, so it helps to have something to jump to—after observing a pattern among dissidents' descriptions of some version of this experience. One concrete example is the work of Leaving MAGA, whose founder, Rich Logis, sat with us for multiple interviews. Logis's self-published 2024 e-book *My MAGA Odyssey* contains helpful details on his life and work, as do the Leaving MAGA website, the testimonials posted there, and Logis's social media posts. Our interview with Stephania Messina, her Leaving MAGA testimonial, and the November 24, 2024, article in *Daily Kos*, "A Former Charismatic Christian Nationalist Tells How She Left MAGA" by Paul Glickman, all contributed to our telling of her narrative. We agreed to protect the anonymity of the attendees of the Leaving MAGA Zoom support group that we observed.

15. Start a Belief Cascade

Our reporting on the Omar Suleiman poster campaign included multiple interviews with Amr Salah, Shady ElGhazaly Harb, and a third prominent Egyptian activist who participated in its planning and execution. Additional details came from contemporaneous coverage by international media, including the BBC and Reuters on September 3, 2010, and the *Los Angeles Times* on September 16, 2010, to reconstruct the timeline. The pseudonymous blog the activists set up to promote Suleiman (omarsoliman.blogspot.com) and weather records from Cairo in August and September 2010 also provided important details. The specifics of El-Ghazaly Harb's subsequent imprisonment came from International Federation for Human Rights reports, *The New York Times*, and ElGhazaly Harb himself. The Egyptian general mentioned at the end of the chapter was the country's production minister, Mohamed al-Assar.

Capturing the societal mood and political environment in Egypt in the lead-up to the Arab Spring and 2011 revolution required a review of both contemporaneous and retrospective reports. For background on the dynamics surrounding the "succession," we reviewed the following articles: Shaimaa Fayed, "Gamal Mubarak Front-Runner in Egypt Succession," Reuters, April 13, 2010; Robert Fisk, "Egyptians Prepare for Life After Mubarak," *Independent*, August 23, 2010; Jon Leyne, "'Mystery Campaign' Backs Egypt President's Son," BBC, August 24, 2010; Heba Saleh, "Group Tests the Waters for Mubarak Son Succession," *Washington Post*, September 8, 2010; Tarek Masoud, "Is Gamal Mubarak the Best Hope for Egyptian Democracy?," *Foreign Policy*, September 20, 2010; and the Congressional Research Service report by Jeremy M. Sharp, "Egypt: Background and U.S. Relations," January 28, 2011.

The human rights abuses and corruption of Hosni Mubarak's regime are well documented. We reviewed Mohammad Fadel, "Public Corruption and the Egyptian Revolution of January 25," *Harvard International Law Journal*, April 2011; Freedom House's Egypt country profile in *Freedom in the World 2005: The Annual Survey of Political Rights and Civil Liberties* (Rowman & Littlefield Publishers, 2005); and two Amnesty International reports: "Egypt: Ten Years of Torture," October 22, 1991, and "Hosni Mubarak: A Living Legacy of Mass Torture and Arbitrary Detention," February 25, 2020.

Our interviews with Salah, now a scholar of Middle East politics, helped put in context the limited liberalization that was underway in Egypt in the early 2000s, as did Bruce Gilley's article, "Did Bush Democratize the Middle East? The Effects of External–Internal Linkages," *Journal of Public and International Affairs* (Winter 2013/2014); and Moshe Efrat, "Hosni Mubarak's Economic and Social Policies in Perspective," Moshe Dayan Center for Middle Eastern and African Studies, August 19, 2015.

A handful of detailed reports allowed us to reconstruct the final days of Mubarak's tenure and place them in the context of the protests that were sweeping the Arab world: "Incidents of Protesters Setting Themselves on Fire Occur Across North Africa," *Los Angeles Times*, January 17, 2011; Ian Black et al., "Egypt Set for

Mass Protest as Army Rules Out Force," *Guardian*, January 31, 2011; "Egypt Army: Will Not Use Violence Against Citizens," Reuters, January 31, 2011; and the retrospective "Timeline: How the Arab Spring Unfolded," *Al Jazeera*, January 14, 2021. In "Comparing the Arab Revolts: The Role of the Military" (*Journal of Democracy*, October 2011), Zoltan Barany explains that both Tunisian and Egyptian soldiers sided with protesters during Arab Spring demonstrations, while forces in Yemen and Libya were "split" and those in Bahrain and Syria fired on demonstrators.

We anchored this chapter in two academic ideas. The first is Timur Kuran's notion of "preference falsification," from his canonical paper "Now Out of Never: The Element of Surprise in the East European Revolution of 1989," *World Politics*, October 1991. In the article, Kuran draws heavily on the writings of Václav Havel, along with his own statistical analysis, to illustrate that repressive regimes forced the people to live in a make-believe world and that the criminalization of publicly voicing dissent left individuals isolated with their own thoughts.

The second idea we incorporated was what Margaret Levi calls the "belief cascade"—the phenomenon of a movement that swells as individuals come to believe that they might be safe in numbers. Levi attributes this idea in part to the work of Dennis Chong, a political science professor at the University of Southern California, who describes these types of action as part of the "assurance game" that movement leaders often need to engage in to motivate broader participation. Chong writes in "Coordinating Demands for Social Change" (*Annals of the American Academy of Political and Social Science*, July 1993): "Until the movement becomes viable, social pressures and psychological incentives to contribute are not strongly felt by the ordinary participant."

16. "Get the Jeep Out of the Mud"

Fred Bauma shared his story of activism and imprisonment in the Democratic Republic of the Congo with us in an interview and in correspondence. To better understand the environment Bauma was navigating during his youth in the eastern Congo, we relied on analysis such as the Amnesty International report of March 31, 2003, "'Our Brothers Who Help Kill Us': Economic Exploitation and Human Rights Abuses in the East"; the Human Rights Watch report "DR Congo: Peace Accord Fails to End Killings of Civilians" (July 17, 2008); and the United Nations High Commissioner for Refugees January 1, 2000, assessment, "The State of the World's Refugees 2000: Fifty Years of Humanitarian Action," which described the Rwandan refugee camps near Goma as home to nearly one million refugees, plagued by cholera, and controlled by military forces. The eruption of the volcano near Goma in 2002 only added to the region's suffering: Estimates of the physical damage come from the Smithsonian Institution's Global Volcanism Program, "Report on Nyiragongo (DR Congo)," edited by Richard Wunderman, *Bulletin of the Global Volcanism Network* (April 2002).

The origins of Lutte pour le Changement (Struggle for Change), Lucha, are beautifully captured in the 2018 BBC Africa Eye documentary *La Lucha: Fighting for a Better DR Congo*; and in Ruby Bantariza et al., "Lucha Continua: The Youth Movement Striking Fear into Congo's Elite," *African Arguments*, May 31, 2017. Zachariah Mampilly also provided context for Lucha among Africa's protest movements through an interview and his scholarship, including "Global Forces, Rural Radicalism, and the Dual Transformation of Urban and Rural Protest in Africa," *African Studies Review*, December 2024.

The Senegalese protest movement Y' en Marre (We're Fed Up!) has been widely profiled, including in a 2016 documentary film, *The Revolution Won't Be Televised*, directed by Rama Thiaw; "The Rappers Who Took Down an African 'Dictator,'" *Huck*, October 27, 2016; and Marame Gueye, "Urban Guerrilla Poetry: The Movement Y' en a Marre and the Socio-Political Influences of Hip Hop in Senegal," *Journal of Pan-African Studies*, September 2013. Our accounting of the Burkinabe protest movement Balai Citoyen (Citizen Broom) relies on the reporting in Robbie Corey-Boulet, "How Burkina Faso's Rapper-Activists Shaped a Year of Upheaval," Institute of Current World Affairs, December 29, 2015.

Documentation of the arrests of the Congolese, Senegalese, and Burkinabe activists in DRC comes from Human Rights Watch, Amnesty International, and the United Nations Working Group on Arbitrary Detention. Fred Bauma's congressional testimony was covered in 2016 by The Enough Project, and he spoke about his post-release advocacy in "The Power of Nonviolence," a speech he delivered at the Oslo Freedom Forum in 2018. Context about DRC President Joseph Kabila's decision to finally step down under pressure comes from news reports, including Sewell Chan, "Joseph Kabila, Congo Strongman, Will Step Down After 17 Years in Power," *New York Times*, August 8, 2018.

The book that establishes the need to have a clear idea of who to blame as an important prerequisite of political protest is University of Notre Dame political scientist Debra Javeline's *Protest and the Politics of Blame: The Russian to Unpaid Wages* (University of Michigan Press, 2003). Javeline's findings are referenced in Peter Cummings's excellent October 2, 2025, talk at Notre Dame, "When Democratic Voices Unite: Global Lessons in Coalition Building," in which the political scientist offered a range of illuminating examples of negative coalitions from around the world.

Some of the other "coalition of no" case studies we mention—including in Brazil and Poland—are mentioned in Maria J. Stephan, "Lessons from Around the World: Engaging 'Pillars of Support' to Uphold and Expand Democracy," *Just Security*, October 9, 2024; additional details are sourced from Daniel Mello, "More Than One Hundred Organizations Sign Manifesto in Defense of Democracy," Agência Brasil, August 5, 2022; and Adam Fefer's write-up, "Polish Judges Resist Attacks on the Rule of Law," for the Horizon Project. Anthony Kunda, "Zambian Churches and Lawyers Oppose Presidential Plan for Third Term," *Christianity Today*, March 1, 2001, offered helpful color on the Zambian case study.

The insight from Stephan on saying both yes and no is from one of our interviews with her. Chenoweth made the "Jeep" comment during a closed-door session in the spring of 2025 at Harvard's Ash Center. We have included it with Chenoweth's permission. The phrase "toxic alliances" is proposed by Duncan McCargo, President's Chair in Global Affairs at Nanyang Technological University in Singapore, and Rendy Wadipalapa, a researcher at the National Research and Innovation Agency in Indonesia, in "Southeast Asia's Toxic Alliances," *Journal of Democracy*, July 2024.

The section on Hong Kong's pro-democracy coalitions drew on our multiple interviews with Nathan Law, as well as additional correspondence about his experiences as an activist and legislator in Hong Kong.

Our summary of Law's disqualification from the legislature and the subsequent introduction of the extradition bill relies on the extensive international reporting about these events, including: Kevin Lui, "Four More Hong Kong Lawmakers Ousted in a Blow to Democratic Hopes," *Yahoo!News*, July 14, 2017; "Hong Kong–China Extradition Plans Explained," BBC, December 13, 2019; Julia Hollingsworth, "Hong Kong Police and Protesters Clash Ahead of 70th Anniversary of People's Republic of China," CNN, September 30, 2019; a summary of the "five demands" published August 28, 2019, by Storm Media Group; "Hong Kong Formally Scraps Extradition Bill That Sparked Protests," BBC, October 23, 2019; and the March 19, 2024, Human Rights Watch report "Hong Kong: New Security Law Full-Scale Assault on Rights." The Hong Kong forum LIHKG and Catherine Thorbecke's "How Tech Has Fueled a 'Leaderless Protest' in Hong Kong" (*ABC News*, October 19, 2019) provide key details about the makeshift technological infrastructure that protesters used to select their demands.

Law's initiative to bring "stories of life under authoritarian regimes" into the classrooms of British middle and high school students is called "Civic Square: Reviving Democracy Through Education." As of early 2026, Law says, the program has worked in eight schools and reached over 1,300 students.

Index

Abbott, Greg, 100
Abortion Beyond the Law (Braine), 127
abortion rights, 125–27, 146–48, 150,
    154–57
academic freedom, 90–94
accompagnateur, 124–25
accompaniment, 124–27
agency, pleasure of, 9, 196
Al-Ali, Nadje, 64–68, 71–75
Alcoholics Anonymous (AA), 114
Alexander, George, 176–79
Algerian War, 173–74
Al-Haj, Jeremy, 115–16
Amen Effect, The (Brous), 82–83
American Airlines, 118–21
American Chemical Society, 92
American colonies, 55–56
American democracy, 2–3, 10
    stress-testing, xi–xiii
American dream, 212
American exceptionalism, 10
Amnesty International, 234–35
"Annals of Autocracy" (Hoffman),
    162–63
"Anthem" (song), 15
anti-Black hate crimes, 152
antisemitism, 72, 151, 152–54, 185
anxiety, 71, 102, 138–39, 140
Apple, 172
April 6th Youth Movement, 222–24
Arab-Israeli war, 104
Arab Spring, 219–24, 227–29
Arch Street United Methodist Church
    (Philadelphia), 119–20

Argentina
    abortion rights, 126, 127
    the disappeared, 38, 40
    Jubilados Insurgentes, 201–5
artificial intelligence (AI), 2, 163
Atkin, Claire, 135–38, 139–42,
    144–45
Atlatszo, 180–81
Australia, and Black Armada, 129
authoritarianism, 3–4, 8, 25, 132, 153,
    200
    evolution of, 10–16
authoritarian leaders, 243–46. *See also*
    specific leaders
    political violence, 148–50, 179–81
    simulation exercise, xi–xiii, 3, 243
    warning signs of, 12, 148–49
    World Liberty Congress, 87

backsliding democracies, 13, 163,
    237–38
Balai Citoyen (Citizen Broom), 232–35
Ball, Patrick, 39–41
Bannon, Steve, 137
Bauma, Fred, 230–35
bearing witness, 31–45
    Eyes on ICE and, 32–37, 43–45
    fighting the long defeat, 41–45
    indigenous Mayan women and
        Guatemala, La Violencia (The
        Violence), 37–41
Beautiful Trouble, 71
Beck, Glenn, 137
belief cascade, 9, 228–29

294 *Index*

Berlin Wall, 95, 248
big data, 2, 12
Black Panther Party, 98, 101
Blackshirts, 149
blame attribution, 236
blankets, bringing the, 113–14
Bloch, Nadine, 71, 207
Blueprint for Revolution (Popović), 183
Bodoky, Tamás, 180–81
Bolsonaro, Jair, 237
Bongino, Dan, 137–38
Boxer, Paul, 92
boycotts, 13, 117, 182, 183, 185, 189–95
Boyd, Coleman, 147–48
Braine, Naomi, 127
Brand, Russell, 137
Brazil, 71, 126, 237
Breaking the Silence, 210–11
Brecht, Bertolt, 190
Breitbart, 136, 215
Brennan Center for Justice, xiii
Brous, Sharon, 82–83
Brown, Elaine, 98
Brown University, 64–65, 67–68
Buckhannon, West Virginia, 128–29,
    130–31
Burma, 54
Bushwick Ayuda Mutua (BAM), 98–104

California Democratic Party, 120
California farmworkers grape strike, 4,
    189–91, 193–95
Cambodia, 149
campesinos, 195–96
Campos, Stephanie, 43–45
Canary Mission, 151–53, 154
Capitol insurrection of 2021, 136–37, 156
Carlson, Tucker, 137–38
Center for Applied Nonviolent Action
    and Strategies (CANVAS), 113,
    159–60
chain reactions, 227–29

Chatterjee, Keya, 198–200
Chavez, Cesar, 193
Chávez, Hugo (Chavismo), 23–24,
    26–28, 164
Check My Ads Institute, 135–38, 139,
    141–42
Chenoweth, Erica, 13, 174–76, 181–83,
    184, 237–38
Chiluba, Frederick, 237
China
    Hong Kong independence, 4,
        110–14, 238–42
    Tiananmen Square protests, 174
Chow, Alex, 111
City University of New York, 159, 165
civil disobedience, 69, 88, 111, 113–14,
    121, 196–97
Civil Rights Act of 1964, 19–20
civil rights movement, 4, 11, 54, 207–8
    Freedom Summer, 196–98, 208
    Lawson's story, 69–71
    Osadebe and housing discrimina-
        tion, 4, 19–22, 28–30
    Royster's story, 116–18, 119–20
Clayoquot protests, 178–79
CLEAR (Creating Law Enforcement
    Accountability & Responsibil-
    ity), 165
climate change, 130, 191–92
Clinton, Hillary, 135
"cognitive liberation," 197
Cohen, Leonard, 15
Cold War, 59, 95, 206
collective intelligence, 6
"collective stubbornness," 181–85
Columbia University, 91–92
communities of fate, 9, 127–31
Congo, Democratic Republic of the
    (DRC), 230–35
"connected criticism," 211–12
conspiracy theories, 135–38
Constitution Party (Egypt), 221

Constitution, U.S., 21, 243
Continental Congress, 55–56
COVID-19 pandemic, 99, 137, 241
COVID-19 vaccine, 215
Cuba, 163
Cummings, Peter, 236–37
curb cut effect, 170–72
Customs and Border Protection (CBP), 103–4
Cytotec, 126
Czechoslovakia, 41–42
    Velvet Revolution, 94–97

Daily Show, The (TV series), 155
dance parties, 199–200
Daniel, Yuli, 30
data-mining, 12
dating apps, 165–66
Dedman, Rachel, 107
"defect," 206
Delano (Dunne), 190
Delano grape strike, 189–91, 193–95
democracy. *See* American democracy
democratic backsliding, 13, 163, 237–38
Democratic Front for the Liberation of Palestine, 106
Democratic National Convention (2016), 118–21
DeSantis, Ron, 215
"Design from the Margins" (movement), 171–72
DHS (Department of Homeland Security), 151–52
"die-ins," 121
digital evidence, 170–72
digital marketing, 135–38
"Dissent as a Personal Experience" (Sinyavsky), 25–26, 30
dissent, taxonomy of, 5–10
dissidents, 1–5, 244–45. *See also specific dissidents*
    being who you are, 25–26
    new reality for, 3–5
    side effects, 9
    two kinds of fear, 22–23
    use of term, 7
dissident communities, 8–9, 244–46
    communities of fate, 9, 127–31
    finding a political home, 84–89
    invitations to, 110–16
    repurposing networks, 90–102
Dobbs v. Jackson Women's Health Organization, 146, 154–55
double thinkers, 9, 205–8
Duke University, 225
Dunne, John Gregory, 190

Earth First!, 177–78
East Germany, 224–25
East Mount Airy Neighbors, 116–18
Egypt, 4, 108, 166–67, 219–24, 227–29
Eisenberger, Naomi, 143
election of 2024, 1–2, 10
ElGhazaly Harb, Shady, 221–24, 228–29
El Salvador, 4, 40, 125, 195–96
Emory University, 56
encryption, 160, 165–66, 167–69
Endora, 156
ENTel Argentina, 201–2
environmentalism, 176–79, 191–92
escuálida, 26–27
Euki (app), 168–69
exposure therapy, 51, 143
Eyes on ICE, 32–37, 43–45
Eyes on the Prize (documentary), 98

facial recognition, 160, 170
Fair Housing Act of 1968, 19–22, 28–30
Faith in Action, 116–18
Fanselow, Michael, 138–39, 142–43

Farabundo Martí National Liberation Front (FMLN), 195–96
Farmer, Paul, 45, 124–25
Fatah, 106
fear, 1–4
    Atkin's story, 135–38, 139–42, 144–45
    Fanselow's research on, 138–39, 142–43
    joy vs., 198–200
    politics of, 47–50, 52–53
    power of accompaniment, 124–27, 131–32
    support networks, 141–45
    Thurman on, 55
    two kinds of, 22–23
    in your body, 138–39
Federal Bureau of Investigation (FBI), 137–38, 148, 152
Feynman, Richard, 6
First Amendment, 74–75
First Nations, 178–79
Florida
    COVID vaccine misinformation, 215
    Parental Rights in Education Act, 150
Fondo Maria, 127
Foreign Affairs, 159
Francis, Pope, 203–4
Francois, Susan, 43
Free Breakfast for Children, 98–99
Free DC, 198–200
freedom, xiii, 54–56, 88–89
    academic, 90–94
Freedom House, 162–63, 203
Freedom: How We Lose It and How We Fight Back (Law), 112
Freedom Summer (McAdam), 197
Freedom Summer (1964), 196–98, 208
free expression, 26, 41–42, 74–75, 95, 227

Front de Libération Nationale (Algeria), 173
FSB (Federal Security Services), 47, 51
Future, The (album), 15

Gandhi, Mahatma, 1, 54, 70, 175
Garner, Eric, 56
gay rights. *See* LGBTQ
Gaza, 104–9
Gaza war, 64–65, 108–9, 212–13
Gel'man, Vladimir, 48, 50
George Mason University, 227
Gessen, M., 85
Goldsmith, Kristofer, 156–57
Goma, 230–35
Gomez, Adriana, 23–25, 26–28
Good Fight, The (podcast), 225–26
Google, 99, 137
Green, Kat, 154–57
green scarves, 127
greenwashing, 191–92
group chats, 44, 98–104, 148
group identity, 206–7
Guatemala
    Commission for Historical Clarification, 38–39
    indigenous Mayan women and La Violencia, 4, 37–41
Guevara, Freddy, 164–65, 166

Haiti, 124
Hamas, October 7 attacks, 64, 108, 212
Hartmire, Chris, 194–95
Harvard University, 12, 59–60, 174, 237
Harwitt, Cecily, 119–20
hate speech, 65, 136
Havel, Václav, 41–42, 95, 96–97
Hayner, Priscilla, 38
Heenan, Palmer, 29
Herron, Maria, 100
Hirschman, Albert O., 197–98

Hoffman, David E., 162–63
Homan, Tom, 63
Homeland Security Investigations
        (HSI), 103–4
Hong Kong independence, 4, 110–14,
        238–42
Hong Kong protests of 2014, 110–11,
        239–40
Hoover, J. Edgar, 11
Hornstein, Erica, 143
Housing and Urban Development
        (HUD), 20–21, 28–30
housing discrimination, 19–22, 28–30
Huerta, Dolores, 193
Human Rights Watch, 166–67, 234
Hungary, 11, 149, 153, 180–81
Hun Sen, 149
Hussein, Saddam, 67
Hynicka, Robin, 119–20

immigration, 1–2
    Al-Ali's story, 64–68, 71–75
    bearing witness, 31–37, 43–45
    Bushwick networks, 102–4
    Canary Mission lists, 151–53, 154
    Eyes on ICE and, 32–37, 43–45
    Lawrence's story, 79–81, 83–84,
        88–89
    Mathis's story, 61–64
Immigration and Customs Enforce-
        ment (ICE), 1–2, 31–37, 43–45,
        61–68, 89, 102–4, 114, 217
Indian independence movement, 54,
        69–70, 159, 175
individualism, 129
Indonesia and Black Armada, 129
inner freedom, 54–56
Instagram, 182
Iran, 170–71, 170–72
Iraq, 64, 67
Israel, 104–9, 175
    Gaza war, 64–65, 108–9, 212–13

Hamas attack of October 7, 64,
        108, 212
    Manekin's story, 208–14
Italy, 149, 179

Jackalope, Remelya, 131–32
Jammi, Nandini, 136–37, 138
Javeline, Debra, 235–36
Jews for Racial & Economic Justice,
        114–15
Johnson, Justin "Yaddiya," 199
Johnson, Lyndon Baines, 19–20
Johnson, Stephanie, 128, 130–31
Journal of Democracy, 238
joy, 198–200
Jubilados Insurgentes, 201–5
Judaism
    Manekin's story, 208–14
    minyan, 81–83
Jummah prayer, 81

Kabila, Joseph, 230–35
kaddish, 82
Kassem, Ramzi, 165
King, Martin Luther, Jr., 19–20, 212
kippah, 209–10
Knight First Amendment Institute, 68,
        72–73, 74
Korean War, 69
Krishnan, Ramya, 72–73
Kuciak, Ján, 179–80
Kuran, Timur, 225–26
Kušnírová, Martina, 179–80
Kuznetsova, Maria, 47–52, 59–60

labor unions, 129–30. *See also* union
        strikes
    drives, 115–16
Lafayette, Bernard, 70
Lancet, The, 126
Lasota, Dominika, 192
Law, Nathan, 110–14, 239–42

Lawrence, Patrice, 79–81, 83–84, 88–89
Lawson, James, 69–71
Leaving MAGA, 214–18
Levi, Margaret, 129, 228
Levin, Jake, 114–15
Levitsky, Steven, 12, 149
LGBTQ, 4, 151, 166–67, 171
    trans rights, 122–24, 131–32
Liberian refugees, 88–89
Life (magazine), 68–69
lily pad theory, 214–18
Lingnan University, 111–12
logging, 176–79
Logis, Rich, 214–16
"lone wolf" shooters, 149–50
López-Uribe, Oriana, 126–27
loyalty, 24, 48, 206, 226
Lutte pour le Changement (Struggle for
    Change), 231–32

McAdam, Doug, 197
McCargo, Duncan, 238
Macri, Mauricio, 202
Maduro, Nicolás, 24, 26–27, 164
MAGA, 151, 157
    Leaving MAGA, 214–18
Maksimovic, Breza Race, 113–14, 116,
    163
Maldives, the, 160–61
Mampilly, Zachariah, 159
Manchuria, Japanese occupation of,
    129–30
Mandela, Nelson, 1, 158
Manekin, Devorah, 184–85
Manekin, Mikhael, 208–14
Maradiaga, Félix, 87
Marcos, Ferdinand, 174
Marea Verde (Green Wave), 127
Marshals Service, U.S., 148
Mathis, Mike, 61–61
Mayan women and Guatemala La
    Violencia, 37–41

Meares Island, 178
medication abortions, 125–27
Menem, Carlos, 202
mentors, 9, 108, 144, 245
Merton, Robert K., 6
messaging apps, 160, 165–66
Messina, Stephania, 216–18
Meta, 172
Mexico, abortion rights, 126–27
Michaels, Jon, 150–51
Middle Eastern Studies Association
    (MESA), 66, 67
middot, 209
Milei, Javier, 203
Milošević, Slobodan, 113–14, 192, 199
Mimoun, Raphael, 169
minyan, 81–83
Mississippi Freedom Summer (1964),
    196–98, 208
Missouri Workers Center, 116
Mitts, Tamar, 184–85
mobile phones. *See* smartphones
"moment(s) of recognition," 85
Moore, Lauren, 122–24, 131–32
moral collision, 8, 19–30, 85, 201
    Gomez's story, 23–25, 26–28
    Osadebe's story, 19–22, 28–30
    two kinds of fear, 22–23
Morris, Aldon, 70
Mosleh, Niveen, 104–9
Mpahlo, Nyasha Frank, 158–62
Mubarak, Gamal, 219–24, 227–29
Mubarak, Hosni, 219–20
Mugabe, Robert, 158–59
Musk, Elon, 185
Mussolini, Benito, 149
Myanmar, 71

Nashville sit-ins, 68–70
Nashville: We Were Warriors (docu-
    mentary), 70
Nathans, Benjamin, 86, 247–48

National Guard, xii, 198
Native Americans, 150, 178–79
Navalny, Alexei, 1, 48–49, 51–52
Nazis, 38, 67, 94, 95, 153, 157
negative coalitions, 236–38
neighbors
    getting in group chats, 98–104
    getting in small fights, 116–18
    support networks, 143–44, 156
Nemtsov, Boris, 49
networks, repurposing, 9, 90–102
    Bushwick Ayuda Mutua and,
        98–104
    Czechoslovakia and Velvet Revolu-
        tion, 94–97
    getting neighbors in group chat,
        98–102
New Yorker, The, 182
New York Times, The, 29, 224
Nexus Moving Company, 123–24,
    131–32
Nicaragua, 11, 87
Nigeria, abortion rights, 126
Nobel Prize, 54, 111, 241–42
Noll, David, 150–51
nonviolent campaigns, 5, 13–14, 173–
    85. *See also specific campaigns*
    Alexander's story, 176–79
    "collective stubbornness," 181–85
    environmentalists and, 176–79
    Slovakia, 179–80, 181
    Stephan and Chenoweth's research
        on, 13, 174–76, 181–83, 184,
        237
    success rates, 184
    3.5 Percent Rule, 182–83
North Atlantic Treaty Organization
    (NATO), 92
"Now Out of Never" (Kuran), 225–26
Nuremberg Trials, 38

O'Keefe, James, 166

O'Leary, Kathy, 32–37
On Tyranny (Snyder), 13
Open Russia, 46–47, 50–51, 52
Opletal, Jan, 94–95
opposition research, 155–57
    watch lists, 151–53, 154
Orbán, Viktor, 11, 149, 180–81, 184
Ortega, Daniel, 11, 87
Orwell, George, 212
Osadebe, Paul, 19–22, 28–30
Oslo Freedom Forum, 235
Oslzlý, Petr, 95–96
Oxford Student, The, 107
Öztürk, Rümeysa, 63, 66, 152–53

Pakistan, 163
Palavecino, Zulema, 201–5
Palestinians, 104–9, 175. *See also* pro-
    Palestinian protests
    flag, 104–6, 107
    Gaza war, 64–65, 108–9, 212–13
    Manekin's story, 209–14
    tatreez, 106–9
panic, 103, 106, 138–39, 140
Peace Brigades International, 125
Penal Colony No. 7, 47, 53–54, 57–59
peregrinación, 190
Philadelphia International Airport
    strike of 2016, 118–21
Philippines, People Power Revolution,
    174
phones. *See* smartphones
Pinckney, Jonathan, 13, 206–7, 226
Pirro, Jeanine, 198
Pivovarov, Andrei, 46–47, 50–54,
    57–59, 60
Pizzagate conspiracy theory, 135–36
Plaza de los Dos Congresos (Buenos
    Aires), 204–5
pleasure of agency, 9, 196
Poland, 183–84, 191–92, 237
police brutality, 56, 113, 241

Policía Federal Argentina (PFA), 204–5
political home, finding, 84–89, 244–45
political satire, 189–95
political violence. *See* vigilantism
Pool, Tim, 137
Popović, Srdja, 183
POWER (Philadelphians Organized
        to Witness, Empower, and
        Rebuild), 119–20
"Power of the Powerless, The" (Havel),
        41–42
practice, 68–75
prayer quorum, 81–82
preparation, 68–75
Preservation of the Soul (Warshavsky),
        211
"Professor Watchlist," 151
pro-Palestinian protests, 64–68
        Al-Ali's story, 64–68, 71–75
        watch lists, 151–53, 154
"protective presence," 125
Prowse, Gwen, 11
pseudonymity, 171–72
Pulitzer Prize, 247
Pussy Riot, 42
Putin, Vladimir, 11, 42, 48–52, 58,
        149, 153
Pythagorean theorem, 6

quantum electrodynamics, 6
Quit India, 175

"racial authoritarianism," 11
racism, 10–11, 150, 152, 184–85
        Osadebe and housing discrimina-
        tion, 19–22, 28–30
Ramirez, Ana Maria, 168–69
Reagan, Ronald, 75
Reconstruction, 11
religious leaders, 117–18, 119–20
resilience, 84, 87, 143
rhythm, controlling the, 73

Rigot, Afsaneh, 170–72
Ríos Montt, Efraín, 39–40
Roe v. Wade, 154–55
role-play exercises, 70–71
Roselle, Mike, 177–78
Rosenwinge, Stephanie, 147–48
Royster, Audrey, 116–17
Royster, Dwayne, 116–18, 119–20
rubber band theory, 240–41
Rumble, 137, 139
Russia, 11, 46–54, 149. *See also* Soviet
        Union
        invasion of Ukraine, 49–50, 58,
        59–60, 153
        Javeline's research on, 235–36
        Kuznetsova's story, 47–52, 59–60
        Navalny's story, 48–49, 51–52
        Pivovarov's story, 46–47, 50–54,
        57–59, 60
        political prisoners, numbers, 47–48
        politics of fear, 48, 49
Rutgers Resolution, 92–94
Rwanda, 87, 230–31

Salah, Amr, 221–24, 227–28
Salas-de la Cruz, David, 90–94
Salfia, Jessica, 129
Salvadoran Civil War, 4, 40, 125,
        195–96
"same Jeep," 238
samizdat, 41–42
satire, 189–95
Schussman, Alan, 115
Schwartz, Barbara, 147
Schwinger, Julian, 6
Second Amendment, 215
"self-deport," 89
Senegal, 232–35
September 11 attacks (2001), 11
Serbia, 113–14, 159–60, 163, 183, 192
Sharansky, Natan, 205–6
Siberia, 50, 52, 59

Sierra Club, 177–78

Signal, 160, 167, 169, 172

Sinyavsky, Andrei Donatovich, 25–26, 30

Sisi, Abdel Fattah al-, 166–67

sit-ins, 68–75

Slovakia, 179–80, 181

small acts of defiance, 194–95, 244

small circles, 84–87

small fights, 116–18

smartphones, 166–69
    curb cut effect, 170–72
    location tracking, 12
    use of encryption, 165–66, 167–69
    videos, 36, 43

Smith, Luther E., Jr., 56

Smol Emuni (the Faithful Left), 211

Snyder, Timothy, 13, 153

social media
    antisemitism and, 152
    conspiracy theories, 135–36
    encryption, 165–66, 167–69
    Messina's story, 217
    overreliance on, 184
    Pivovarov and Russia, 60
    surveillance, 12, 41, 162–63, 165–66
    3.5 Percent Rule, 182

social welfare, 98–99, 143

Solidarity movement, 183–84

Somerville, Massachusetts, 61–64, 152–53

Soros, George, 138, 153

Soule, Sarah A., 115

South Africa apartheid, 4–5, 15, 40

Soviet dissidents, 4, 85–86, 247–48
    samizdat, 41–42
    Sharansky and, 205–6
    Sinyavsky and, 25–26, 30

Soviet Union. *See also* Russia
    collapse of, 15, 85–86, 224–25, 247

Stalin, Joseph, 25–26, 30, 52

Stand Together for Higher Ed, 93

Stanford University, 129

Star Wars, 198

Stephan, Maria J., 13, 174–76, 181–83, 237

storytelling, 189–95
    Delano grape strike, 189–91, 193–95
    Valdez and *actos*, 189–91, 193–95

stress-testing American democracy, xi–xiii

structural racism, 184–85

Student Nonviolent Coordinating Committee (SNCC), 207–8

Sulafa Embroidery Centre, 106–7, 108–9

Suleiman, Omar, 221–24, 227–28

Sullivan, Leon H., 117

sumud, 107–9

support networks, 114, 141–45

"swatting," 157

Swiss cheese theory, 9, 169

Tagore, Rabindranath, 54

Tahrir Square (Cairo), 223–24, 227

Takedown Tesla, 185

Tate, Andrew, 137, 217

tatreez, 106–9

tawrith, 220–21

taxonomy of dissent, 5–10

tech surveillance, 2, 11, 12, 86

Telegram, 49–50

Tella (app), 169

Tennessee, transgender school laws, 150

Tesla, 185

Texas
    Heartbeat Act of 2021, 150
    immigration, 100
    Uvalde school shooting of 2022, 215

Thailand, 162–63

thobe, 107

3.5 Percent Rule, 182–83

Thurman, Howard, 5–6, 54–55, 56
Tiananmen Square protests of 1989, 174
TikTok, 43, 182, 217
Tomonaga, Sin-Itiro, 6
totalitarianism, 85, 97, 205
"toxic alliances," 238
traje, 39–40
Transcendence Care Network, 132
transgender rights, 4, 122–24, 131–32, 150
tree spiking, 176–78
Trilling, Claire, 13
Trump, Donald
    authoritarianism of, 2, 3–4
    election of 2024, 10
    immigration policy, 75
    Inauguration Day (2025), 3
    university research funding, 91–94
Tupamaros, 149
Turning Point USA's "Professor Watchlist," 151

Ukraine, Russian invasion of, 49–50, 58, 59–60, 153
UndocuBlack Network, 88–89
unemployment, 118, 231
union drives, 115–16
union strikes, 129–30
    Delano grape strike, 189–91, 193–95
    Philadelphia International Airport strike of 2016, 118–21
    West Virginia teachers' strike of 2018, 127–31
United Farm Workers strike, 189–91, 193–95
United Nations (UN), 37, 38
    Working Group on Arbitrary Detention, 234–35
University of Arizona, 115
University of California, Los Angeles (UCLA), 138, 143
University of Colorado, 174

University of Notre Dame, 235–37
University of Pennsylvania, 86, 247
University of Redlands, 54–55
University of Texas, 206, 226
university research funding, 91–94
Unspeakable Truths (Hayner), 38
Uruguay, 149
Usmanova, Tatiana, 57–59
Uvalde school shooting of 2022, 215

Valdez, Luis, 189–91, 193–95
Velvet Revolution, 94–97
Venezuela, 4, 164–66
    Gomez's story, 23–25, 26–28
Victoria and Albert Museum, 107
Vigilante Nation (Michaels and Noll), 150–51
vigilantism, 11, 146–57
    time of lists, 148–54
Violence Against Women Act of 1994, 28
violent resistance, 7, 176–77

Wadipalapa, Rendy, 238
Walzer, Michael, 211–12
"War in the Woods" (1993), 176–79
war of persuasion. *See* nonviolent campaigns
Warshavsky, Dvir, 211
"war zones," 85
Washington-Leapheart, Naomi, 121
Washington Post, The, 162, 224
watch lists, 151–53, 154
Weaver, Vesla M., 11
West Bank, 104–9, 209–14
West Virginia teachers' strike of 2018, 127–31
WhatsApp, 163, 167, 171, 172
whisper networks, 126–27
Why Civil Resistance Works (Stephan and Chenoweth), 13
Winstead, Lizz, 154–55
witness. *See* bearing witness

Wong, Joshua, 110, 111, 241–42
Wood, Elisabeth Jean, 196
world building, 140–42
World Liberty Congress, 87
writing down your people, 141–42

X (Twitter), 136, 152, 163

Yale University, 196
Y'en A Marre (We're Fed Up!), 232–35

Young, William G., 74–75
Yousafzai, Malala, 1
YouTube, 182

Zambia, 237
Zelenskyy, Volodymyr, 153
Ziblatt, Daniel, 12, 149
Zimbabwe, 158–62
Zion Baptist Church (Philadelphia),
    117

About MARINER BOOKS

Mariner Books traces its beginnings to 1832 when William Ticknor co-founded the Old Corner Bookstore in Boston, from which he would run the legendary firm Ticknor and Fields, publisher of Ralph Waldo Emerson, Harriet Beecher Stowe, Nathaniel Hawthorne, and Henry David Thoreau. Following Ticknor's death, Henry Oscar Houghton acquired Ticknor and Fields and, in 1880, formed Houghton Mifflin, which later merged with venerable Harcourt Publishing to form Houghton Mifflin Harcourt. HarperCollins purchased HMH's trade publishing business in 2021 and reestablished their storied lists and editorial team under the name Mariner Books.

Uniting the legacies of Houghton Mifflin, Harcourt Brace, and Ticknor and Fields, Mariner Books continues one of the great traditions in American bookselling. Our imprints have introduced an incomparable roster of enduring classics, including Hawthorne's *The Scarlet Letter*, Thoreau's *Walden*, Willa Cather's *O Pioneers!*, Virginia Woolf's *To the Lighthouse*, W.E.B. Du Bois's *Black Reconstruction*, J.R.R. Tolkien's *The Lord of the Rings*, Carson McCullers's *The Heart Is a Lonely Hunter*, Ann Petry's *The Narrows*, George Orwell's *Animal Farm* and *Nineteen Eighty-Four*, Rachel Carson's *Silent Spring*, Margaret Walker's *Jubilee*, Italo Calvino's *Invisible Cities*, Alice Walker's *The Color Purple*, Margaret Atwood's *The Handmaid's Tale*, Tim O'Brien's *The Things They Carried*, Philip Roth's *The Plot Against America*, Jhumpa Lahiri's *Interpreter of Maladies*, and many others. Today Mariner Books remains proudly committed to the craft of fine publishing established nearly two centuries ago at the Old Corner Bookstore.